TABLE OF CONTENTS

LEARNING IN K-3 CLASSROOMS

by Carla Gull, EdD, Suzanne Levenson Goldstein, EdD, and Tricia Rosengarten, PhD

Gryphon House

Gryphon House, Inc.

www.gryphonhouse.com

Introduction

Have you ever wondered why children are so drawn to playing with sticks, rocks, and cardboard boxes? These items are examples of open-ended materials in the environment, or *loose parts*. As educators, parents, grandparents, community leaders, and researchers, we have explored the importance of loose parts in classrooms. We've learned that, given the opportunity to experiment with loose parts, students grow socially, emotionally, physically, and cognitively.

Our intent with this book is threefold: to help you become acquainted with the loose-parts philosophy by developing a loose-parts mindset, to show you how you can apply loose parts in your educational setting, and to continue refining your teaching practices using loose parts.

The use of loose parts is a mindset that supports invention, promotes imagination, inspires innovation, instills problem-solving skills, and builds confidence. As authors, our goal is to provide tools and resources to help you develop, apply, and teach using this mindset.

Understanding and exploring the use of loose parts in early elementary classrooms allows for greater implementation and meaningful conversations around the topic. Creative and imaginative play fosters the development of learning in all students, especially in early elementary children. Having a deeper understanding of loose parts allows for more diverse application and use of this theory in our classrooms and schools. Developing and applying a loose-parts mindset promotes an engaging class and enhanced learning.

How This Book Is Organized

We offer a variety of tools and resources to refine your thinking and planning and to help you share the vision with others. This is one of the main goals of our book; we want to arm you with research, tools, resources, specific examples, and activities to justify your implementation and use of loose parts in your elementary classrooms.

In section 1, Developing and Implementing a Loose-Parts Mindset, we walk you through the research that defines and supports the use of loose parts in the classroom. We describe the benefits and potential uses of loose parts and examine common myths and challenges about using loose parts in educational settings. We look at obtaining buy-in from all the stakeholders: administration, teachers, and families. We also examine the realities of planning lessons to meet educational philosophies and standards while allowing flexibility. As you read, we hope that you will make your own connections and see how you might use these principles and examples in your own classroom and school.

In this section, we outline a strategy for getting started, growing a loose-parts plan, repurposing what you already have, finding more loose parts, and utilizing housekeeping ideas for maintaining your materials. We discuss safety and the use of loose parts, and we address the role of the educator in a loose-parts environment.

In section 2, Applying and Teaching a Loose-Parts Mindset, we apply this mindset to the elementary classroom and address how to use a variety of approaches to loose parts and learning across learning domains. We use a science, technology, reading, engineering, arts, and math (STREAM) framework, recognizing the interconnectedness of disciplines and learning, and we offer specific suggestions and ideas for using outdoor spaces and transforming indoor environments and routines to allow for more playful moments. And, in chapter 15, we share a plethora of ways to celebrate loose parts in the classroom, including special days to investigate. In section 3, we offer tools and resources to help you get started and assessment options to help you document the learning that's taking place.

Thank you for your work in connecting students to a loose-parts mindset. Each step you take to allow students choices and a voice within the educational setting makes a difference. Expanding the borders of our classrooms to embrace the schoolyard and beyond allows access to more loose parts and opportunities.

Please use this book as a smorgasbord of ideas—no teacher can "do all the things," but choose the ones that work for you, your students, and your community, and adapt them as appropriate. Realize that as educators we are never done or perfect in our educational approach. We will continually evaluate and apply what we learn through this loose-parts journey. We are all on this adventure to apply loose parts in our learning situations more fully. Please connect with us on the Loose Parts Learning Facebook group and share what you learn and experience.

We hope these suggestions and options will be springboards for where you and your students can go with a loose-parts mindset. One beauty of loose parts is that it allows exploration and experimentation and provides additional connections and opportunities for building knowledge. Take time to reflect on your understanding of loose parts and how your students might benefit from them in the classroom. Dabble, try, and experiment with the concepts, words, and ideas that come up in the classroom. Apply that process of a loose-parts mindset to your own teaching practice and personal interests. Not one of us is too old for a little loose-parts play.

· SECTION 1 ·
DEVELOPING
AND
IMPLEMENTING
A LOOSE-PARTS MINDSET

· CHAPTER 1 ·
An Overview of Loose Parts

Loose parts are often associated with play, but they are also vital components to learning and growth. As philosopher and education reformer John Dewey (1942) states in his book *The School and Society*, "Education is a social process. Education is growth. Education is not a preparation for life; education is life itself." The distinction between educational learning and play begins to vanish as we allow learning and development to take place with the use of loose parts.

Using open-ended materials is an age-old practice, starting from the first time a human picked up a rock or stick and used it in a creative way. Today's older generations often mention that playing with found materials—scavenging for natural and discarded objects outside for play and inventing—is just how they grew up. Additionally, theories and practices by education thinkers, including Friedrich Fröebel,

> "To me, it is the experimentation and process that make loose parts, rather than the actual stuff."
> —Dr. Carla Gull

Maria Montessori, and John Milton, had roots in manipulating objects as part of learning, as did the adventure-playground movement after World War II.

Open-ended materials create opportunities to interact and manipulate with both natural and manufactured items and challenge children to think, build, and create. As educators, it is important that we "encourage children to take risks, explore, and investigate while engaging in active, sensory, collaborative, and dramatic play" (Carr et al., 2017).

Loose parts can intrigue and captivate students at any age and in any subject. Dewey argues that education and learning is an interactive, experiential, and engaging process. The experiential approach to education is founded on the idea that growth takes place when students are actively (physically, socially, intellectually, emotionally) involved in their learning rather than just being receivers of information (Stanchfield, 2016).

Exploring the Theory and Intent of Loose Parts

While many educational theories and practices have influenced open-ended play, architect Simon Nicholson coined the term *loose parts*. Nicholson's perspective, which he explains in his 1971 article "How NOT to Cheat Children—The Theory of Loose Parts," is that "in any environment, both the degree of inventiveness and creativity, and the possibility of discovery, are directly proportional to the number and kind of variables in it." Nicholson believed that children can be creative and imaginative when incorporating loose parts in their play and learning. In his article, he defines *creativity* as "playing around with the components and variables of the world in order to make experiments and discover new things and form new concepts."

> *"Give the pupils something to do, not something to learn; and the doing is of such a nature as to demand thinking; learning naturally results."*
>
> **—John Dewey**

Peter Gray (2013), author of *Free to Learn*, admits that "play would be more respected if we called it something like 'self-motivated practice of life skills,' but that would remove the lightheartedness from it and thereby reduce its effectiveness." Of course, many life skills and personal qualities are essential to students' future academic, personal, and professional success. Loose-parts explorations support important skills such as divergent thinking, decision making, creativity, problem solving, self-confidence, adaptability, self-direction, and motivation.

Divergent thinking is a process of creating many ideas and solutions related to a concept a person is attempting to understand or a problem she is trying to solve. Unlike convergent thinking, the divergent approach encourages students to think cognitively, critically, and creatively. Using loose parts in classrooms supports this learning process and creates "a spontaneous, fluid, non-linear mental approach based on curiosity and nonconformity. In fact, it is also a type of thinking very common in children, where joy, imagination, and a fresh perspective make their reasoning more free" (Exploring Your Mind, 2018).

Play is an essential aspect of the learning process. As Gray (2013) puts it, play is how students can learn to take control of their learning and lives. What important skills do children learn from play? In his 2019 article, "The Decline of Play—Peter Gray," Ying includes the ability to solve problems with creativity, imagination, and innovation; getting along with peers; social and emotional skills; and risk taking in the list. Along these lines, Nicholson (1971) suggests that loose parts move beyond playing with sticks and cardboard boxes (although both are important!) to a more complex understanding of engagement in education.

We pulled ten principles from his theory to rethink Nicholson's intent:

1. Limit the restrictions.

2. Involve children in using, planning, and building spaces and learning.

3. Blur the lines between inside and outside.

4. Create a lab-like environment.

5. Solve real-life problems.

6. Allow children to learn through experimentation.

7. Use a variety of approaches to loose-parts play.

8. Just add water.

9. Use what you have.

10. Play

Limit the Restrictions

How can we have a "yes" mentality in classroom and outdoor learning? We put many restrictions on children throughout the day, as Nicholson points out: "Young children (often) find the world incredibly restricted—a world where they cannot play with building and making things, or play with fluids, water, fire, or living objects and all the things that satisfy one's curiosity and give us the pleasure that results from discovery and invention." While children may not be playing with fire in our classrooms, there are ways we can lessen the restrictions and say yes more often to children's curiosity and experimentation.

Involve Children in Using, Planning, and Building Spaces and Learning

Nicholson advocates for making children a part of the planning and environment of the learning space. He says that if environments such as schools, playgrounds, day-care centers, and museums do not work, it is because the adults (artists, landscape architects, planners) have had all the fun playing with materials, concepts, and planning alternatives—all the fun and creativity been "stolen." Children *can* be part of the design process of our classrooms. We can give that creativity and fun back and allow them to be integral in creating learning spaces. Children can give suggestions on class layout and how a space is used if we offer them choices both within the classroom and outside on the school grounds.

Blur the Lines between Inside and Outside

We often just think that learning only occurs in our individual classrooms; however, we might extend education to our entire school building, the schoolyard, and beyond. Nicholson suggests switching things up, allowing learning to take place outdoors and fun and games to occur indoors. He advocates letting the distinction between education and recreation begin to disappear. Think of the outdoor spaces in your school—the courtyards, school gardens, playgrounds, asphalt, and green spaces. Integrate nature into your classroom, and incorporate loose parts into outside recess. Think of ways to use outdoor spaces for learning and to bring more play inside.

Create a Lab-Like Environment

If we turn direct-teaching lessons into experimentations where students can explore and produce their own understandings, Nicholson says children can "enjoy and find out things for themselves." This laboratory-like space can be more than just the physical aspect and include exploration and experimentation in the learning process. For example, an outdoor space might become a mud kitchen. Inside, consider having a nature table to explore. Offer a makerspace, which is a prime example of a lab-like environment.

Solve Real-Life Problems

Meaningful learning is often tied to investigating and solving problems in our environment. As educators, we can pose problems and use place-based education practices to promote creativity. Nicholson points out, "Children greatly enjoy playing a part in the design process. This includes the study of the nature of the problem; thinking about their requirements and needs; considering planning alternatives; measuring, drawing, model-making and mathematics; construction and building; experiment, evaluation, modification and destruction." Project- and place-based education centered on solving a problem allow children to be fully immersed in the learning process.

Allow Children to Learn through Experimentation

While it's great to study information and gain knowledge, hands-on experience goes a long way in learning. Nicholson shares an example of how loose parts can connect with experimentation and learning, referring to the generally accepted idea that children like being in small, cave-like spaces. He then expands on that idea to say, "when children have the opportunity to play with space-forming materials in order that they may invent, construct, evaluate and modify *their own* caves . . . we have a perfect example of variables and loose parts in action . . ." Students can use loose parts—and all the possibilities they offer—to construct their own knowledge and learning, connecting play and experimentation.

9

Psychologist James J. Gibson (1979) developed his theory of affordances to describe how humans perceive materials and other aspects of their environment, and how they explore the possibilities offered, or *afforded*, by those materials and aspects. In her 2011 article "The Place of Outdoor Play in a School Community," Emily Stanley relates Gibson's theory to children's learning: "An affordance can be thought of as an 'action possibility' for an individual in relation to the environment, dependent on that individual's capabilities." For example, a collection of materials—wooden boards, rope, water, rocks, sticks, and so on—in the eyes of children offer an almost endless supply of possibilities. Each child will perceive the loose parts in their own way and will respond to the materials in their own way. Perception drives action in student learning. The use of loose parts in classrooms and schools enables our students to explore and develop divergent thinking.

Use a Variety of Approaches to Loose-Parts Play

Nicholson goes well beyond tree cookies and cardboard boxes in defining loose parts. He includes a variety of materials and shapes, smells, sounds, electricity, magnetism, gravity, gases, fluids, music, motion, chemical interactions, cooking, fire, other people, animals, plants, words, concepts, and ideas. He says, "With all these things all children love to play, experiment, discover and invent and have fun. All these things have one thing in common, which is variables or 'loose parts.'" The classroom can be a great place to explore these many variables. Using a variety of approaches, loose parts allow us to meet both learning standards and the needs of our students.

Just Add Water

Nicholson describes water as one of the easiest and best ways to transform a space: "Loose parts at work—water, ripples, reflections, slush, floating and living objects. Many curriculum units are based on experiments with water; here is the quickest, cheapest way to introduce variables into an asphalt/chain-link environment." Water can be a powerful variable to explore properties of matter while having fun. Water has many states and aspects to explore. Nicholson mentions the need for "human interaction and involvement with water—its refraction, beading, noise. Liquids, gases (waterfall, wind tunnel) afford classic examples of how loose parts permit experimentation, creativity." Water experimentation can be a staple of classroom learning.

Use What You Have

Nicholson notes, "In the simplest possible terms, the most interesting and vital loose parts are those that we have around us every day." Using what we have around us can be very powerful. Children have long scrounged for scraps to use in play; these same bits and bobs can become part of their learning process.

Play!

What actions happen in your program? Nicholson uses a variety of verbs that can give educators many options for learning actions in the classroom: *build, construct, play, experiment, invent, explore, discover, evaluate, modify, study, think, consider, measure, draw, model-making, calculate, destruct, slide, fold, hide, paint,* and *bounce.* He says, "In early childhood there is no important difference between play and work, art and science, recreation and education . . ." Blurring those lines and embracing a variety of verbs for play and learning allows us to profoundly widen our students' experiences and deepen their understanding.

Sharing Current Definitions and Research

In addition to Nicholson's theory, research provided many definitions of loose parts over the years. In their article "Let the Children Play," Natalie Houser and colleagues (2016) define loose parts as "materials that are variable, meaning they can be used in more than one way so that children can experiment and invent through play. " Victoria Carr and colleagues (2017) assert in their article "Nature by Design" that loose parts "encourage children to take risks, explore, and investigate while engaging in active, sensory, collaborative, and dramatic play." Jennifer Kable and Juliet Robertson (2010) define loose parts as "materials that can be moved, carried, combined, redesigned, lined up, and taken apart in multiple ways." Stuart Lester and Wendy Russell (2010) conclude that loose parts provide many possibilities for learning and play, and Mary Jo Sutton (2011) notes that loose parts provide an effective yet playful way for students to form connections. Sutton also offers a definition and explanation: "Loose parts can be any collection of fully movable elements that inspire a person to pick them up, to re-arrange or create new configurations, even realities, one piece or multiple pieces at a time. They can be small or large enough to require multiple hands or full bodies to move them. Loose parts require the hand and mind to work in concert; they are catalysts to inquiry. Loose parts are the flexible edge of an inviting open-ended interactive environment that allows participants to make an imprint of their intention."

We conducted a formal research study to further explore this important learning component and created our own working definition and understanding of loose parts. We analyzed more than two thousand articles to investigate the current span of literature available on loose parts and to allow for more diverse application and use of the loose-parts theory. Based on our expansive review of current information on this topic, we created a working definition of loose parts:

> Loose parts are open-ended, interactive, natural and manufactured materials that can be manipulated with limitless possibilities. Interaction with loose parts includes experimentation, exploration, and playful interactions with variables through creativity and imagination. Participants have the freedom to explore variables, combine materials, and react to complex themes and ideas that emerge. Facilitators encourage participants, make loose parts available, stimulate discovery, provide opportunities, allow for open-ended play, and prompt meaningful connections and experiences. Through loose parts exploration, participants develop imagination, creativity, and collaborative skills. Process is more important than the end product, fostering overall growth and development (Gull, Bogunovich, Levenson Goldstein, and Rosengarten, 2019).

This loose-parts definition and research allows us to more fully embrace the concept and apply it to the children we serve. We'll explore how to do this in more depth in the subsequent chapters.

Addressing the Challenges and Myths of Loose Parts in the Elementary Classroom

Using loose parts in a classroom offers proven benefits; however, reservations, myths, and challenges with understanding the purpose and use of loose parts persist. In addition to teachers, many school administrators and families have objections and fears when it comes to using loose parts as a learning tool. Inspired by a 2020 article we wrote for *Exchange*, "Bridging Research and Practice: Seven Loose Parts Myths Busted," let's take a look at a few common myths surrounding using loose parts that relate specifically to learning in the classroom:

- Loose parts are for play.
- Loose parts are expensive.
- Loose parts must be loose or moveable.
- Loose parts are messy.
- Loose parts should be organized, arranged, and displayed in divided trays.

Loose Parts Are for Play

Some educators view the use of loose parts as ineffective and a waste of time, but it's important to realize that loose parts are an effective source of learning. Open-ended materials are not just "stuff" in a child's backyard or bedroom but can also be a vital tool in the classroom.

Loose Parts Are Expensive

A common myth is that collecting and buying loose parts is a complicated and expensive process. "While some loose parts items may be expensive, loose parts can adapt to any place, budget, and situation" (Gull, Levenson Goldstein, and Rosengarten, 2020). You can find most loose parts with little effort or cost, locating many just by looking and asking around. A quick review of your current classroom, school storage closets, cafeteria supply room, outdoors, and your own personal home and garage can produce a wealth of loose parts at no cost. And you have the satisfaction of cleaning and organizing your home and classroom—that's a win-win situation!

The Importance and Benefits of Loose Parts in Early Elementary Classrooms

Loose parts are often associated with play, intriguing and captivating children at any age, but they can also be a vital component to learning. This chapter describes the benefits and potential uses of loose parts to help you understand how to implement this teaching mindset effectively with your students. In addition, we will examine common myths and challenges surrounding the use of loose parts.

Developing a Loose-Parts Mindset

Have you heard the term *loose-parts mindset*? What does this mean? How can we understand and embrace this concept? How can we develop a loose-parts mindset for our students in our classes, school, and community?

In her article "The Arts, Loose Parts, and Conversations," Sheryl Smith-Gilman (2018) asserts that loose parts is "a mindset, a process-oriented approach whereby meaningful conversations emerge unexpectedly and add significantly to

"Children need the freedom to appreciate the infinite resources of their hands, their eyes, and their ears, the resources of forms, materials, sounds, and colours."
—**Loris Malaguzzi**

learning." Christine Kiewra and Ellen Veselack (2016), in their article "Playing with Nature," state that learning with loose parts is a way for students to "explore their process, to problem solve together, to negotiate and debate and to have support from a caring adult."

Sheryl Kerr (2017), author of "Why Is Elementary Education So Important?" reminds us that "elementary school is the most important stage for every child, since the child may evolve from a young child to a self-conscious person." Using loose parts to promote engaging play and active learning provides the opportunity for young students to develop and increase their ability to perform better in school and later in life when they face personal and professional challenges. As educators, we need to use the theory and research on loose parts to form our own loose-parts mindset. We need to make sure we present materials, methods, and concepts so that our students can comprehend the topics. We need to find a way to motivate children.

With younger students, many activities need to start as teacher-led instruction; however, students eventually need to become active participants in learning. Engaging children in their own learning increases their focus, motivation, and excitement. A constructivist approach to teaching promotes learning by encouraging students to question, research, explore, assess, and understand. Research from educators across the globe has demonstrated that a student-centered approach lets students fully embrace the class objectives and enjoy the learning process. Using this approach, students "construct their own understanding and knowledge of the world, through experiencing things and reflecting on those experiences" (WNET Education, 2004). By understanding, applying, and teaching a loose-parts mindset, we can help students learn critical subjects and skills and meet standards.

Benefiting from Loose Parts in the Elementary Classroom

Based on our research and experiences in the classroom, we recognize five key benefits of using loose parts in our elementary classrooms:

- Supporting curriculum and connection to standards
- Developing critical-thinking, problem-solving, and decision-making skills
- Fostering imagination, curiosity, creativity, and wonder
- Improving communication skills and social interactions
- Expanding knowledge and learning

Learning with loose parts provides students the opportunity to think imaginatively and discover different solutions to problems. Students begin to gain an understanding of new concepts through their engagement, experimentation, and curiosity with open-ended items. Loose parts provide "ample opportunities with a wide array of materials to encourage and provoke children in meaningful experiences" (Veselack, Miller, and Cain-Chang, 2015).

Loose-parts play encourages children to explore, experiment, design, create, and construct. It gives them the opportunity to figure out that there are different ways of doing things. It teaches them to be critical of their own creations and to be flexible and resilient when things don't work out. Loose-parts play encourages independent play, self-motivation, and creative thinking (Maes, 2015).

"Children learn most readily and easily in a laboratory type environment where they can experiment, enjoy, and find out things for themselves."
—Simon Nicholson

There really is no "wrong" way to play with loose parts. Allowing children to freely play with objects is a very pure form of this type of play, though other applications may include provocations, outdoor classrooms, nature art, and so on. Nicholson mentions verbs as part of loose parts. The possible actions are varied and include experimentation, building, inventing, and exploring. These explorations may even include deconstruction—knocking over blocks, ripping cardboard, and so on—at times.

When children can freely explore and create on their own, they are processing what they are learning. They can experiment, test their own hypotheses, and understand the properties of materials. Children are naturally drawn to this age-old principle of interacting with their environment through playful approaches.

The Importance and Benefits of Loose Parts in Early Elementary Classrooms

Loose parts are often associated with play, intriguing and captivating children at any age, but they can also be a vital component to learning. This chapter describes the benefits and potential uses of loose parts to help you understand how to implement this teaching mindset effectively with your students. In addition, we will examine common myths and challenges surrounding the use of loose parts.

Developing a Loose-Parts Mindset

Have you heard the term *loose-parts mindset*? What does this mean? How can we understand and embrace this concept? How can we develop a loose-parts mindset for our students in our classes, school, and community?

In her article "The Arts, Loose Parts, and Conversations," Sheryl Smith-Gilman (2018) asserts that loose parts is "a mindset, a process-oriented approach whereby meaningful conversations emerge unexpectedly and add significantly to

> *"Children need the freedom to appreciate the infinite resources of their hands, their eyes, and their ears, the resources of forms, materials, sounds, and colours."*
>
> —**Loris Malaguzzi**

13

learning." Christine Kiewra and Ellen Veselack (2016), in their article "Playing with Nature," state that learning with loose parts is a way for students to "explore their process, to problem solve together, to negotiate and debate and to have support from a caring adult."

Sheryl Kerr (2017), author of "Why Is Elementary Education So Important?" reminds us that "elementary school is the most important stage for every child, since the child may evolve from a young child to a self-conscious person." Using loose parts to promote engaging play and active learning provides the opportunity for young students to develop and increase their ability to perform better in school and later in life when they face personal and professional challenges. As educators, we need to use the theory and research on loose parts to form our own loose-parts mindset. We need to make sure we present materials, methods, and concepts so that our students can comprehend the topics. We need to find a way to motivate children.

With younger students, many activities need to start as teacher-led instruction; however, students eventually need to become active participants in learning. Engaging children in their own learning increases their focus, motivation, and excitement. A constructivist approach to teaching promotes learning by encouraging students to question, research, explore, assess, and understand. Research from educators across the globe has demonstrated that a student-centered approach lets students fully embrace the class objectives and enjoy the learning process. Using this approach, students "construct their own understanding and knowledge of the world, through experiencing things and reflecting on those experiences" (WNET Education, 2004).

By understanding, applying, and teaching a loose-parts mindset, we can help students learn critical subjects and skills and meet standards.

Benefiting from Loose Parts in the Elementary Classroom

Based on our research and experiences in the classroom, we recognize five key benefits of using loose parts in our elementary classrooms:

- Supporting curriculum and connection to standards

- Developing critical-thinking, problem-solving, and decision-making skills

- Fostering imagination, curiosity, creativity, and wonder

- Improving communication skills and social interactions

- Expanding knowledge and learning

Learning with loose parts provides students the opportunity to think imaginatively and discover different solutions to problems. Students begin to gain an understanding of new concepts through their engagement, experimentation, and curiosity with open-ended items. Loose parts provide "ample opportunities with a wide array of materials to encourage and provoke children in meaningful experiences" (Veselack, Miller, and Cain-Chang, 2015).

Loose-parts play encourages children to explore, experiment, design, create, and construct. It gives them the opportunity to figure out that there are different ways of doing things. It teaches them to be critical of their own creations and to be flexible and resilient when things don't work out. Loose-parts play encourages independent play, self-motivation, and creative thinking (Maes, 2015).

"Children learn most readily and easily in a laboratory type environment where they can experiment, enjoy, and find out things for themselves."
—**Simon Nicholson**

There really is no "wrong" way to play with loose parts. Allowing children to freely play with objects is a very pure form of this type of play, though other applications may include provocations, outdoor classrooms, nature art, and so on. Nicholson mentions verbs as part of loose parts. The possible actions are varied and include experimentation, building, inventing, and exploring. These explorations may even include deconstruction—knocking over blocks, ripping cardboard, and so on—at times.

When children can freely explore and create on their own, they are processing what they are learning. They can experiment, test their own hypotheses, and understand the properties of materials. Children are naturally drawn to this age-old principle of interacting with their environment through playful approaches.

Addressing the Challenges and Myths of Loose Parts in the Elementary Classroom

Using loose parts in a classroom offers proven benefits; however, reservations, myths, and challenges with understanding the purpose and use of loose parts persist. In addition to teachers, many school administrators and families have objections and fears when it comes to using loose parts as a learning tool. Inspired by a 2020 article we wrote for *Exchange*, "Bridging Research and Practice: Seven Loose Parts Myths Busted," let's take a look at a few common myths surrounding using loose parts that relate specifically to learning in the classroom:

1. Loose parts are for play.

2. Loose parts are expensive.

3. Loose parts must be loose or moveable.

4. Loose parts are messy.

5. Loose parts should be organized, arranged, and displayed in divided trays.

Loose Parts Are for Play

Some educators view the use of loose parts as ineffective and a waste of time, but it's important to realize that loose parts are an effective source of learning. Open-ended materials are not just "stuff" in a child's backyard or bedroom but can also be a vital tool in the classroom.

Loose Parts Are Expensive

A common myth is that collecting and buying loose parts is a complicated and expensive process. "While some loose parts items may be expensive, loose parts can adapt to any place, budget, and situation" (Gull, Levenson Goldstein, and Rosengarten, 2020). You can find most loose parts with little effort or cost, locating many just by looking and asking around. A quick review of your current classroom, school storage closets, cafeteria supply room, outdoors, and your own personal home and garage can produce a wealth of loose parts at no cost. And you have the satisfaction of cleaning and organizing your home and classroom—that's a win-win situation!

Loose Parts Must Be Loose or Moveable

Another myth about *loose* parts is they must be just that: loose. Of course, many loose parts that we use in the classroom are loose and moveable, but they do not have to be. Fixed items in our classrooms, outdoor playgrounds, parking lots, and school gyms can serve as open-ended materials and are a powerful addition to the learning process.

Loose Parts Are Messy

Many educators—even those who are not "clean freaks"—are often hesitant to implement the use of loose parts in the classroom because they believe it is just not worth the mess. A common myth is that loose parts are simply junk piled in a corner, overwhelming to look at or motivate children to use, and difficult to clean up. Let us reassure you: With organization and student involvement, cleanup can be a breeze.

Loose Parts Should Be Organized, Arranged, and Displayed in Divided Trays

Who doesn't love loose parts that are attractively displayed and neatly organized? Sure, it is great to have a designated area with plenty of space. Having shelves, storage bins, carts, wall hooks, and display areas is wonderful, but that is often neither possible nor necessary. Getting open-ended materials out, letting children to pick out what they want to use, and cleaning up afterward can be part of the learning process and fun. "While invitations and provocations can certainly have a place in early childhood settings, how we allow children to interact with these [materials] can make a huge difference in discovery and invention as children are permitted to experiment in their own ways" (Gull, Levenson Goldstein, and Rosengarten, 2020).

Sharing Realities of Using Loose Parts for Learning

"Teachers around the world consider elementary education the most important part in every person's educational life" (Kerr, 2017). Do you agree? What can you do in your class and on your school grounds to ensure every student is building the skills necessary to excel?

Our goal is to spark interest and find ways to make classrooms fun and engaging. As educators, we need to capture the attention and interest of our students; this can be a frustrating challenge for both teachers and students. School administrators, fellow teachers, and families may question and dispute the idea that learning can also include play. This is often a reality teachers face when using loose parts—or any other fun, new, and different teaching method.

The benefits of using loose parts, we believe, outweigh any negatives. Divergent thinking can be an obstacle that educators face when implementing new tools or approaches to learning.

Divergent behavior is often discouraged in school when students are scared to say or do the "wrong thing" in class. This system of overt convergence is reinforced by a grading culture that systematically penalizes students for being "wrong" and by allowing a school environment in which students tease those who exhibit nonnormative behaviors (Goodman, 2015).

Opening space for different ideas in the classroom fosters divergent thinking and creativity. Making student learning fun and engaging is an ongoing challenge, but when this approach is successful, the rewards are limitless. Loose parts can be an integral aspect of this process.

CHAPTER 3

Obtaining Stakeholder Buy-In and Building a Loose-Parts School Culture

When you are incorporating loose parts into your teaching practices, you will need administrative support, parental buy-in, and a school community that embraces the concept. To help stakeholders understand loose parts as integral to your approach, you may need to consider professional development and family events that explain the value of honoring different learning approaches and locations, of affordances, and of encouraging divergent thinking.

As teachers, we play a critical role in developing, supporting, and embracing a positive school environment and a culture that benefits all who are a part of that environment. In his blog post "11 Real Ways to Build a Positive School Culture," Justin Raudys (2018) suggests ideas that, we believe, fit perfectly with a loose-parts mindset:

- Create meaningful parent involvement.

- Celebrate personal achievement and good behavior.

- Establish school norms that build values.

- Set consistent discipline.

- Model the behaviors you want to see in your school.

- Engage students in ways that benefit them.
- Create rituals and traditions that are fun for students and teachers.
- Encourage innovation in the classroom.
- Provide professional development for teachers.
- Maintain the physical environment of your school.
- Keep tabs on your school's culture and adjust when necessary.

We are sure most of you already use many of these techniques to create an enriching school environment and culture. Let's consider these techniques through a loose-parts lens and apply them using loose parts to strengthen the culture and values in our schools.

Obtaining Support from Colleagues

Getting support for innovative ideas or concepts from fellow educators, school staff, and administrators can be challenging, especially if you want to expand beyond your classroom walls and share your efforts and ideas with the entire school. Not only is it necessary to obtain this approval and support, but it is also important to promote and seek collaboration.

Invite administrators to see how loose parts are used in your classroom, and provide information on the theories and research behind this approach. Offer ideas and examples of how this learning technique can be applied in other classrooms and throughout the school.

To help employees at her school begin to understand the loose-parts approach, Tricia made loose-parts "gifts" for them. She and the students created items to showcase the students' work with loose parts—a technique that can go a long way. Each week, the class would plan, collaborate, create, and then distribute gifts to

the principal and school staff. In addition, the students designed table decorations for the cafeteria out of loose parts. The students were so excited to come to school, knowing that in the afternoon they would build and display their creations. Some of the staff took breaks at an old picnic table behind the school; the children created

a table decoration for that space too. The staff appreciated this small act of kindness—so much so that they became advocates and collectors of loose parts for the classroom. Who better to collect wonderful materials for your classroom projects? Staff saved egg crates, jars, empty containers, cardboard boxes, cans, old pots and pans, utensils, empty paper-towel rolls, tools, office supplies, and outdoor items in a box that was waiting for the students each week. The children would open the box, discuss how they could use the items, and decide where and how they would store them until needed. On special holidays, the students would also create items that they could easily take home and share with their families.

Enhancing Playful Elements in the School

Rotating and sharing loose-parts items throughout the school can enhance playful and appealing elements and can help maintain (and even improve) a positive culture. The school library, an extra classroom, an empty office or lounge, the media center, or an outdoor area might serve as a central area to collect, store, and check out loose-parts materials. Consider having one person in charge of the space who can help organize and distribute materials. Create a sign-up system for using certain spaces and materials. You can fill tubs of smaller loose parts and rotate them among classrooms to keep the inspiration fresh. Store larger sets such as Rigamajig building sets or a wind tunnel as well as bins of outdoor loose parts so that teachers can check them out for use with their students.

The entire school can also support experimentation in many ways, such as through makerspaces, pop-up play, adventure days, and enhancing the environment. For example, designing a makerspace that the entire school can use goes a long way toward enhancing the environment and promoting a positive culture. "The beauty of a makerspace is that the space is never 'done.' This space should grow with our students, always pulling in new materials and technology so that our students can continually be pushed in their making abilities" (Heavin, 2018). What an exciting way for students in your class and the entire school to share their ideas and creations.

Lego bricks, in particular, can be engaging option that the entire school can use and participate in creating. Consider having a Lego wall in the school common space, on a hallway wall, or in an open space in the library to offer a collaborative space for all to use, add to, and create. If possible, make the Lego wall wide enough to allow several students to work on it at once. Simply attach Lego base plates to a wall with adhesive strips or adhere the base plates to plywood with construction glue. Hang the plywood on a wall and frame it as a continually developing and changing art piece. Smaller Lego walls can also be nestled in a classroom under a chalkboard or on the back of a portable shelving unit. You can put magnetic base plates on a whiteboard or other magnetic surface, and the children can take them off for individual work. These walls can be used for any subject, design challenges, or for family nights. Read on for suggestions to consider for other spaces at your school.

Outdoor Classrooms

Some schools are also taking their classrooms outside as part of the normal school day through a variety of approaches, such as Kinderforest, nature kindergartens, outdoor classrooms, schoolyard walks, school and community gardens, or lessons in the forest. At Merry Lea Environmental Learning Center of Goshen College in Goshen, Indiana, kindergarten students visit the outdoor facility for one full day ten times over the school year. The program integrates the use of sit spots, where students daily spend five to fifteen minutes sitting in the same observation spot in nature. In addition, the program embraces discovery learning, in which students use inquiry to build and discover knowledge, implements unstructured outdoor time (full of natural loose parts), and makes connections to the indoor classroom. Student researchers at the college observed the children and documented

eighty-six connections to English and language arts, science, and math academic standards within just one to one-and-a-half hours of observation. Students met multiple academic standards in physical science, life science, and engineering though the simple activity of making, exploring, and experimenting with mud at the learning center's outdoor facility (Stoltzfus, 2019).

What may look like outdoor play also meets the needed standards of an academic early elementary program. Schools might reserve one day a week, month, or quarter to spend the entire day outside as part of a formal school program. Look around the school property and local neighborhood to find locations to discover and use loose parts. Get to know the school grounds and nearby greenspaces. Are there neat natural hideouts and other spots to visit with students? A quick walk can break up the day, support a specific curricular topic, help get the wiggles out, and facilitate options for learning.

After School

After-school clubs can also be a good option for focusing on play and exploration in elementary schools. After-school loose-parts activities might include explorations such as the following:

- Robotics
- STEM/STEAM
- Tinkering
- Makers club
- Art
- Outdoor play

While these explorations are naturally connected to loose parts, open-ended experiences could be included in any type of after-school programming.

At the Parish School in Houston, Texas, they host an after-school adventure play, which is child-directed play with loose parts. The students oversee their own time, assess what is important to them, learn from their mistakes, and tackle their own challenges. The play is about the experience, not the outcome. During this time, children have the freedom to use teamwork and collaboration to try new things without the timeline and structure of a classroom. When teachers and families take a step back, students realize they need one another and begin to collaborate and create together (Wood, 2020).

Gardens

School and community gardens also can support learning in many ways. Students learn where their food comes from and are often more open to try foods they have grown. They have opportunities to develop their understanding of pollination and other growing processes, and can build persistence and grit (Gull, 2020d).

23

Establishing Family Relationships and Support

Like all new concepts and activities, it is important to inform families and seek their buy-in. Most of the time, they are our biggest advocates and helpers; however, they can also be a stressor when they are not properly informed and do not understand the goal, intent, and meaning behind your use of loose parts (or any teaching concept or technique). Having children go home and state that they played with sticks, empty paper-towel rolls, tiles, or buttons can set off alarm bells for parents who do not understand loose-parts learning. We're sure most of you already have an established method for communication with families, but sending an email, providing information in a newsletter, or bringing it up at a parent/teacher meeting can be effective methods to share your implementation of loose-parts learning. Another effective way that we have used in our classrooms is to have a "Brown-Bag Lunchtime" with parents once a month to inform them about curriculum, philosophy, and application in the classroom. Prior to the meeting, families send in their questions and concerns. We then take time to research, find out answers, and develop our responses. These brown-bag meetings create a cohesive group of parents that can positively inform other families about the classroom activities. As we know, if the parents are happy, the teachers and administrators are happy!

In addition to informing families, it is helpful to celebrate our success and our students' hard work. Allowing families to see the positive outcomes that can occur will enhance the parent-teacher relationship. Make sure you show off student creations as they inspire creativity and learning with other students, grades, and fellow peers. We will explore ideas for celebrating children's work in chapter 15.

CHAPTER 4

Getting Started: Sourcing, Storing, and Managing

Many early elementary educators face challenges in incorporating loose parts and applying a loose-parts mindset in their classrooms. In this chapter, you'll learn how to overcome these obstacles by assessing what you already have; collecting new materials to get you started; and implementing strategies for storing, organizing, and cleaning up.

> "In any environment, both the degree of inventiveness and creativity, and the possibility of discovery, are directly proportional to the number and kind of variables in it."
>
> —Simon Nicholson

Children will naturally interact and explore the materials available in any setting. Typical loose parts available in homes, the outdoors, and classroom settings may include blocks, scarves, natural items, and manufactured items. Think of how a cardboard box and stick can become many things, and both are quite intriguing to a child. Children often find scraps or junk to create their own play. Interacting with loose parts encourages creativity, imagination, exploration, engineering, and artistic expressions.

Plant and Grow a Loose-Parts Plan

Many educators wonder where to start with loose parts, how to collect items, and where and how to store and manage these materials. As you consider adding loose parts to your classroom, think first about your goal, and then think about the distinct phases of planting and growing a loose-parts plan. This approach can be used in any content area to add loose-parts learning to a specific standard, subject matter, or topic. In their blog post for *Inside Outside Michiana*, Carla Gull and Chris Whitmire (2015b) describe how to think through the details.

First, consider your goal:

- Why do I want to do this?
- Who will benefit?
- How does it fit into our work and philosophy?
- Where will children use the materials?

Next, think of the items that children can explore. Create an inventory of what you already have, and then prioritize your needs and explore potential resources:

- What specific items am I looking for?
- What is the purpose?
- What are the safety concerns and risks?
- What materials do I currently have for this purpose?
- What are the most important items to gather first? Why?
- Which items will have the most impact?
- Where can I source loose parts in my community?

As you consider how to grow your collection of loose parts, look at your plans from a practical point of view:

- What costs are involved for these materials?

- Can I find a free source?

- Do I need to develop a budget for higher-cost materials?

- How do I keep the materials ready for use and store them appropriately?

- How will I need to manage and refresh this type of material?

- What needs to be adjusted, changed, or removed from my list of materials?

- What is working well?

Consider Your Goal

In the following example, Carla Gull wanted to expand the outdoor loose-parts options around math with her students.

- **Why do I want to do this?** To have more options to explore and experiment with mathematical concepts in a playful way outside

- **Who will benefit?** The students

- **How does it fit into our work and philosophy?** Math is a required subject, and many adults are afraid of math. If we introduce math concepts through loose parts, students can begin constructing a relationship with math through their natural explorations.

- **Where will children use the materials?** Outside in the outdoor classroom

Create an Inventory, Prioritize Needs, and Explore Resources

Carla inventoried her materials. She went through math bins, outdoor play equipment, her garage, and bookshelves. She found she had some materials but was lacking others.

- **What is the purpose?** The children will be able to explore mathematical concepts through loose parts in a variety of ways.

- **What are the safety concerns and risks?** While supervision is needed, no major safety issues are posed; however, care should be taken in checking materials that might be broken. Choosing more durable materials for outside would also be helpful.

- **What materials do I currently have for this purpose?** Rulers, number charts, rocks, clothespins with numbers, balancing scale, number and clock puzzles, pattern blocks, a garden trellis, large circles, a variety of arrays, dominoes, large wooden dice, mud play materials including measuring cups and spoons, numbered cubes, poker chips, applesauce pouch lids, shapes, mark-making materials

- **What specific items am I looking for?** Carla wanted more math-related tools, such as ten frames, scales, mirrored symmetry books, mirrors, additional arrays, small manipulatives, and books.

- **What are the most important items to gather first? Why?** Carla noticed students had been involved in mud play outside, so she wanted to add mathematical support to this play. Adding measuring spoons and cups, recipes, mark-making materials, and books that talk about numbers and cooking (such as *Feast for Ten*) could really enhance this mathematical play. These items are easy to add, and she already had some available, making it easy to check something off the list and see success.

- **Which items will have the most impact?** The children in Carla's room like to work with large loose parts paired with smaller manipulatives. Carla found inexpensive large, wooden triangles and circles at a school sale. Paired with natural loose parts and a lid collection, Carla thought these items would have the greatest impact.

- **Where can I source loose parts in my community?** Carla thought of the many ways she could source materials—garage sales, online shops, her math cupboards and bins, outdoor play area, her garage, and friends on social media.

Look at Your Plans from a Practical Point of View

After creating an inventory and a list of items she would like and places she could get them, Carla looked at her plans and got practical.

- **What costs are involved for these materials?** Carla wanted scales for the outdoors; she found some on Amazon for $25–$35 each. She wanted a fund that would allow her to purchase inexpensive items at thrift stores and garage sales. She also bought a couple of books.

- **Can I find a free source?** Carla had a lot of things already and just needed to find and repurpose them for this situation. She also put a shout-out on social media for a few things—clean tin cans with smooth edges, takeout containers, button collections, and loose game pieces. Friends also helped collect sticks and applesauce pouch lids.

- **Do I need to develop a budget for higher-cost materials?** She decided that the total should be less than $100, to stay within the amount of the Amazon gift cards she had.

- **How do I keep the materials ready for use and store them appropriately?** Carla made some loose-parts math kits that she kept in repurposed backpacks, which she could easily bring out anytime they go outdoors. She also stocked the outdoor cart with math tools, books, and materials.

- **How will I need to manage and refresh this type of material?** Carla thought she would want to rotate materials every few weeks to introduce additional materials. Additionally, she watched for broken items that needed to be fixed or thrown away. She could also easily change out the math kits for new options.

- **What needs to be adjusted, changed, or removed from my list of materials?** While it would be nice to have a permanent natural scale outdoors, it's not easy to leave things like that outside. Carla bought a hanging scale that she could put up outside and store inside the outdoor cart when not in use.

- **What is working well?** The measuring cups and spoons were a hit. Children have been talking about different fractions and measuring different items outside, such as water, soil, or rocks.

Getting Started with Loose Parts

Time to Create!

- Grab 5–10 random items nearby.

- Explore your materials.

- Note the textures, weight, colors, and possibilities.

- Manipulate and explore this combination of items in some way.

- Sketch and share your creation!

What materials did you use?

What did you notice about your process?

What questions do you have about loose parts?

Did anything surprise you?

What is your takeaway of the loose-parts mindset?

(adapted from Gull, 2020a)

Repurpose Materials You Already Have

Most elementary schools have many items that can serve as loose parts, such as blocks, manipulatives, playground equipment, art supplies, outdoor nature, scarves, and more. For example, you can create manipulative kits for experimentation and play. Go through the classroom closets, check the shelves, and inventory the contents of storage sheds for potential loose parts. What is available on the school grounds that could work? Consider items such as pinecones, sticks, discarded cicada exoskeletons, shells, and pebbles. You can eventually rotate these items into center work, morning bins, and class zones for easier student access. Educators in the Loose Parts Play Facebook group (2020) that Carla Gull administers have shared their observations on using loose parts in the elementary classroom. Here are a few ideas from seasoned educators across the world:

> Cassie Marsh suggests collecting caps, erasers, paper clips and magnets, binder rings, binder clips, and brad fasteners. She says, "I love to keep the spiraled wire from notebooks! I also take apart old pens that no longer work—the ones that click have really interesting parts."

Nicole Gay reflected on her time as a kindergarten teacher, noting that she had all sorts of interesting materials that she reserved for use as math manipulatives. "How I wish . . . I [had] provide[d] those resources for my students to use at their disposal!" She suggests allowing students more access to resources on shelves rather than hiding resources in cupboards. "There were valuable storage areas that could have been used as open shelving with baskets of loose parts and provocations. I think 'old me' was concerned about the mess of so many pieces. Though, when I used the manipulatives for centers, the children did just fine with them as they had a task to accomplish or had been shown how to use them. 'New perspective me' knows there is no 'right' way to learn through loose parts."

Karen Begley's definition of loose parts opens up all sorts of possibilities: "When I think about school supplies, I think of [measuring sticks], ribbons, strings, wooden beads meant for threading, chalkboard erasers, pencils and erasers, metal fasteners, leftover bits of laminating plastic, poster tubes, anything found in the back dusty corners of resource closets—outdated game pieces, puzzle pieces to puzzles missing other pieces. And the gym—safety cones, skipping ropes, balls, bean bags . . ."

As Tracy Rowe shifted to a loose-parts mindset, she realized the flexibility offered by her classroom materials. ". . . EVERYTHING that I had stored in my classroom could have been used in a different way. I would advise just looking at objects from a different perspective."

So, go look through your classroom cupboards, storage rooms, gym, and teacher lounges to see what you can find. When you've gathered some interesting items, feel free to take baby steps and make just a few things available at a time as you try out this approach.

Collect Items to Support a Loose-Parts Mindset

One of the beauties of loose parts is that the materials are often free or low cost. That's a win in our book! From time to time, we also choose to invest in quality items that can be reused repeatedly. Consider being intentional in collecting loose parts; however, having a stash of items without an intended purpose can open additional possibilities. Here are options adapted from a blog post (Gull, 2018a) inspired by the Loose Parts Play Facebook group, with additional ideas by Suzanne Levenson Goldstein and Tricia Rosengarten.

Free and Found Items

Shop your home. You probably have plenty of loose parts right where you are. Items to look for include the following:

- **Craft supplies:** fabric, ribbons, pompoms, buttons, and so on

- **Kitchen items:** stainless-steel bowls, canning-jar rings, silicone muffin cups, muffin tins, ice-cube trays, and so on

- **Electronics:** Old electronics can be taken apart and then used as loose parts.

- **Containers:** baskets, divided trays, old cookie containers

- **Recyclables:** clear plastic containers, lids, egg cartons, plastic packaging, boxes

- **Garage or basement items:** balls, tools, rope, nuts and bolts, washers, and so on

- **Decorations:** seasonal items, potpourri, vase fillers

- **Landscaping materials:** rocks, mulch, sticks, and so on

Often, local businesses will donate items for classroom use. Suzanne used to get tiles of all sizes from the local tile stores for her kindergarten classroom. Many owners are happy to donate their discontinued supplies. Cardboard, too, is something businesses will often donate.

Consider doing a swap with other educators! There are many ways to organize this, such as asking each participant to donate five of a particular type of loose part (wooden items, nuts, bolts, washers, screws, and so on). Then, the participants meet and swap with others. You can easily coordinate this swap online as well.

Put out an ISO (In Search Of) on social media, with specific details on what you are looking for. Community members will often deliver. For example, when we were collecting items to create more engaging outdoor spaces, we asked for tree stumps, landscaping materials, and crates. You can put an alert in many applications to get notified when these things are listed.

We put a free ad in our local community paper for "nature stuff" for children to play with. We were contacted about buckeyes, pheasant feathers, specialty rocks, furs, and more. What a great way to meet people in the community and collect stuff!

Before any family gathering at your school, consider reaching out to family members to solicit loose parts and new ideas. Family members, both inside and outside of your household, can be helpful in adding to your collection. Inform them of your goals, and share specific ideas of what you need. Family can provide an ongoing source of materials. For Tricia, this has become a holiday tradition (and fun contest) for family to give creative and plentiful loose parts.

Know friends who are decluttering? With so many people going the minimalist route, be alert to what they are getting rid of. For example, seniors moving to smaller residences are often happy to know they can pass along useful items.

Carla Gull has a friend, Annette, who is a great scavenger. She loves keeping things out of the landfill and has gathered baskets and baskets of bits and pieces for loose-parts play. We never know what she will bring, but it's always a pleasure to figure it out!

Be open to what others might have available in quantity. Place a box near the entrance of the classroom or school where families can drop things off. Or send home a bag with each child and follow Topal and Gandini's (1999) *Beautiful Stuff!* approach to collecting supplies and for special projects.

Many educators have found success in asking families for specific items needed for a loose-parts project. Cardboard is cheap and plentiful. Families can send in cardboard, or you can check with school staff to ask for some. Cardboard can be used in art, engineering, tinkering, and basically any loose-parts application. When Suzanne taught kindergarten, she often sent letters to families asking them to send in empty paper-towel rolls, broken appliances, plastic tubs, and anything they thought the children would enjoy using to create. When one class made magnetic cardboard games, the teacher supplemented what he had with donations of sturdy cardboard, wood scraps, recyclables, and assorted objects from families. Additionally, families may have unique skills to offer. (See page 235 for a sample letter to parents.)

Nature is a wonderful place to find loose parts, and they're all appropriate to your location. In the United States, we typically can collect fallen leaves for short-term use, bark, sticks, sweet gum balls, acorns, conkers, buckeyes, nuts of all kinds, and so on. We can make tree cookies, slices of tree trunks cut with a chop saw or chain saw. We sometimes find something special, such as a butterfly wing! Steer clear of toxic natural items, such as poison ivy, hemlock, and

33

other toxic plants. Also, in the United States, most bird feathers and nests are protected, so let those be. Think of what is available in your area, as each biome will afford different items.

Get to know the rhythm of your local area to understand what might be available each season. In the fall, for example, consider collecting gourds, pumpkins, straw bales, corn stalks and cobs, acorns, sunflowers and stalks, garden clippings, leaves of all shapes and sizes, and mums. While some may be composted, others might be collected, displayed, or stored for future options.

Low-Cost Items

Whatever you call them, garage sales, yard sales, tag sales, and boot sales are great sources of loose parts. We look for wooden items, baskets, gardening tools, scoops, books, bowls, arts supplies, scarves, decor that has many pieces, blocks, frames, and so on. Often, toward the end of the sale's last day, sellers want to get things moving, so they are more willing to bargain.

Thrift stores are also good places to look for lost-cost items. Watch for their seasonal collections, such as after-Christmas offerings. Raid the kitchen area for mud kitchen and art items and sorting trays, and consider games and toys as well. They often have half-off days to make items even cheaper.

Building-reuse thrift stores, such as Habitat for Humanity ReStores, can offer interesting items. We never quite know what to expect when we stop at a ReStore. We can typically find tiles; molding, which can be cut down for ramps or decorative elements; cabinet doors, which we use as frames or signs or trays; lots of nuts and bolts and other metal items; signs and sign lettering; fake flowers; and much more!

Some areas have local nonprofits that collect donations and castoffs from artists, businesses, and community members. In Indiana, for example, there is a teacher "store" that K–12 educators can visit once a month for free. In addition to notebooks and school supplies, they collect packaging and other items that teachers can use in their classes. If you do not have a local creative reuse store, plan to visit one when you travel. We have collected plenty of inexpensive, unique odds and ends by driving twenty minutes extra on our vacations. Just look up creative reuse stores in the area you're planning to visit.

Discount stores, variety stores, five-and-dimes—whatever you call them in your area—are inexpensive sources of seasonal items, rocks, glass pebbles, felt pieces, containers, tongs, trays, and so on. We often check the seasonal section, children's toys, party supplies, and the kitchen area.

Craft stores, such as Michael's and Hobby Lobby in the United States, will have table scatter (the festive, often acrylic, items scattered on party tables), seasonal items, peg people, wooden cutouts, glass pebbles, shells, rocks, clay, and much more. They typically have large bags of inexpensive wooden miscellaneous items too. Check the clearance and after-holiday sales, and use a coupon to get a significant percentage off. Online stores and craft sites sell all kinds of things, such as tree cookies, wooden acorns, animals, wooden cutouts, and so on. A few stores, such as Casey's Wood Products and Woodcrafter, specialize in wooden products. Oriental Trading Company also sells many unique items.

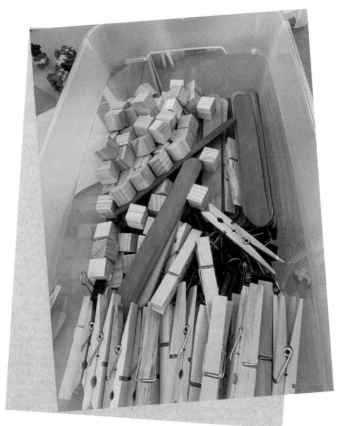

When you have something specific in mind, or you know you will need a material repeatedly, consider making or growing it. Carla asked for a chop saw for Christmas one year so she could make tree cookies whenever she wanted. Consider investing in some basic tools (even a hand saw will do) so you can make some of the loose parts you desire. With the help of a volunteer, Carla made ramps for an outdoor classroom for about thirty dollars when they typically cost more than three hundred dollars for a set.

Some loose parts can be grown in your personal or school garden. Think of sunflowers, pumpkins, gourds, flowers, and so much more! Some community gardeners and friends may be willing to let a class borrow dried beans or corn to shell.

Higher-Cost Items

If you need something that it a bit more expensive, budget for it. There are many catalogs that are starting to sell higher-quality loose-parts materials. Watch for after-season sales and use grant funds for those items. Use our Plant and Grow worksheet on page 233 for ideas on planning for grants and getting funding for higher-ticket items.

· CHAPTER 4 ·GETTING STARTED: SOURCING, STORING, AND MANAGING

Review Your Loose-Parts Collection

As you gather items and receive donations, consider how you might put these loose parts into rotation and how you will store and manage them. Consider a regular time for intake, such as once a month or once a quarter. Then gather your educator friends and colleagues, and share the workload and joy of discovery. The following suggestions are adapted from a podcast episode by Carla Gull (2019), with additional comments from Suzanne Levenson Goldstein.

Designate a Collection Place

Having a specific spot to corral items is so helpful. As already mentioned, you can place a box at your classroom door or at the front of the school where families can put donations. Carla sometimes uses a large, clear plastic jar to collect small loose parts. She sorts the contents later or uses it as a junk-jar resource. Suzanne asks families to bring in donated items in large trash bags and put them in her classroom workroom for sorting later.

Inspect and Clean Donated Items

Before you offer materials to the children, inspect the items for safety hazards and applicability. Enlist parents and other volunteers to help do safety checks. Look for sharp edges, pointed objects, or other items that may pose an issue, and put any that might be dangerous into the recycle bin. You may decide that some items are not suitable for use in your classroom, even though they are not dangerous; these can go in a box to donate to a more appropriate cause. Other items may be recycled or go right in the trash.

Many items will need cleaning. Have a quick soap-and-water wash available in the classroom sink, and set up a drying area. Use a mesh bag for smaller loose parts and run them through the dishwasher.

Sort the Materials

Sort the items into broad categories tailored to your classroom needs; for example, we often use wood, metal, plastic, or specific uses for the classroom. As you sort the items, put them in containers that allow you and the children to see the contents. For example, large plastic animal-cracker containers allow you to see the contents and have lids. You could use several empty boxes with the top flaps cut off. Some educators like empty tennis-ball cans; take the label off, and you have clear storage for small items. Clear plastic shoeboxes and drawer organizers are great for storage. Suzanne has used clear candy bins (found in grocery stores) to sort and display loose parts. Teachers are often very resourceful with tubs and containers—use what works in your classroom.

Consider Storage Strategies and Options

Storing and organizing loose parts in the elementary classroom can take many forms, and we have used almost all of them. The easiest are the natural loose parts in the outdoor classroom or play yard that children find. No need to store or organize—just let children find and play with them!

As much as possible, store loose parts where they will be used; for example, store blocks in the building area. Consider a loose-parts corner or area. One area of the classroom or "zone" could be the spot where loose parts are freely available. These might be stored on open shelving in baskets or bins for easy access throughout the day. You could create additional centers or zones tied to a specific curricular or interest feature, such as materials to explore magnetism or electricity. Children could use and store the corresponding loose parts in large tubs in those areas. One educator has a loose-parts shelf where items are within in reach but not out on the tables; children can access the materials if needed. She says, "I do try and help sort out that area because I want it to look inviting and appealing, and I want everyone to see what's there and feel welcome to use it."

If you have a central storage area for multiple classrooms, rotate and share loose parts with other classes. If you're lucky enough to have a large pantry or storage space attached to your classroom, you could store the materials there. Some schools set aside an extra classroom for a "game" room or other ideas. Why not make it a loose-parts or experimentation area? Try rolling carts for mobile loose parts, and use sheds for outdoor storage.

Manage the Collection

Once you have built up your loose-parts collection, think about which materials will have the most impact on your class, and make those accessible on open shelving. Organize the materials around usage, or categorize them around STREAM. Consider keeping a master list of the items to track what is available.

Consider your maintenance plan. Regularly review the loose parts available for safety, cleanliness, and suitability for your program. Let go of items that no longer serve your classroom needs or are ready for the trash or recycling can. Include students in taking care of the loose parts.

Build on Children's Schemas

Consider the concept of *schemas*, which are repeated behaviors allowing children to explore and develop ideas. Children naturally use a variety of play schemas, including:

- **Trajectory:** exploring how things and themselves move, such as building a ramp and trying to get different objects to go down or up the ramp

- **Rotation:** curiosity in things that spin or rotate, such as drawing circles or finding things that spin

- **Enclosing:** creating enclosed spaces, such as building a fort out of desks and fabric in the classroom to read inside

- **Enveloping:** wrapping items with material such as fabric, paper, paint, or scarves

- **Transporting:** moving items from one space to another, such as a child who carries a small bucket filled with nature treasures from spot to spot outside

- **Connecting:** connecting or joining things together, such as using boxes and tape or dot to dots

- **Positioning:** careful placement of objects in lines or patterns, such as when sorting objects by different characteristics or lining them up

- **Orientation:** looking at objects from different viewpoints or angles, such as using a mirror to investigate a tree or using magnifying glasses to see things up close (Baker-Jones, 2010)

Children often use loose parts in connection to these repeated behaviors. For example, dumping and pouring is a typical early childhood activity, and offering loose parts to scoop and pour facilitates this natural exploration tendency.

Children will show different play schemas during their sessions with loose parts. Pay attention to the ideas they are developing so you can plan materials to support this type of play. In the Loose Parts Play Facebook group, educators gave examples of supporting schemas in the classroom. Sheila Schaffer advises, "Observe your group. Are they into things that spin? Provide items with wheels or lazy Susans that provide a spinning action. Then sit with the children and ask the questions why, how, and what if. Ignite their curiosity so they see something more than just the item. It's amazing when you take the time to build on the philosophy of loose parts and not just think you have to put out a ton of stuff." Amy Muir says, "Sometimes it's a tornado in here. It depends on where the play takes us, really. Sometimes my kids like to set up amazing creations and then a 'storm' comes. Destruction. Everywhere. But that's just part of it." Crystal Black suggests, "When a dumper dumps a basket of loose parts, provide them with a cardboard tube or piece of gutter, and encourage them to slide the pieces back into the basket. Making the cleanup as fun as the dumping might help."

Manage the "Mess"

One challenge that often comes up with loose parts is the "mess" that happens because of the play, interaction, and experimentation. But is it really a mess? Some describe it as play residue, evidence of play, play aftermath, or play debris. It's all in how you look at it. No matter what you call it, consider the following cleanup tips, as recommended in the Loose Parts Play Facebook group and as reported in a blog post by Carla (Gull, 2018e), with additional tips by Suzanne.

- Start small.
- Make it fun.
- Use defined spaces.
- Use tools to help with cleanup.
- Make cleanup part of the process.
- Be aware of phrasing and wording.
- Consider having a "dump" basket or bin.
- Leave some to come back to.
- Use spaces to your advantage.
- Consider your educational philosophies.

· CHAPTER 4 · GETTING STARTED: SOURCING, STORING, AND MANAGING

Start Small

Consider using larger loose parts outside as a starting point. Encourage children to develop good habits with cleanup before you move these materials inside. Slowly add loose parts into the classroom, as children become more accustomed to the idea of using these materials in open-ended ways. Limit the amount to what is manageable for your students. Allow playful experiences, then gradually increase the amount of materials available as children show responsibility and care in handling them.

Make It Fun

Cleanup can be an enjoyable part of the play and learning process. Some educators only have one major cleanup each day, designating certain children to clean up areas, pulling all items into a central location for sorting into bins, playing I Spy to help children focus on items to put away, actually throwing the items into the bins, and making cleanup part of the transition. Put a fun song on during cleanup time; for example, Suzanne had the children sing the "Clean-Up Song" as they straightened the classroom.

In the Loose Parts Play Facebook group, many educators shared advice on making cleanup fun. Cara Ruffo learned a technique from her dad. She designates one or two items as "secret magic scraps" during pickup. The student who picks up a secret magic item might win a prize or get a chance to shoot a basketball at the class hoop. She also might add another magic scrap if she sees an especially hard worker. Dee Ann Perea asks students if all of the "fun" is back in its place and ready for more exploring tomorrow.

Use Defined Spaces

Many educators limit the space used for loose-parts play and learning. A rug, a large tray or pan, or a table can define that space. Use different levels, trays, and surfaces to define spaces for exploration. Keeping the materials in one zone can make cleanup easier.

Use Tools to Help with Cleanup

Using child-sized tools, such as a broom and free-standing dustpan, allows students to sweep items into one place, sort, and put them away. Some teachers use a small garden rake to gather items or even use a shop vac with a sock on the hose end for collecting items for sorting. Provide appropriate containers for the items as well.

Make Cleanup Part of the Process

While some see loose parts as a "mess," creating class routines to use, put away, and retrieve loose parts can be a way to allow the creativity and problem solving of using loose parts in the classroom while also having a system to use the materials. Work with students to set and maintain expectations. In the Loose Parts Play Facebook group discussion, Shelli Patt mentions, "Instead of trying to control the loose parts mess, make clean up a meaningful part of the activity. The children were just as engaged with sweeping up the pompoms as they were with taking them out to begin with." In her Explore Inspire EC blog post, Shelli also encourages us to notice the learning taking place during this process.

> What looked like a mess to my teacher eyes at the beginning was her process. Her organization, and her plan. If I used my adult power to stop her process, and put my process in its place, what would I be teaching? That my ideas and my plans are more important than hers? That her concepts and problem solving aren't valued? Or maybe, that she shouldn't even seek solutions in the first place, because a person in power will simply direct her (Patt, 2018).

Cleaning up can be part of that valuable learning process for children.

Be Aware of Phrasing and Wording

Transitional phrases can be helpful to encourage tidying up. In the Loose Parts Play Facebook group discussion, educators suggested the following transitional phrases. Nina Moench mentions, "It looks like you want to move on to . . ." to help children think about what's next. Then she reminds them that the blocks need to go back the baskets before they move on to the next activity. She offers to help them put materials away. Another educator, Sherryl Allen, uses the term *reset* to remind students to put the classroom back to its typical standard state so the environment is ready for play. Similarly, Mads Ferris uses, "It's time to refresh our environment." Annie Hosking says she "frames cleaning up as getting ready for the next thing, e.g. clearing away stuff from a table because we need to get it

ready for lunch. Finding the right home for an object so that we know where to find it next time. Clearing the floor so we have room to sit for a story." If you find that a child is having a tough time letting go of something she has built, offer to take a picture of the creation; this can be good for documentation purposes as well.

Consider Having a "Dump" Basket or Bin

Do loose parts always need to be sort out in individual baskets? Provide an "extras" box or bin for the bits that can be more thoroughly sorted once a week. Having a big bin of things not sorted allows for the "hunt" for the perfect item they will need and for exploring a variety of objects. In the Loose Parts Play Facebook group, Julie Crouch mentions, "We always end up with a box of odds and ends that got missed as we have to tidy and pack away each day, and it usually ends up being their most interesting box to look through the next morning."

In outdoor spaces, some elementary schools have the children put the loose parts back in any order in large rolling garbage pails at the end of recess. This allows the students to optimize play and have a quick cleanup (Almon, 2017).

Leave Some to Come Back To

Some projects will take ongoing commitment rather than just one play session. Consider designating a works-in-progress shelf or area, or make signs that children can put by projects that they are still working on. In the Loose Parts Play Facebook group, Shelli Patt advises, "There's also the process of teachers helping children figure out the difference between an ongoing work that they're coming back to, and something they aren't. Those conversations are all part of the process of children learning problem solving and planning skills."

Use Spaces to Your Advantage

Consider the setup of your classroom or outdoor space, as educators suggested in the Loose Parts Play Facebook group. Sue Gray suggests, "Have a look at the layout of your environment. See what [loose parts] seem to gravitate to where. A few tweaks in room layout really helps. We have a construction area next to the den. They often build walls to enclose themselves. A lot of our small loose parts are under/next to a ridged table, so the children tend to use this for creative mandalas and pictures, and natural items are close to sand and water. They are free to move things around but seem to have organised themselves."

Megan Burrows likes to have specific routines and labels. She relates, "Everything needs a place, maybe with photo label. I definitely think you need to be doing it a couple of times thru the day—maybe before lunch and at end of day because too much clutter and mess is overwhelming and creates chaos. We delegate areas and put on a song, which gets everyone going."

Consider Your Educational Philosophies

We each have different educational philosophies that affect how we clean up our classrooms. Consider your own philosophies that shape your management style and how you might enhance this even more, as educators remind us in the Loose Parts Play Facebook group. Natasha Kocher relates that she let go of the idea that the space "needs to be tidy all the time." Shelli Patt reminds us to consider "what it is that draws you to use loose parts with children, and what your intent is that the children will do with them. As you can see from the variety of comments, what is considered a 'mess' is related to educational philosophy and framework and perspectives about teacher['s] and child's roles in the environment."

Some educators, such as Cynthia Nahia, follow a Montessori approach: "Work in a designated area . . . when they are done they put it back." Amy Muir believes in letting children take an active role. She relates, "If I ask one or two children to be in charge of [a classroom] area, they do a wonderful job putting things where they think they should go. They seem to be working on sorting things in different ways. And whatever system of organization they use, everyone is able to find everything next time. So I try not to be particular in this kind of thing."

Cathy Chalklin notes, "Cleanup needs to be balanced between necessity and respect. Every environment is different in terms of factors that limit or control what needs to happen. Shared space, inclement weather (if outdoors), multi-age settings, need of space to be cleaned (carpet or floors), etc." She advises that if it's possible to leave a structure or work in progress where it is, then do so. "We need to guide and support them in the same way we do their play . . . [c]hoice, time, opportunity, and with developmentally appropriate expectations," Chalklin says.

Sue Gray says, "I look on the tidying away as part of the learning process and also an area in which the staff can interact with the children, developing all aspects of learning. Sorting, separating, counting, noticing and discussing as you do so—always allow extra time for this aspect."

Marc Armitage shares, "The playwork answer to this would be, just tidy up as you go! We don't ask children to tidy up after themselves, for various reasons—we see it as our job and, therefore, we tidy as we go." He also suggests just starting play with random piles rather than carefully arranged materials, noting, "[N]eatness and tidiness are the enemies of self-directed play, and therefore this is always going to be tricky!" Playwork is rooted in the adventure-playground movement, in which children are encouraged to use scrap materials to build whatever they can dream up. Playwork principles recognize children's inherent capacity for development when given many opportunities and play options. The principles list that all children need play, play should be freely chosen, playwork supports play, playworkers advocate for play over adult agendas, playworkers support children in building a space for play, playworkers are aware of how they affect the space, and playworkers intervene as needed in ways that will help enhance and extend play (Playwork Principles Scrutiny Group, 2005). What can we learn from the playwork philosophy to use in our classrooms?

There are many "right" approaches to cleanup time. Mel Staff suggests, "It often comes down to what suits an individual group too. You have to find what is best for your group. From year to year, I find a difference in what I can make available for each group." Use appropriate strategies according to the children's interests, what is happening in the classroom, and how much you can tolerate the creativity.

Think about Next Steps

As you finish reading this chapter, consider your situation. What might work for your space and your students? Take a minute to list a few ideas you are already doing, some you might like to implement soon, and others that would be helpful to keep in your back pocket for future use. Use the Planning for Loose Parts form on pages 233–234 in the appendices to note your ideas.

CHAPTER 5

Safety in a Loose-Parts Environment

Researchers Rebecca Spencer and colleagues (2019) considered the perceptions of educators on the benefits and challenges of loose-parts play. They found that one of the potential challenges is educators' apprehension, especially when they first introduce loose parts.

Children's safety is so important. It is critical at home, but even more care and responsibility are required and necessary with a classroom full of students. Although exploring boundaries and taking risks may be learning tools, we must be safe and compliant with our use of loose parts—especially in elementary classrooms. General safety concerns apply to the use of loose parts with all students; additionally, specific concerns based on your location and school, the grade you teach, and the subject under consideration will apply. The goal of loose parts is to provide different and diverse "stuff," but as you know with elementary-aged students, they will find a way to taste, touch, throw, and tear apart anything put in front of them!

Do the benefits of using the loose parts outweigh the risks? To ensure safety using the loose parts, teachers can complete a benefit-risk form, which takes into consideration any risks while reinforcing the benefits to the children. We adapted our benefit-risk assessment from a risk-benefit form (Ball, Gill, and Spiegal, 2014) available on Play Safety Forum's Playlink website (https://playlink.org/risk-benefit-assessment-form.html); you can make adjustments to fit your circumstances. In addition, Playlink offers other risk-benefit assessment forms.

BENEFIT-RISK ASSESSMENT FORM

Benefits:
specific, positive outcomes;
consider social, physical, emotional,
educational, psychological, and so on

Risks:
- hazards
- potential injury
- environmental factors

Local factors:
- accessibility
- relevant site-specific issues
  (supervision, access, size of site,
  and so on)
- policies
- strategies

Precedents and/or comparisons:
consider similar situations and
how those educators deal with the
situations

Decision:
- proceed
- adjust
- cease

Actions taken:
- none
- remove activity
- increase supervision
- monitor benefits/risks
- meet with parents

Ongoing management and monitoring
(attach additional sheets as needed):
- maintenance schedule
- inspection protocol
- reviews of accidents/injuries
- user feedback

Additional expertise:
- if needed
- risk management

Practical tips for using loose parts safely include the following:

- As adults, we need to spend time playing and experimenting with the options before we offer them to the students.

- We must make sure to have enough space, choosing a different area or scaling loose parts smaller, as necessary.

- We should tape or rope off a designated area where students may explore riskier loose parts.

- We must leave plenty of time for children to explore. Don't make loose-parts explorations a one-day experience.

- We must be patient.

- We need to give children time and space to solve problems and figure things out (Gull, 2020k).

Safety Tips

When creating activities, make sure you evaluate the loose parts you provide to ensure they are not dangerous, and make sure you monitor all use. Student-led learning does not mean that you are not an active participant and mentor in students' learning. It is important to teach the students how to safely use each item and the expectations that go along with it. Here are a few safety tips to evaluate loose-parts activities.

- **Know your students.** Gradually introduce additional loose-parts options as you know the interests and capacities of your students. Some teachers may start with fewer options and add more as students show their capacity to use the loose parts in safe ways. Be aware of students who may still mouth materials, and limit smaller items around those children. No list of safety suggestions can replace understanding your students' specific capacities and needs; know your students' allergies and medical needs.

- **Choose developmentally appropriate loose-parts options.** Be aware of where students are developmentally to choose options that may be appropriate. Younger children may not be ready to use more specific tools. Older children might be ready to explore more, with proper training and supervision.

- **Share expectations and boundaries.** If using loose parts outside the classroom, identify boundaries of where the children and loose parts may go, using visual cues to help designate the space. For instance, use tree tape or brightly colored cones to show the space allowed. Or simply say the children must always be able to see the teacher and the teacher must always be able to see the child. While we typically choose more rugged materials for play, delicate items may require that you set expectations on the treatment of the material. Consider having some consumable materials that could be used for destructive exploration or self-initiated craft projects. Options may include dried leaves, cardboard, newspaper, or decomposing stumps. Specific items may need specific guidelines; for example, sticks need to hit other sticks rather than people if used in this context. We often say "stick to stick" as a reminder.

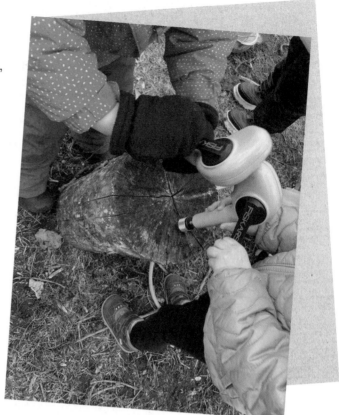

- **Plan ahead for group conflict.** As a class, set general expectations of being respectful of the materials, space, and other people. Strategically plan groups as needed for specific loose-parts projects. Consider using cooperative learning techniques or roles as the need arises.

- **Teach students how to use tools.** As Theresa Casey and Juliet Robertson (2016) mention in the *Loose Parts Play: A Toolkit*, tool use allows children to open additional options in creativity, gain skills, and increase self-assurance. Tools might be used for cooking, gardening, tinkering, textiles, or constructing items at school. Educators should understand how to use the tools and should consider the interests of students and their ability to use the tools. Generally, introduce tools gradually, manage and store tools and materials regularly, and implement a benefit-risk assessment plan (Casey and Robertson, 2016).

- **Use care when tinkering.** If your class is using old appliances to take apart or to reuse resources, be sure to cut off the electrical cords before giving them to the children. Use disposable gloves or wash hands after interacting with materials that might contain lead.

- **Use proper safety gear.** Some activities may need safety gear, such as hand coverings or safety glasses. Activities that involve pounding or sensitive chemicals should include eye protection. Monitor all use and activities.

48

- **Consider having one teacher monitoring one risk.** When higher-risk activities such as using tools are taking place, have a specific teacher monitor the activity. One adult would only supervise the tool use; another adult would supervise other children.

- **Use designated areas for riskier options.** For example, if children are using ramps and balls or small catapults to explore velocity, use cones or rope to partition off that area and direct the play so the projections go to a space away from other children. Periodically stop the play to give the children time to collect their projectiles.

- **Do a benefit-risk assessment.** For items that may have a bigger risk factor, do a deeper analysis of using the item with the students. Complete a list of benefits of using the item, any potential risks, and ways to mitigate the risks. For example, if you're considering using tools, think about the benefits, such as learning skills, students being able to express themselves, sense of accomplishment, and building confidence.

  Consider potential hazards, such as eye injury, cuts, smashed fingers, and so on. List ways to mitigate the hazards, such as having a designated area to use the tools, training on using the tools, having close supervision of tool use, using eye or hand protection, and having an emergency plan in place in case something more serious happens.

- **Help children assess risk on their own.** Children often can negotiate their own risks. Our vocabulary can help them think through potential danger. The Child and Nature Alliance of Canada (2017) has a great list of phrases and questions to use in the six categories of risky play: great heights, high speed, dangerous tools, dangerous elements, rough-and-tumble play, and locations where children can disappear or get lost. They suggest asking questions such as, "What's your plan with that big stick?" or "Before you throw that rock, what do you need to look for?" Backwoods Mama (2018) also offers a list of phrases to foster awareness, including "Notice how," "Did you see . . .?" and so on. She suggests phrases to encourage problem solving such as, "What can you use?" and "How will you. . .?"

- **Evaluate for broken pieces, excessive use, and items that cannot be cleaned.** Do a regular maintenance check with students, and discard or mend any items that have sharp points, are worn out, or are past the point of cleaning.

- **Clean and sanitize regularly.** Some materials will need regular cleaning and sanitizing, depending on your needs, materials, amount of use, and so on.

49

- **Seek classroom safety tips and feedback from fellow teachers.** When trying out a new loose- parts option with your students, seek common concerns and tips for safety from other educators who have used these materials with their students. For example, when Carla worked with a group of children making magnetic cardboard games, she noticed how the teacher set up a designated cutting area where he was the only one allowed to use the cutting tools. He used painter's tape to mark off the area, and no children were allowed inside. Use online groups and teaching forums to ask questions and seek feedback.

- **Be aware of hazards.** Minimize choking, strangulation, and suffocation hazards for younger children through careful selection of items and clear supervision. Remove button batteries, small magnets, allergens, poisonous plants, sharp points, and broken items. Regularly check items, and supervise play to ensure safety. If possible, clear poison ivy and other plant irritants in regular outdoor play spaces, and teach children to identify and avoid these while visiting other areas. With older children, use some items, such as button batteries, only at designated times. If you plan to send these items home, alert families and remind them to supervise.

- **Prepare for a possible emergency.** Have a plan if there is an emergency. For example, when we go outside, we always take a small first-aid kit, a cell phone, and emergency numbers. Follow the standard emergency protocol for your setting.

Accidents can happen in any setting, no matter how many rules we have in place. Use a commonsense approach of knowing your students, conducting regular maintenance checks, being sensitive around or avoiding hazardous materials, and being prepared for emergencies. While we cannot bubble wrap students, we can help them grow in their skills, awareness, and capacity to negotiate risk in their lives and loose-parts interactions.

A helpful resource available online is the "Health and Safety Recommendations for Natural Materials and Loose Parts in Childcare Settings" (2018) from Alberta Health Services (https://www.albertahealthservices.ca/assets/wf/eph/wf-eph-recommend-natural-materials-childcare.pdf). A quick online search can also produce many tools and checklists you can use or tweak to fit your goals for student learning.

In the next chapter, we offer suggestions for the role of the teacher in supporting loose-parts explorations, and we look at methods of evaluation and assessment techniques.

CHAPTER 6

Refining the Role of the Educator

For teachers, running into former students and discovering they are successful, hardworking people is especially gratifying. Has a former student ever reached out later in life to thank you or seek your advice? Have you had the opportunity to teach the children of your former students? Although it might make us feel a bit old at first, it is such a rewarding feeling to know the positive impact we can have.

Our role as educators is vital to the development of our students. It is our responsibility and privilege to mentor children and help them to develop the skills necessary for academic, personal, and professional success. We help to cultivate children to become the best possible version of themselves. In addition to teaching basic facts and information on a variety of subjects, we are also responsible for teaching students critical-thinking, decision-making, and problem-solving skills. As Rebecca DeLuccia-Reinstein (2020) puts it, "[T]he teacher's role incorporates a multifaceted sense of purpose intended to encourage a child's social development." Our work is important! Teachers encourage wonder, experimentation, and exploration. Rachel Carson (1956) affirms the important role of adults in children's learning: "If a child is to keep alive his inborn sense of wonder, he needs the companionship of at least one adult who can share it, rediscovering with him the joy, excitement, and mystery of the world we live in."

The Role of an Educator in Loose-Parts Play

Four key elements help to instill and develop knowledge in students: space, time, materials, and teachers. We have control over these elements, and it is important that we embrace and apply our role as educators. As highlighted in the STREAM content chapters (chapters 9–14), there are many options for providing interactive and informative learning experiences using loose parts. Successful loose-parts play in both the indoor and outdoor classrooms should include flexible spaces, multiple options for exploration, maximum discovery time, and abundant loose-parts materials. In addition, teacher support (not direction) is an important aspect of learning with loose parts.

When implementing experiential lessons, it is helpful to monitor and evaluate our own teaching techniques and roles as educators to ensure student success. Researchers Christine Kiewra and Ellen Veselack (2016) stress that too much direction can hinder creativity: "There are many supporting roles that educators take with children, ranging from observing from a respectful distance to being fully immersed in the child's play. The most supportive role is one that balances the two extremes." Additionally, Kiewra and Veselack describe the following qualities and practices of an educator in a loose-parts environment:

- Asks open-ended questions that further scientific inquiry

- Allows ample time for deep exploration

- Observes children's play to see and document learning

- Supports student processes and thinking to enhance learning

- Follows children's lead without taking over

- Trusts students to make decisions

- Promotes children to view other perspectives and learn about problem solving

- Supports a sense of wonder

- Offers an abundance of loose parts

- Allows flexibility and freedom to use spaces and materials in unintended areas or ways

Eric Nelson (2012), in his book *Cultivating Outdoor Classrooms*, adds the following roles:

- Monitor

- Intervener/adjudicator/protector

- Facilitator

- Information provider
- Mentor/guide
- Provocateur (asker of *What if?* questions)
- Supporter/supplier
- Program organizer/designer

Nelson advises that we can support child-created activities by recognizing and accepting through careful observation and listening, by identifying children's needs through proximity and asking questions, and by fostering self-support. Teachers can supply material support, information, and psychological support. We can describe what we observe, pose provocative questions, and respond to the children's questions (Nelson, 2012).

Cas Holman (2020) says that guiding and supporting play and investigation requires observation, resisting the temptation to take over or fix things, and encouraging students to be documenters and recorders of their work. We need to scaffold children's learning by sharing language and rules around using loose parts in the classroom, creating time and space for reflection on what works, and challenging students with questions and deeper exploration.

Evaluating and Assessing Loose Parts in the Classroom

It is important to evaluate and assess the use of loose parts by your students. "In all areas of education, and in other sectors, we are being asked to demonstrate 'impact,' to produce evidence of student learning" (Bamber and Stefani, 2015). As children use loose parts to spark imagination and creativity, teachers need to assess the knowledge gained. In his book *School and Society*, John Dewey (1942) discusses the value of open-ended materials in supporting children's curiosity, planning, persistence, and imagination:

> *Take the example of the little child who wants to make a box. If he stops short with the imagination or wish, he certainly will not get discipline. But when he attempts to realize his impulse, it is a question of making his idea definite, making it into a plan, of taking the right kind of wood, measuring the parts needed, giving them the necessary proportions, etc. There is involved the preparation of materials, the sawing, planing, the sand-papering, making all the edges and corners to fit. Knowledge of tools and process is inevitable.*

By going through the exercise of building a box, the child follows his own interests, develops perseverance, exercises discipline, overcomes obstacles, and learns about the world (Dewey, 1942).

Nicholson (1971) asks,

- What did children do with the loose parts?

- What did they discover or rediscover?

- What concepts were involved?

- Did they carry their ideas back into the community and their family?

- Out of all possible materials that could be provided, which ones were the most fun to play with and the most capable of stimulating the cognitive, social, and physical learning processes?

Here are a few more reflective questions to consider when evaluating loose parts in your classroom:

- Are students engaged?

- Are they learning the concepts?

- Are they expanding their knowledge and understanding?

- Are they meeting standards and the 4Cs (collaboration, creativity, communication, and critical thinking)?

- Are they fulfilling goals and objectives?

For example, a group of four children has created a block city including other loose parts, such as little people, trees, houses, and cut-up paper labeling the various parts of the scene. In addition, two other children have written a script for a skit, using the block-city scene and other props. We used Nicholson's questions to evaluate the learning.

- **What did children do with the loose parts?** The children created a block city and wrote a skit.

- **What did they discover or rediscover?** They discovered how to work collaboratively. When they created the hills in the city, they explored gravity. They also noticed spatial relationships.

- **What concepts were involved?** Creating the block city, using unit blocks, meeting language arts standards in listening, speaking, reading, and writing

- **Did they carry their ideas back into the community and their family?** Yes, some of the children in the group had their family members take pictures of their creations at home.

- **Out of all possible materials that could be provided, which ones were the most fun to play with and the most capable of stimulating the cognitive, social, and physical learning processes?** This question can be asked of the children.

In another application, two children used a bin of loose parts and wrote math problems. The bin held various loose parts, including pompoms, sticks, stickers, ribbons, and chenille stems. The children discussed how to use the parts to create addition problems that equal ten. For example, they chose and laid out two ribbons, four pompoms, and four stickers. Then, they wrote the equation $2 + 4 + 4 = 10$. Suzanne evaluated the learning with Nicholson's questions.

- **Are students engaged?** Yes, the children were engaged for fifteen minutes.

- **Are they learning the concepts?** Yes, the children wrote five equations that equal ten.

- **Are they expanding their knowledge and understanding?** Yes, the children used two sets to add together to equal ten. In addition, the children used three sets to add to ten.

- **Are they meeting standards and the 4Cs (collaboration, creativity, communication, and critical thinking)?** Yes, the children worked collaboratively and communicated to write the equations that they created. They used critical thinking to think of the problems.

- **Are they fulfilling goals and objectives?** Yes, the first-grade math standards were addressed.

Assessment Options

Learning can be assessed in a variety of ways. Assessment doesn't always have to be in the form of a test or a paper-and-pencil activity.

- **Observations:** When children are engaged in play, observe and write notes. Suzanne likes to use index cards on a clipboard. She uses an index card for each child, and when she sees something, she writes it down. Carla often uses label stickers or sticky notes on a clipboard for each child and writes down her observations. You can also use an assessment form, such as Nature Notes from Nature Explore, which has space for a sketch of the loose-parts creation, a check box for the zone of the outdoor classroom, and room to record a summary of the interaction and specific quotes from children (Kiewra and Veselack, 2016).

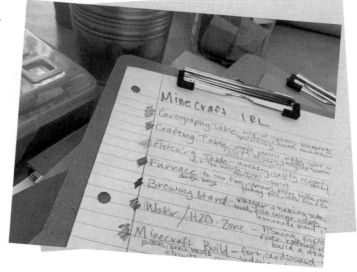

- **Presentations:** When children do presentations, have the learning standards for the grade level written on a piece of paper. (See the recording sheet on page 58 for an example.) Check off the completion of a standard as it occurs. For example, speaking is typically one of the language arts standards, so that one can be checked off when a child does a performance or a presentation.

- **Projects:** Like presentations, projects offer opportunities for noting the standards met. For example, when learning about reptiles, children created a reptile out of many different loose parts. Then, each child wrote some facts about the reptile and shared that information with the class. Suzanne checked off each language arts standard as a child demonstrated mastery.

- **Experiments:** Observe the children in their play and experimentation with loose parts.

- **Simulations:** Let students use an online program to test their ideas electronically. For example, PBS Kids has an app called Play and Learn Science. Students can digitally create a simulation of a ramp series and test it out. The teacher can check the simulation to verify that it works, and students get immediate feedback on their designs.

- **Open-ended questions:** Ask the students lots of open-ended questions, such as how they came up with their plan, how they collaborated with other students, and what they might improve or change for next time.

- **One-on-one discussions:** Suzanne likes to have one-on-one discussions with students to allow them to explain their loose-part creations. She usually asks questions such as, "What materials did you use?" "How did you think of that idea?" "What did you discover?" and so on.

- **Authentic assessment:** Observe the children in their play and experimentation with loose parts. Again, know the grade-level standards so you can check off mastery of applicable standards for each child. This is an effective form of authentic assessment.

- **Student self-evaluation:** Students often enjoy sharing their loose-parts creations with the class. They can describe their creation, how they made it, what their inspiration was, what challenges they encountered, and so on. The other students can then ask questions of the student who is sharing. Group assignments work similarly; Suzanne gives each student a grade-appropriate rubric and the students do a self-evaluation on their project.

- **Video recording:** Ask the students to write reports about their research for their projects. Afterward, they can deliver the reports orally. Record all of their oral reports to create a video. Review the video and evaluation and assess the standards met by each student.

- **Written composition:** Use the check-off list of standards, and check the mastered standards as children share stories, plays, or word problems they have written.

- **Assessment form:** Create your own assessment forms listing the standards that you are required to teach. As children master those standards, mark them off.

- **Student portfolios:** Encourage the children to keep samples and photographs of their explorations in portfolios. In Suzanne's school, teachers keep most of the children's writing in a portfolio. At the end of the year, the children choose the three samples that they want to pass on to their next teacher. This approach can be adapted to your local needs.

Assessment Form

The following is an example of a recording sheet that can be used to assess students based on standards. This document reflects the Common Core English/Language Arts Standards in the Literature strand. You can alter this document by simply replacing the standards, grade-level goals, and district objectives you need to assess.

Grade 1 English/Language Arts Standards: Literature

Name:_____ Date: _____

Type of assessment used:_____

STANDARD	LOOSE PARTS USED	PROJECT COMPLETED	NOTES/ OBSERVATIONS
1.1 Ask and answer questions about key details in a text.			
1.2 Retell stories, including key details, and demonstrate understanding of their central message or lesson.			
1.3 Describe characters, settings, and major events in a story, using key details.			
1.4 Identify words and phrases in stories or poems that suggest feelings or appeal to the senses.			
1.5 Explain major differences between books that tell stories and books that give information, drawing on a wide reading of a range of text types.			
1.6 Identify who is telling the story at various points in a text.			
1.7 Use illustrations and details in a story to describe its characters, setting, or events.			
1.9. Compare and contrast the adventures and experiences of characters in stories.			
1.10 With prompting and support, read prose and poetry of appropriate complexity for grade.			

(National Governors Association Center for Best Practices and Council of Chief State School Officers, 2010)

The following is a sample assessment form using the book *The Gingerbread Man* (any version). Note that not all of the standards are mastered using this book. However, the same assessment can be used at another time for the student to master other English/Language Arts standards.

Assessment Form for Grade 1 English/Language Arts Standards: Literature

Name: _____Margaret_____ Date: _December 15, 2021_

Type of assessment used: _____Authentic_____

STANDARD	LOOSE PARTS USED	PROJECT COMPLETED	NOTES/ OBSERVATIONS
1.1 Ask and answer questions about key details in a text.	Felt, paper-towel tubes, googly eyes, markers, chenille stems, yarn	Holding up the student-created puppets, the child could answer questions about the story.	Child was able to answer questions about the story.
1.2 Retell stories, including key details, and demonstrate understanding of their central message or lesson.	Paper-towel tubes, felt, googly eyes, markers, pipe cleaners, yarn	The students created puppets to go along with the book *The Gingerbread Man*. The student retold the story, using the puppets.	Child created all of the characters from loose parts. Child retold the story using the same story sequence, expression, and vocabulary.
1.3 Describe characters, settings, and major events in a story, using key details.	Shoe box, construction paper, leaves, sticks	The children created the setting of the story with loose parts.	The child asked other children to collaborate on the setting.

Student Self-Evaluation Form

The following is an example of a record sheet a student can use as a self-evaluation form. This form would be used after a child has completed a project.

Student Self-Evaluation Form

Name:_____Date: _____

Today I made_____.

I made it during_____.

Here is my picture:

I used these items:

_____

_____

I feel proud that I

_____

Next time I will

_____

I discovered

_____

The following is a sample self-evaluation form using the book *The Gingerbread Man* (any version).

Student Self-Evaluation

Name:_____ *Margaret* _____ Date:_____ *December 15, 2021* ____

Today I made_____ *The Gingerbread Man puppets and the scenery* _____.

I made it during_____ *reading time* _____.

Here is my picture:

I used these items:

_____ *Felt, Googly eyes, Paper scraps, Shoebox, Construction Paper,* _____

_____ *Scissors, Buttons, Glue, Leaves, Sticks* _____

I feel proud that I

_____ *I feel proud that I made all of the puppets with the help from Mason. We worked together.* _____

Next time I will

_____ *Next time I will ask Jorge and Shanelle to help me too.* _____

I discovered

_____ *I discovered that it was a lot of work but we worked on it for a week.* _____

Recording Sheet

This recording sheet can be used and adapted for any subject or observation of children. Note the loose parts that the child/children use, any specific standards or schema, quotes of what the child/children say, and notes to describe what learning is taking place. Consider making one specific with the standards for a topic in a subject matter, such as geometric concepts within math, that you could observe as the child/children interact with loose parts.

RECORDING SHEET				
Student Name	Loose Parts Used	Schema/ Standard	Quotes	Notes

(Gull, 2020a)

The following is a sample recording sheet used to note the learning of four children, each exploring different loose parts and investigating different concepts and skills.

RECORDING SHEET

Student	Loose Parts Used	Schema/Standard	Quotes	Notes
Jake	Leaves, wind, body	Rotating	"I'm flying away!"	Look of joy on the child, spinning round and round in the sea of leaves and wind
Carsten	Sticks, tweezers, clothespin, array, acorns, acorn caps	One-to-one correspondence, positioning, fine-motor skills	"I have 3 acorns in three rows. That's 3x3. 3+3+3. I have 9 acorns!"	Used tweezers to put sticks in holes on array, gathered acorns in outdoor play space, lined up acorns in rows
Eden	Blocks, cardboard tubes, marbles	Orientation, slope, speed, velocity, perseverance	"My marble falls off the ramp at the corner. I have an idea—what if I put something so it doesn't roll out?"	Kept adjusting the angles of her tubes to get the marble to the end, placed and experimented with a block to bounce the marble back into the next tube
Lydia	Sticks, dirt	Fine-motor skills, literacy, mark making, self-identification	"I can write my name! L-y-d-i-a!"	After playing with a stick, she found she could make marks in the dirt. She drew an L and then continued with her name.

Exceptional Needs and Loose Parts

Another important aspect in our role as educators is to assess potential mental, physical, and behavioral concerns. "Learning and development disorders are conditions that interfere with a child's ability to process information and acquire skills in language, speech, reading, and/or mathematics" (Child Mind Institute, 2020). Loose parts can help identify exceptional needs that may go undetected. Loose parts can also be a great tool for noticing concerns, challenges, learning disorders, and trauma our students may be facing, as well as for noticing the special needs of gifted children.

For example, an educator noticed a child in her class repeatedly lining items up or repeatedly running loose parts over the grate in the classroom. This behavior was a cue to observe these behaviors in more depth, consult with the family, and start a formal special-needs referral. While repeated behaviors are typically not a concern, in some situations they can give insight into a child's possible exceptional needs.

By evaluating and assessing student behaviors and actions, we can identify risk factors and overall developmental delays that might interfere with positive learning and development. Additionally, loose parts allow students to interact with materials in developmentally appropriate ways for the child, allowing a good match for all children in the classroom.

In the following chapters, we explore how to apply a loose-parts mindset to our classroom and STREAM subjects, and we offer ideas for celebrating the children's loose-parts explorations and sharing their work.

· SECTION 2 ·
APPLYING
AND
TEACHING
A LOOSE-PARTS MINDSET

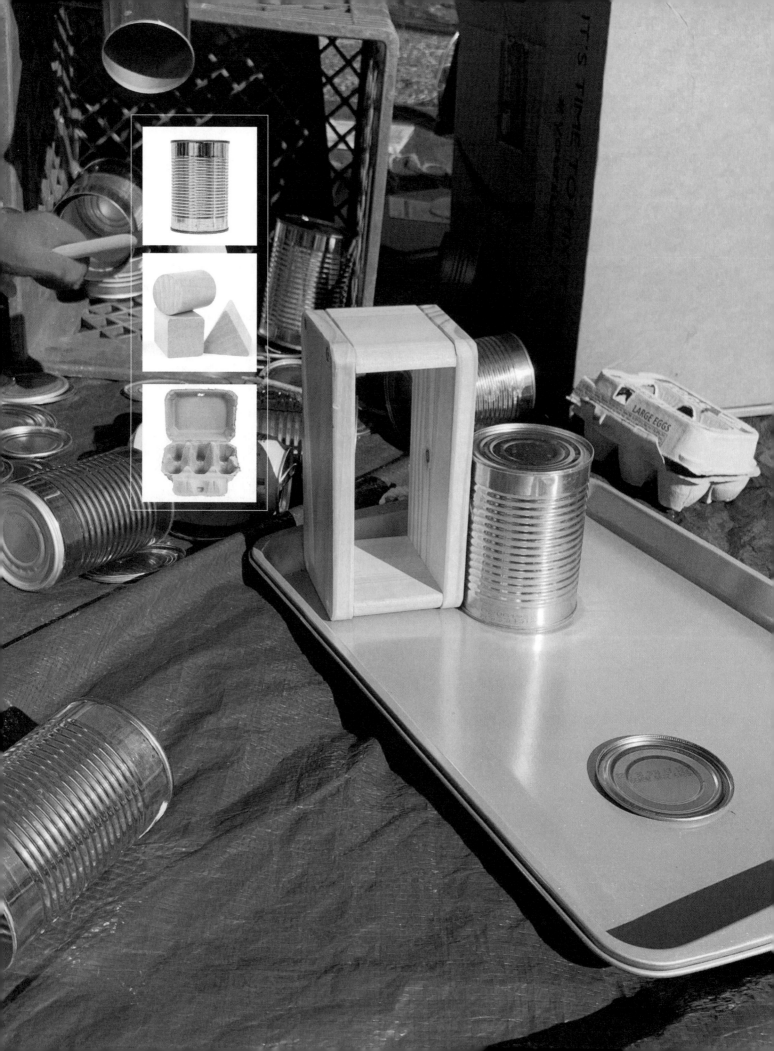

Loose-Parts Applications

Education requirements and standards continue to evolve and change, so it is critical that we expand our teaching methods to meet, and even exceed, expectations. Teachers often say that they don't have time for play or loose parts in their early childhood classrooms. We assure you that loose parts can be an integral part of the classroom, enhancing the curriculum and meeting state standards. Researcher Leigh Roche (2018) explains that providing an appropriate learning environment, materials, and experiences for the young child that correlate with the curriculum standards will create quality early childhood programs.

"The wider the range of possibilities we offer children, the more intense will be their motivations and the richer their experience."

—Loris Malaguzzi

This chapter demonstrates how to connect a loose-parts mindset to curriculum standards and how to use a variety of approaches to loose parts and learning. We explore the various educational philosophies in which loose parts can be easily integrated into lesson plans, how to address STREAM in the classroom, and how to transform sample lessons to a loose-parts approach.

67

Connecting a Loose-Parts Mindset to Standards and Approaches

When considering using loose parts in your classroom, you might think to yourself, "If I integrate loose parts into the mathematics curriculum, how am I going to guarantee that I am teaching the required standards?" Using a workbook from the school district or state-adopted math or reading series doesn't ensure that your students are mastering the standards. Good teaching requires that multiple teaching methods be used to enable all learners to achieve the standards. When teachers use a variety of visual, auditory, kinesthetic, and tactile activities, students with various learning styles will have an opportunity to master the required grade-level standards or objectives. "As teachers prepare to instruct, they need to consider many factors: the content, their students' previous knowledge and learning styles, their own teaching styles, and so on" (Wolfe, 1987).

As you become familiar with the concept of loose parts and consider them in the context of your grade-level standards and course objectives, you will probably start brainstorming about many materials that you can collect to enhance learning. It is exciting to think beyond the worksheet while integrating loose parts into content-area lessons.

Many different learning theories can easily include loose parts. Please use the philosophies that suit you and your school district, and adapt accordingly. We include the following for your consideration:

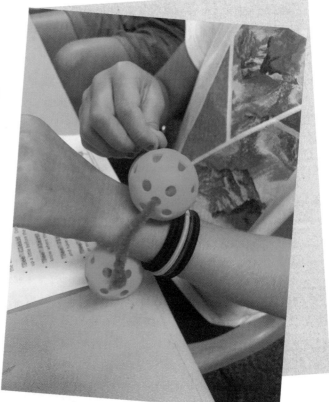

- Constructivism

- 5E instructional model

- Place-based education

- Problem-based learning

- Project-based learning

- Inquiry-based learning

- Emergent curriculum

- Direct-teaching model

These learning theories offer students "some choice, time, and measure of autonomy to support deeper, meaningful learning that leads to skills and knowledge critical for the modern student and world citizen" (Buchanan, Harlan, Bruce, and Edwards, 2016). In addition, we include the Madeline Hunter Direct Instruction lesson plan, which can be adapted for use with loose parts in the content areas.

Constructivism

Many philosophers have developed constructivist, active-learning, student-centered educational theories that support the love of lifelong learning. Jean Piaget (1923/1926) posited that children learn through experience. John Dewey (1942) expounded that children learn by doing. The Reggio Emilio philosophy developed by Loris Malaguzzi promotes the idea that learning should be student centered, where students construct their own knowledge, are self-directed communicators and collaborators, while the class environment is a key component (Edwards, Gandini, and Forman, 1993). Malaguzzi expressed that active learning and play is important for learning. Maria Montessori (1912) believed that children learn best by actively exploring materials independently.

In her article "Benefits of Constructivist Learning Design," Grace Dover (2018) agrees: "Constructivism is a learning theory that emphasizes student agency through self-guided exploration, reflection, and evaluation." The following list describes the benefits of constructivist curriculum design:

- It's active.

- It promotes student agency.

- It develops advanced skills such as critical thinking, analysis, evaluation, and creation.

- It promotes diverse viewpoints.

- It encourages students to reflect, evaluate their work, and identify intermediary skills to acquire based on their needs.

- It reflects our modern world's vast access to content (Dover, 2018).

In a constructivist classroom, the focus tends to shift from the teacher to the students. The classroom is no longer a place where the teacher "expert" pours knowledge into passive students, who wait like empty vessels to be filled. In the constructivist model, the students are urged to be actively involved in their own process of learning (University College Dublin, n.d.). When loose parts are included in the lesson plan, the students are empowered. Students can use their knowledge and test new ideas while experimenting in class activities.

5E Instructional Model

The 5E instructional model "promotes collaborative, active learning in which students work together to solve problems and investigate new concepts by asking questions, observing, analyzing, and drawing conclusions" (Lesley University, n.d.). The five *Es* are *engage, explore, explain, elaborate,* and *evaluate.* Loose parts fit easily in the explore phase of this type of lesson plan.

Place-Based Education

Loose parts can be incorporated nicely into place-based education, which emphasizes hands-on learning. This philosophy can be integrated into the content areas across the curriculum (Getting Smart and Teton Science Schools, 2017). Place-based education—also referred to as place- and community-based education or place-conscious learning (Smith, 2017)—is an approach to curriculum development and instruction that directs students' attention to local culture, phenomena, and issues as the basis for at least some of the learning they encounter in school.

Problem-Based Learning

"Problem-based learning is open-ended and encourages students to engage with a real problem that is often led by student interests and curiosities" (Getting Smart and Teton Science Schools, n.d.). Students are provided a topic, work collaboratively with others, and solve problems for which sometimes there is no one correct answer (Campbell, 2014). Loose parts can be an integral part of this approach.

Project-Based Learning

In this type of learning, students experience structured teaching that leads to a project in which they consider a real-world problem, set goals, and participate in finding information and developing a solution. Loose parts can fit easily into this approach. "Students explore real-world problems and find answers through the completion of a project. Students also have some control over the project they will be working on, how the project will finish, as well as the end product" (Campbell, 2014).

Inquiry-Based Learning

Inquiry-based learning (IBL) is another philosophy that lends itself well with using loose parts. "IBL allows students to make determinations about . . . problems, challenges, and issues they investigate, helping move students toward meaningful engagement and deeper learning" (Buchanan, Harlan, Bruce, and Edwards, 2016). The parts of this approach are design, interaction, clarification, and questioning. The interaction segment can be the perfect stage to include loose parts.

Emergent Curriculum

Loose parts can fit in a classroom where emergent curriculum is the philosophy. The University of Toronto (2017) describes emergent curriculum as ". . . based on the premise that children are most successful at learning when curriculum experiences account for their interests, strengths, needs, and lived realities." In this curriculum, learning is based on children's interests and active participation. For example, if some children are interested in airplanes, then the teacher can provide many different loose parts for children to create their own airplanes. In addition, the teacher can add airline uniforms, trays, seat belts, headsets, and other props and open-ended materials to the dress-up area so children could create a dramatic play with the planes they make.

Hunter's Seven-Step Lesson Plan

Educator and psychologist Madeline Hunter developed an approach to creating lesson plans built around seven steps (Hunter, 2004), which represents a direct-teaching model:

1. **Anticipatory set:** What is the "hook" to draw the students into the lesson?

2. **Objective/standard:** State the objective and/or standard for the lesson.

3. **Input, modeling:** Impart new knowledge and model a concept using loose parts.

4. **Check for understanding:** Ask students how they will use loose parts to investigate a concept and develop understanding.

5. **Guided practice:** Practice understanding using a different loose part.

6. **Independent practice:** Have the students use loose parts to complete the lesson.

7. **Closure, recap:** What did you do or learn?

For example, when a teacher demonstrates during the input stage of the lesson, she can use loose parts. Then, during guided practice and independent practice, students can use loose parts to demonstrate understanding of the concept or objective.

- **Anticipatory set:** What is the "hook" to draw the students into the lesson?

  In groups, have a tub of magnets, nonmagnetic items, and magnetic pieces of metal for the children to explore for five minutes. Ask the students what they notice about the magnets and how they interact with materials around them. Allow them to make observations and ask questions about the magnets.

- **Objective/standard:** State the objective and/or standard for the lesson.

  3-PS2-3. Ask questions to determine cause-and-effect relationships of electric or magnetic interactions between two objects not in contact with each other.

  3-PS2-4. Define a simple design problem that can be solved by applying scientific ideas about magnets (Next Generation Science Standards, n.d.).

- **Input, modeling:** Impart new knowledge and model a concept using loose parts.

    Scaffolding on observations from the "hook," share concepts and vocabulary around magnets with examples. Consider watching a video on magnetism to understand these concepts.

    Terms to use: *repel, attract, north pole, south pole, magnetism, ferromagnetic material, magnetic field lines, compass*

- **Check for understanding:** Ask students how they will use loose parts to investigate a concept and develop understanding. Have students show the concepts and vocabulary with the magnets and loose parts at their tables. Share with a partner.

- **Guided practice:** Practice understanding using a different loose part. Show how a magnet can connect two different magnetic metals, using table or chair legs and other magnetic materials in the classroom. Allow students to try this as well. Show how a magnet can help move magnetic materials from one place to another. Allow students to try this.

- **Independent practice:** Have students identify problems or issues in the classroom where magnetism could help. Allow them to explore and experiment to come up with a magnetic option to solve a problem in the classroom. Options will vary but might include using magnets to create a game, move things from one space to another, move items without touching them, leave a note on the pencil sharpener, position posters on the whiteboard, create a lunch check-in on the back of the metal door, create a magnetic sculpture to add beauty to the room, or other needs the children identify

- **Closure, recap:** What did you do or learn?

    Travel the room and ask students to share how they solved a simple classroom issue with magnets, reiterating vocabulary and concepts as needed.

Addressing STREAM in the Classroom

We hear a lot about science, technology, engineering, and math (STEM) in the elementary classroom. However, many educators are looking to include reading and art to create STREAM. We feel that both reading and art are important content areas to include in creating a balanced curriculum. In addition, all these subjects can benefit from a loose-parts mindset. We approach STREAM in the context of this book as separate subjects, organized by chapters; however, STEM concepts are interdisciplinary. Learning with loose parts is not a siloed approach to one subject; instead, using loose parts often includes a holistic approach to learning, making, and doing.

It is important to allow the students to manipulate different materials and discover concepts on their own. For example, if you know that one of your grade-level standards is to teach sorting and classifying, letting the students discover ways to sort and classify loose parts is more exciting and engaging than doing a workbook page. Children discover important concepts as they manipulate materials, and learning comes to life!

It is easy to adapt a lesson plan to include loose parts. You can choose from among a variety of lesson plans; just be sure to use the lesson plan that is approved for your school and/or school district. First, become familiar with your grade-level standards and objectives. Next, write out your lesson plans according to your school's or district's requirements. Look for opportune places where loose parts can be integrated to allow for different learning modalities. Try it out and integrate slowly into one content area. When you feel comfortable, try expanding using loose parts to another content area. Continue to add loose parts to each content-area lesson plan you implement. Consider using the following planning sheet to adapt a lesson plan.

Standard:

Objective:

LOOSE-PARTS CYCLE PLANNING SHEET	
Stage	**Observations and Decisions**
Ask: What is the problem? What can I explore? What can I do? What am I curious about? What is this? How can I use this?	
Imagine: What are the possibilities?	
Play: Try various options.	
Experiment: Test your solutions.	
Improve: How can you make it better?	
Share: Share and celebrate.	

(Gull, 2020a)

Set the stage with a variety of dramatic-play materials in bins for each group in class—fabrics, scarves, costumes, props, and simple accessories. The following is a cycle planning sheet used to develop a lesson plan around retelling a story, which is a Common Core English/Language Arts Standard.

SAMPLE LOOSE-PARTS CYCLE PLANNING SHEET

Standard: CCSS.ELA-LITERACY.RL.1.2
Retell stories, including key details, and demonstrate understanding of their central message or lesson" (National Governors Association Center for Best Practices and Council of Chief State School Officers, 2010).

Objective: Retell a story.

Stage	Observations and Decisions
Ask: • What is the problem?	In groups, students talk about how they might explore and retell the story *Stone Soup*, with the props.
• What can I explore?	As students discussed the story, they realized other options in the room might be good for retelling their story. They grabbed a pot and wooden spoon from the cart with outdoor items.
• What can I do?	The children started testing the materials to see how they might work for the portions of their story. They tied fabric around their waists and found objects to represent the various vegetables.
• What am I curious about?	The students started thinking about how to have wood for their fire. They remembered there was newspaper from the recycle bin and wondered what they might do with it.
• What is this?	The children explored the newspaper—opening, folding it, and rolling it.
• How can I use this?	They realized rolling the newspaper made it seem like the round logs they see when making a campfire.

SAMPLE LOOSE-PARTS CYCLE PLANNING SHEET

Standard: CCSS.ELA-LITERACY.RL.1.2
Retell stories, including key details, and demonstrate understanding of their central message or lesson" (National Governors Association Center for Best Practices and Council of Chief State School Officers, 2010).

Objective: Retell a story.

Stage	Observations and Decisions
Imagine: What are the possibilities?	While students had basics of how they might use the items, they also needed to imagine how they might retell the story, what details they should include, what the main point is, and so on. They chatted about different ways of moving their bodies and using their voices to retell the story.
Play: Try various options.	They played around with the materials and their ideas, trying a few ways of expressing their story. Someone thought they should all be animals like in one version of the story, so they tried to see if they could make it work. They settled on one approach after experimenting with several options.
Experiment: Test your solutions.	They did a trial run with their teacher, retelling the story of *Stone Soup* with their props, materials, and imaginations. The teacher liked their use of materials and asked them to think of how they might make it better, specifically asking about their stone.
Improve: How can you make it better?	The children knew the stone was an important part of the story, almost magical. Before they just put a small stone in the pot. They thought about ways to make it seem magical, such as wrapping it up, saying special words when introducing the stone, or coloring it in a special way. They decided to use special fancy fabric to wrap the stone up to signify its importance.
Share: Share and celebrate.	The children retold their improved story to other students in the class, highlighting the moral of the story, emphasizing the importance of the stone while making soup and then picking up another stone as they left town. The teacher recorded the story and was able to share with families to celebrate the students' success.

It is worth the time and effort to integrate loose parts into STREAM content areas. You will see highly engaged, active, and empowered learners. Our suggestion is to take it slowly; perhaps concentrate in one curricular area at a time. Take one area where you feel proficient and choose that subject as a starting place for integrating loose parts into the content-area lessons. Once you are feeling comfortable using loose parts in that area, expand to another, and then another.

It takes a little adjustment and creativity to think about ways to include loose parts across the curriculum. But once you do, you will see that the possibilities are endless.

CHAPTER 8

The Class Environment

The class environment sets the stage for the mood, tone, and learning of our students. Many aspects of the class environment transcend grade and subject matter and can be great vehicles to promote loose parts, creativity, and imagination in our classrooms. In this chapter, you will find a smorgasbord of options for enhancing your classroom with loose parts, including morning baskets and tubs, a loose-parts shelf or area, a Beautiful Stuff project, junk jars, provocations or stations, block and other play zones, and ideas for homework options. Many of the suggestions in chapter 3, such as a Lego wall or makerspace, will work well at the classroom level as well.

Loose-Parts Zone

Some educators set up a shelf or zone of loose parts within the classroom. These items may be used in any subject across the day, as part of free-choice time, for early finishers, or for indoor recess. A loose-parts zone could simply be a shelf with baskets of rocks, sticks, blocks, shells, metal pieces, plastic items, and textiles. You could rotate the items as needed or set them out all year. Additionally, other zones or areas within the class can always include loose parts.

Loose-Parts Starts

Some classrooms are moving away from morning worksheets to morning baskets or tubs. These can be connected to a topic that the class is studying and filled with loose parts for exploration and experimentation. Carla started making "loose-parts starts" that students can use in whatever way they prefer, strengthening creativity and diverse thinking (Gull, 2020f). They are easy to put out and put away again and are great for easing transitions.

Carla creates loose-parts starts containing magnets and magnetic and nonmagnetic items, wooden pieces with recyclables and mixed-up building toys, and traditional brain toys such as Plus-Plus. She suggests breaking down larger sets of materials into smaller groupings and using manipulatives and items already on hand. Also, consider gathering rocks and random items, small cups, and dollar-store craft items. These loose-parts starts can be theme based and include, for example, miniature items for small-world play and arts-and-crafts materials. For example, Carla has several bins of small items where students can create an outdoor playscape. The bins include miniature characters, blocks, crates, building logs, fabric scraps, food pouch lids, trees, corks, Lego windows, ribbons, chenille stems, craft sticks, and so much more. In groups, children work together to use the items to re-create a scene, tell a story, design a playground, or experiment with materials. You can even create individual options that will fit into plastic pencil boxes, which are easy to transport, fit easily on a desk, and hold a good amount of personal materials.

To get them started each morning, first-grade teacher Christina DeCarbo gives her students about eight to ten minutes to "explore, create, build, and, dare I say it, play" with containers of loose parts—which she calls "brain bins" (DeCarbo, 2021). Her routine, based on ideas by Montessori, Erikson, Piaget, and others, is an easy way to set the stage for great thinking. This approach allows young children to be children, build creativity, practice social skills, develop critical thinking, and enhance language skills. To manage the brain bins, she rotates six bins each morning in her classroom and switches the materials approximately every six weeks. Options for the brain bins include Dado Squares, Brain Flakes, Magformers and other magnets, Bristle blocks, Squigz, pattern blocks, Keva planks, Lego bricks, and playdough (DeCarbo, 2021). As the children explore the materials, they have a chance to listen to the morning announcements and get ready to think and learn during the day in a stress-free way.

Valerie, author of the All Students Can Shine blog, suggests simply putting out a different tub for each group every morning and allowing the children to choose a table where they can sit as they get warmed up. She asks that the children choose a different group each day. When a timer set for ten minutes dings, the students quickly put everything back into the storage tubs and put them away. She uses TinkerToys, tangrams, snap flakes, magnet sticks and balls, cups, dominoes, K'nex, geoboards, and other items for her bins (All Students Can Shine, 2017).

Another teacher, Catherine Reed, author of the Brown Bag Teacher blog, noticed that her students exhibited more divergent thinking and used math manipulatives in unique ways when they used the manipulatives as loose parts. While some educators are worried about the time it takes to use the bins, Catherine noted that her students are excited to play as they enter the room and quickly go through routines, so they don't waste learning time. In this class, bins are often filled with math and literacy manipulatives, and students can explore them in a variety of ways. This nonthreatening approach allows time for exploration and experimentation without "getting it right." Students build communication skills as they collaborate and work together for a short time each morning while also building skills in the content areas. Magna-Tiles, story cubes, letter tiles, base-ten pieces, marbles/marble runs, plastic links, and other items can be great options for the bins. The morning tubs also become instant indoor recess options as well (Reed, n.d.). Additionally, experiment with random loose parts and/or natural items in bins and see what the children do with the materials inside. The options are endless.

Class Rewards and Inside Recess

Many classes use class rewards, movies, or special activities to celebrate an achievement or offer an incentive. Why not turn these into options for play and loose-parts exploration? Use materials from the morning tubs, bring out the cardboard, or try an open-ended STEM challenge in place of a passive reward or recess options. For example, when an educator observes the students doing something good, such as helping clean up, the teacher can give the class a letter (writing it on the whiteboard or pinning a cutout letter to a bulletin board). As the teacher observes more positive behaviors, she can give another letter and then another. Eventually the letters spell the word *cardboard*. The class then celebrates with cardboard activities. Another idea to implement when students earn extra recess might be to take out bins of fabric, wood scraps, and other loose parts for part of the play. During rainy day recess, allow students to use the loose-parts starts as part of their play. If a lesson is finished early, children can access the loose-parts options in the classroom. Additionally, brainstorm with the students for their ideas on including loose parts in classroom rewards.

Junk Jars

One approach to loose parts is to simply have a large, recycled jar for bits and scraps of stuff. Junk jars are classic loose-parts play as we think of children scrounging for scraps of stuff from which to create. The jar might be filled with old marker caps, repurposed packaging waste, scrap wood or fabric, chenille stems, ribbons, corks, home-improvement samples, clothespins, and so on. The jar can be available for collecting items in the classroom as well as used for creating and building. It could be a part of a tinkering station, a center or station used during free-choice time, or morning baskets, or as an option for early finishers. The open-ended nature of junk jars means the materials will work for a variety of situations, from creating art and visual stories to helping solve math problems. Consider having several junk jars to allow one per table or group.

Sensory Bins

While there are many great sensory-table options, a sensory bin can also be a large wooden or plastic tub, an empty drawer, a kiddie pool, or an underbed storage container. You can fill sensory bins with a variety of items, such as pea gravel, sand, soil, or water, and keep things interesting by adding in three or four types of items, such as plastic animals or characters, glass pebbles, tree cookies, pinecones, or sweet gum balls. Include one or two types of tools for the children to use, such as small buckets, paintbrushes, scoops, measuring cups, or plastic or paper tubes.

Sensory bins can be incorporated into centers or stations. A sensory bin might be correlated to a particular concept or standard within the classroom. In kindergarten, sensory bins can be part of a math center, with measuring cups and other tools to use to explore volume, length, and so on. A science sensory bin in a first-grade classroom could be a container of nuts, bolts, washers, and other magnetic and nonmagnetic items, along with a variety of strengths of magnets. Bins can also be seasonal or holiday based, or they can connect to a story by including letters, words, and items mentioned in the story. The possibilities are endless and allow open-ended discovery and exploration.

Block Play

Blocks, and the loose-parts add-ons the children can explore with them, can be a great option past preschool. Block play can help children nurture and develop a variety of other skills that are important to their overall development and success. The skills listed below are just a few examples of the learning opportunities block play provides children (Kaplan Early Learning Company, 2021).

- **Social-emotional skills:** working with others, taking initiative, respecting others

- **Language and literacy skills:** learning new vocabulary, exchanging ideas, naming buildings

- **Social studies skills:** learning about the community, understanding people and their work, role playing

Blocks are such a versatile learning tool, spanning subjects from mathematics to literacy. Keep block areas in elementary classrooms as long as possible. As one teacher put it:

I LOVE when children make a connection between what we are learning in the classroom and their exposure to certain materials! My kindergarteners are learning about castles and all that entails—crenellations, drawbridge, portcullis, watchtower, keep, and so on. Some of my students built [a castle] using unit blocks yesterday! They then labeled the parts of the castle using sticky notes! It is so exciting to see learning in action! (DeLanghe, 2019)

Homework Choices

While many schools are moving toward minimal or no homework, if you do assign homework, giving open-ended choices centered on loose parts and experimentation can be a great idea Consider offering a homework choice board related to loose parts.

LOOSE-PARTS HOMEWORK CHOICES

We LOVE loose parts! How many choices can you do? Remember these are starting points—make it your own! Snap a picture and share it with your teacher.

Make a face with found objects. Try it another way.	Fill a shallow bin with water. Add scoops and other utensils. Play!	Build your own fort! Will you use blankets, pillows, boxes, sticks, or something else?	It's Not a . . . Choose an object and brainstorm new uses. Try an idea!	Take apart an old appliance (with permission). Have an adult cut off the cord first.
Find the biggest box you can! How might you use it?	Experiment with the wind. What might you need? Perhaps string, ribbon, or a paper bag?	Dig into the recycling bin! What can you make?	Pull out the blocks. What else can you use with them?	Create our own nature art. Look at art by Andy Goldsworthy or Chelsea Bahe's Take 'Em Outside Facebook page for inspiration.
Combine toys or building sets. What happens with new combinations?	Make a musical instrument from nature or things you use in our space.	Experiment on your own! What can you do with objects around you?	How many ways can you use a stick? Write a list.	Can you make a ramp for something to slide or roll down? Is there another way you might do this?
Find rocks! Can you tell a story with them?	Read a loose-parts-inspired book! Try *Rosie Revere, Engineer*; *Not a Stick*; *Not a Box*; or another book about loose parts.	What can you make with cardboard?	Make your own junk jar! Gather random "extras" from around your space to use in creations.	Grab a flashlight. Experiment with shadows. Try another option.
Pull out the button jar! Explore!	How many ways can you use playdough outside? Be sure to leave no trace.	Find pieces of nature on the ground—sticks, leaves, rocks, seedpods, and so on. How might you use these?	Time to experiment with sound! Try mason jars, utensils, water, and stainless-steel bowls. What else?	Make a math equation with loose parts, or sort items you find outside.

(adapted from Gull, 2020e)

Provocations and Stations

Many early childhood classrooms already use stations and provocations. These can be slightly adjusted to have more of a loose-parts vibe. They can be subject, standard, or theme specific and allow for open-ended exploration of the materials available. The key is to treat these options as a starting point or invitation to explore and make meaning out of the materials.

Facilitating a "Beautiful Stuff" Project

The book *Beautiful Stuff! Learning with Found Materials* by Cathy Topal and Lella Gandini explains one classroom's journey to collect, categorize, and use loose parts in their classrooms. The educators sent each child home with a paper sack and a request for donations of found items. Back in class, the students sorted the items; talked about them; and used them in art, play, and learning. The teacher facilitated observations, recorded categories, and encouraged conversations around the materials. The students put the items in clear containers so they could easily view and use the loose parts as part of a laboratory for thinking. The materials were left out for regular interaction and inspiration. Children used the materials in creating and documenting creations, having paper and mark-making materials nearby to sketch and write about their creations (Topal and Gandini, 1999).

Students are often drawn toward creating shapes, designs with symmetry, and mandalas with loose parts. They might also tell stories with the items, explore circles and colors, and work on materials over time. Having an "in process" or "in progress" shelf can help, as students may need more time to manipulate the materials. Eventually students may use the materials to create and connect to other possibilities. For example, a teacher may challenge children to use the materials to create puppets; however, how they make puppets is completely open to the students' imaginations and the loose parts available. Or a teacher may challenge the children to study their own and other faces in the classroom before making representations of the faces using the materials however they like. Or children might create characters out of collage materials and draw and write to document their characters (Topal and Gandini, 1999).

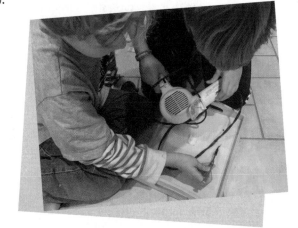

Students in the Beautiful Stuff project were encouraged to make color wheels of found objects and then add more color and additional materials to their sculptures. Consider providing children with wood scraps (sanded to prevent splinters) as well as other materials, such as corks, craft sticks, small dowels, toothpicks, and other wooden objects, to use in creating sculptures. Encourage the children to explore and sort the materials, make connections, and find possibilities of how they might use the loose parts. For example, they might create three-dimensional objects, with the option of gluing them together eventually or leaving them free for use in another project.

Whatever beautiful things the children create, encourage them to document their process. The students in the Beautiful Stuff project wrote stories to explain their sculptures and took photos and drew pictures to document and reflect on the creative and problem-solving process. The sculptures were then displayed for the school community to explore. Moving beyond the materials into documenting with drawings, writing, and displaying is a powerful way for the children to connect and broaden their ideas and learning (Topal and Gandini, 1999).

Promoting Loose Parts Outside the Classroom

Most things that can be done inside can also be done outside the room. If you have flexible spaces in the school, utilize them to provide room for projects that may require larger or different spaces than the typical classroom offers. For example, a multipurpose area can be a great place for students to spread out for larger projects. Some classes even spread out into their hallways for more space to work. You can also consider creating an outdoor classroom in your schoolyard. Carla often follows the Nature Explore certification (https://certified.natureexplore.org/) process for these, including a mix of research-backed areas that meet the needs of the whole child. There may be areas for building, art, music, large-motor activities, messy materials, gathering, and other areas to support students' learning. Having implemented and used one of these in a nature center setting, Carla found that the outdoor classroom provided a great backdrop for natural observations, mathematical connections, and reading outdoors. Required standards can be met in these spaces as well.

Almost all the loose parts we describe in this book include materials that will work well outdoors. In addition, consider the following list of common outdoor loose parts that can further enhance skill development and the overall learning process.

- Dirt, soil, and mud
- Rocks, stones, and gravel
- Sand
- Flowers, herbs, nontoxic weeds, grass, and other plants
- Water, ice, and snow
- Trees, limbs, branches, bark, and leaves
- Tree cookies
- Nuts
- Garbage cans and lids

- Containers (plastic and wood)
- Crates (plastic and wood)
- Building blocks
- Buckets
- Insects (if handled gently)
- Seedpods
- Gardening tools
- Recycled materials
- Cardboard boxes
- Outdoor fabric

- Tires
- Plastic cones
- Balls and sports equipment
- Benches
- Tables
- Parking lot
- Sandbox
- Brick walls and structures
- Barrels
- Playground equipment

(adapted from Gull et al., 2019)

Take time to consider what outdoor areas and open-ended materials you have available on your school property. You can gather and use outdoors materials that are unique and expansive, based on your geographic location and educational setting.

California has adopted the 4Cs (creativity, critical thinking, communication, and collaboration). Kristin Shepard, of Orange County in Southern California, has brought loose parts into recess time. She states, "Recess Revolution likes to use tires, cardboard boxes and tubes, wood planks, fabric, clothespins, linoleum, rope, netting, buckets, spools, hoses, crates and more" (Recess Revolution, n.d.). Their slogan is "Enriching environments, engaging minds." One educator experiments with loose parts in physical-education classes, bringing loose parts to schoolyards. The teacher notes, "Children just love to play. When I go to schools, I give a short speech about how play is good for the brain and that it helps us develop creativity, communication, collaboration, and critical thinking skills. These 4Cs are a part of the Common Core Standards, so school administrators eat it up. They feel like they need to justify using the time to play, so I help them" (Almon, 2017).

· CHAPTER 8 · THE CLASS ENVIRONMENT

Playpods

Recess options might include a playpod—an outside storage structure filled with loose parts as described by Joan Almon (2017). She suggests that, while longer sessions of thirty to sixty minutes are ideal, even the typical twenty-minute recess can offer great loose-parts play opportunities. With a little training for the recess aides and inexpensive and repurposed loose parts, schools have transformed their recess options. She also recommends seeking community donations and discounts from local business to help provide the needed materials. For example, one school spent $3,500 (gathered from donations) in startup costs for a metal storage building, shelving, and trashcans on wheels. Each year after the first, they spend $300 to restock their playpod. The teachers are delighted with the success of the space and the children's enthusiasm:

"They jumped right in, pulling items from bins, constructing, imagining, and building with a joyful, collaborative spirit. Just as our research indicated, playground conflicts are significantly reduced when the playpod is open. Children are happily engaged and very busy. Every day we see new creations and inventions" (Almon, 2017).

Almon (2017) suggests the following tips for managing outdoor loose-parts areas:

- Use rolling trashcans and medium bins for materials. There is no need to label or sort.

- Maximize playtime by allowing students to clean up materials into any bin.

- Post basic rules in the playpod area, such as focusing on fun, safety, sharing, physical boundaries, and cleanup expectations.

- Allow sufficient time for play by leaving materials out between groups and letting classrooms use the materials outside of recess.

- Designate one trained staff member to supervise the playpod area.

- Introduce the playpod with a video of play possibilities in action and related picture books in classrooms.

If you want to try a slower, incremental approach to outdoor learning, Carla suggests the following steps to creating temporary and mobile play spots outdoors.

1. Define spaces and materials if needed.

2. Consider the affordances of your space. What is naturally available?

3. Use bags, totes, carts, or crates to make the loose-parts materials portable—just grab and go.

4. Designate a few floater volunteers to supervise the play.

5. Review playwork principles for how adults might interact during play sessions.

6. Consider the ages and stages of the children. Keep in mind, however, that most children will find the right developmental fit for their play experiences.

7. Have a question or sign describing what might happen in the space, but keep the space open ended. Invitations should not be limitations of children's play but rather starting points.

8. Cultivate a variety of approaches to nature play to meet the needs of many participants.

9. Consider setting up a temporary outdoor classroom with spaces for art, movement, building, and so on.

10. Use folding tables as needed for workspaces (Gull, 2018h)

Additionally, you can tie various standards to natural play spots, noting through observation and other assessment options which standards the play and explorations are meeting.

Ideas for Outdoor Loose-Parts Play across the Curriculum

Creating spaces outside for loose parts can be helpful. As you figure out what might work in your space, you might try mobile or temporary options to see how children respond and what fits your school style. These spaces can be used for recess or free time outside, for specific content- area work, or for special occasions. Often, children display skills and learning across the content areas during these playful interactions.

- **Natural adventure play:** Designate an area for outdoor play in the schoolyard, bringing in logs, soil, hay bales, sticks, burlap, tree cookies, and so on. Add additional layers of twine, chenille stems, paint, chalk, small shovels, and stainless-steel bowls and muffin tins. Allow children to create and explore!

- **Pop-up adventure play:** This is similar to the previous option, with a mix of other materials. Pop-up adventure play can be done inside or out. Gather a variety of boxes, fabrics, rope, duct tape, paint, recyclables and let participants create! The organization Pop-Up Adventure Play has a free kit to help you get started on this.

- **Book extensions:** Use a variety of natural and loose-parts-related books as a starting point for play. For example, read the book *Leaf Man* by Lois Elhert outside in the fall. Encourage children to make their own leaf creations during outdoor time. After reading *Not a Stick* by Antoinette Portis, children can use sticks outside in a variety of ways, from suggestions in the book to their own creations.

- **Dramatic play:** Bring a bag of scarves, fabrics, feather boas, ribbons, costumes, and other dramatic-play items outside for storytelling and open-ended play. Tie the play to a specific standard or watch the standards unfold as you observe students build literacy skills through play.

- **Fairy and gnome gardens:** Carla keeps a basket of "fairy" stuff we have made over time; although, most children just love creating their own huts and such while in the woods.

We like making fairies and gnomes with clothespins, fabric, natural materials, and hot glue. You can easily take the fairy basket outside or use what is naturally available in your space.

- **Mud play/mud kitchen:** Bring a crate full of cast-off dishes, pans, utensils, digging utensils, and so on. Put the materials outside near a section of dirt. Have water in cooler jugs available. Consider setting up a simple area with wooden planks and stumps or concrete blocks to use for small tables or benches.

- **Nature art:** Bring out picture frames in a variety of sizes and a basket of natural and found objects. Let children scavenge for natural stuff to create their own nature art. For inspiration, share examples of the work of artists such as Andy Goldsworthy, Marc Pouyet, Chelsey Bahe, and Patrick Dougherty.

- **Painting in nature:** In an area surrounded by nature, string up a clear shower curtain between trees with rope. Set out paint and painting tools and encourage the children to find natural materials to paint with. This creates a quick and inexpensive outdoor easel that allows students to see nature through the curtain. Allow students to experiment with ways of painting with nature outside. Wash the shower curtain and utensils between uses.

- **Natural weaving:** There are many ways to do this! On hikes or during outdoor time, create cardboard and yarn frames, and weave found objects from nature into the frame. Experiment with other weaving options.

- **Nature play kit:** Make a kit with the basics, such as magnifying glasses, bug jars, nets, field guides, and so on, to explore nature. Allow students to explore and share their finds with each other. Let any bugs or insects go before returning to class.

- **Seed dispersal:** Bring in cattails and dried milkweed pods, or find dandelions in seed in the outdoor play space. Windborne seed dispersal is so exciting to explore. Carla has seen children experiment with seeds and wind for over an hour!

- **Scavenger hunts:** Use scavenger hunts to connect to the outdoors. Children might create their own or use Fundanas (https://www.fundanabandanas.com/) or printables. They can hunt for specific natural loose parts and then make something with what they have found.

- **Fort building:** Gather clamps, rope, bungee cords, tarps, fabrics, sheets, and so on to make forts among the trees, along the fence line, or wherever the student architects decide.

- **Obstacle courses:** Using an open space, bring tubs and crates of cones, wooden planks, rope, expandable tunnels, tires, ladders, pool noodles, large plastic hoops, and so on. Add in stumps, logs, mud patches, hay bales, and more. Encourage the children to change up the course to their hearts' content.

- **Pulleys, rope, and buckets or baskets:** Explore pulley play by draping a rope over a branch and/or attaching a pulley to a tree branch. Use a basket attached to the rope to transport items. Children love this and can explore simple machines and transportation firsthand.

- **Ramps and balls:** Use ramps (wood planks, gutters, PVC pipes cut in half, and so on), crates or stumps, and a variety of balls and natural spheres, such as acorns or walnuts, to explore physics. How can students move the ball along their course? What needs adjustment or engineering to allow the ball to travel from the beginning to the end of the ramp?

- **Sticks and chenille stems:** Allow students to build with bamboo poles or tall, thin branches. They might build structures and use chenille stems, twine, Velcro, and/or Sticklets to connect the sticks.

92

- **Tools in nature:** Have a designated area to use tools, such as garden clippers, vegetable peelers, and microplanes, in nature. Children can explore using the tools with tree cookies, sticks, and branches. Teach safety explicitly, and have direct supervision. Establish a small zone for this type of play with direct teacher supervision.

- **Water walls:** Create a temporary area where students can experiment with water. Allow them to attach different items to an existing chain-link fence. Consider having funnels, water tubing, L and T connectors, and recyclable plastics, and provide zip ties and/or chenille stems for children to use to attach the items to the fence. Provide pitchers, water, tubs, and tools (scissors, hand drill, knife, and so on) for children to use to create pathways for water exploration. (Gull, 2018h)

By taking the class outside, you can make learning more engaging and relevant while still meeting standards—with the added benefit of fresh air, nature therapy, and moving your bodies! Allowing students to expand their thinking and physical location can nurture imagination and creativity, provide new learning opportunities, and develop their interest in the surroundings and environment. Expose children to unlimited resources and opportunities, and they will learn through play and experimentation (Hesmondhalgh, 2011).

· **CHAPTER 8 · THE CLASS ENVIRONMENT**

Overcoming Hurdles to Loose Parts

Now it's your turn. Consider the hurdles you might face to implementing a loose-parts mindset in your school. List each one, and think of some possible solutions. Then choose a solution to try.

HURDLES TO LOOSE PARTS		
Hurdles	Possible Solutions	What I Will Try

(Gull, 2020a)

· **CHAPTER 9** ·

Science

Children naturally gravitate toward science! Scientific discovery happens all the time. Whether it is rolling rocks down a ramp, rolling balls through a tunnel, weighing objects on a balance scale, or discovering information about bugs and animals, children are curious and engaged. It is wonderful to see the "lightbulb" turning on in their brains. Children experiment with scientific concepts using loose parts, and they are empowered as they discover scientific principles. In their 2014 article for *Review of Science, Mathematics, and ICT Education*, Despoina Desli and Anastasia Dimitriou state, "The active involvement of children in experiments and the use of materials as well as the knowledge integration into daily life situations seem to be the most appropriate approaches for successful science teaching and learning."

Many schools align the curriculum with the Next Generation Science Standards (n.d.) and teach lessons in physical sciences, life sciences, earth, and space sciences. Early childhood–aged students learn about cause and effect, patterns, scales, proportion, quantity, systems and system models, energy and matter, structure and function, stability and change, analyzing and interpreting data, obtaining, evaluating, communicating information, and planning and carrying out investigations. This chapter illustrates many examples of ways to use loose parts that integrate into the Next Generation Science Standards (NGSS). In particular, we highlight ideas related to magnetism, simple machines, chemistry, plants, animals, and wind exploration.

"There is evidence that all children love to interact with variables such as materials and shapes; smells and other physical phenomena, such as electricity, magnetism, and gravity; media, such as gases and fluids; sounds, music, and motion; chemical interactions, cooking, and fire; and other people, and animals, plants, words, concepts, and ideas. With all these things, all children love to play, experiment, discover, and invent and have fun. All these things have one thing in common, which is variables or 'loose parts.'"
—Simon Nicholson

96

The following list includes our suggestions along with some adapted from Jill Hauser's (1997) book *Super Science Concoctions*. This isn't a complete list of all the materials you could use for science explorations. This is really just a beginning!

Salt

Baking soda

Vinegar

Gelatin

Food coloring

Liquid dishwashing soap

Paraffin

Medicine dropper

White glue

Hot glue

Corks

Plaster of Paris

Art paper

Paint

Markers

Chenille stems

Craft sticks

Sidewalk chalk

Plastic spoons

Glitter

Beads

Plastic tubing

Measuring cups

Measuring spoons

Straws

Water

Ice cubes

Stove

Plastic containers with lids

Coffee filters

String

Trays

Spices

Jars

Scissors

Pencils

Paper clips

Toothpicks

Baking pans

Cookie sheets

Egg cartons

Ice-cube trays

Coffee cans

Pots

Pitcher

Yogurt containers

Tweezers

Tape

Blender

Paper towels

Waxed paper

Rocks

Dirt

Flowers/petals

Plant parts

Discovering Magnetism

Children are intrigued by magnets! Why do magnets attract at certain places and then, conversely, why do they repel at others? Magnetism is a perfect unit for incorporating loose parts based on NGSS. For example, the third-grade science standard (3-PS2-3) encourages students to be able to apply understanding of magnetic interactions, determine the cause and effect of magnetic interactions, and define a simple design problem that can be solved with magnets (Next Generation Science Standards, n.d.). As Carla explains in her blog, "[Magnetism] also models how exploring items and properties of materials can be a part of loose parts play within elementary school and higher before buckling down with designing an experiment and such. We need time for discovery" (Gull, 2017a).

Magnetic Games

This exploration

- emphasizes the process over the product;

- allows for unique end products that have the children's voices;

- focuses on key elements of the project, such as experimentation; and

- spotlights an interdisciplinary approach, often working on more than one standard at a time.

Materials

Plastic baggies

Variety of magnets, such as Tegu Blocks, Magna-Tiles, Magformers, magnetic rods, magnetic horseshoes, nuts, bolts, magnetic slime,* and magnetic pieces *Note: You can find recipes for magnetic slime online.

What to Do

Be sure to have many different types of magnets available to explore.

You can provide the students with baggies of different magnets and then let them walk around the classroom to independently discover which items are attracted to the magnets and which items repel.

The students can then become scientists and write down their discoveries in an open-ended science journal. The younger learner can draw pictures of the items that attract and that repel. The emerging writer can draw and label the picture. The more confident writer can write sentences to record the findings, just as real scientists do. Students learn vocabulary words such as *observation*, *hypothesis*, *prediction*, and *results*. The more advanced writers can use the steps of the scientific method to record their findings.

As an extension, children could explore magnetism outside the classroom on the school grounds. In addition, for homework the children could investigate magnetism in their home surroundings. Be sure to have the students record their findings like true scientists!

SUGGESTED BOOKS ON MAGNETISM

Use this list as a springboard for creating your own list of science books that are appropriate for your grade level. Add to your list as you find other books that are rich with scientific vocabulary, beautiful illustrations, and loose parts.

Adler, David. 2018. *Magnets Push, Magnets Pull.* New York: Holiday House.	This simple book explains the world of magnets along with several experiments. Encourage the children to test various items, such as coins, toy cars, cans, paper clips, paper, and iron filings.
Alpert, Barbara. 2011. *A Look at Magnets.* North Mankato, MN: Capstone.	This book introduces students to the science of magnetism. Encourage them to use different magnets and loose parts, such as magnetic filings, a compass, and so on, to discover magnetism.
Beaty. Andrea. 2016. *Ada Twist, Scientist.* New York: Abrams Books for Young Readers.	This book is great for inspiring explorations with loose parts. The main character, a budding scientist, starts with her first question, "Why?"
Fowler, Allan. 1995. *What Magnets Can Do.* San Francisco: Children's Books Press.	In this book, young students discover magnetism with connections to solids, liquids, and gases. As you read, ask critical-thinking questions. Encourage the students to do hands-on experiments with magnetic north and south poles on loose parts such as pens, thumbtacks, nails, toothpicks, a rubber ball, plastic dice, string, paper clips, and a compass.
Hughes, Monica. 2015. *Magnet Max.* Dallas: Brown Books.	Trying to understand the magic of magnets, Max and his friend Nick experiment to understand how magnets work. Encourage the students to discover and play with magnets and loose parts, such as a teapot, tin cans, a metal bowl, a toaster, scissors, tools, safety pins, utensils, nuts and bolts, paper clips, a toy horse, and a refrigerator. Perhaps go on a magnetic walk to see what might be magnetic in your environment.

Using Simple Machines

According to Generation Genius (2021), "Simple machines make work easier. They have few or no moving parts, and they work by changing the direction of a force or the amount of force needed to do something." Levers, axles, pulleys, inclined planes, wedges, and screws are all simple machines. Children enjoy experimenting and creating their own simple machines and then experimenting to see if they work. Loose parts, such as craft sticks, rubber bands, paper-towel tubes, straws, plastic spoons, cups, string, plastic soda caps, balls, and clothespins, fit nicely with this experimentation.

Consider taking or using simple machines outdoors where there can be more space and opportunities to experiment. A temporary or permanent outdoor classroom can help define spaces to explore these concepts in more depth. Simple machines themselves can be used as loose parts in a variety of ways: open loose-parts play, tools exploration, as part of the outdoor offering and in zones of the outdoor classroom, in engineering challenges, at gathering time, and in skill building. When using simple machines as loose parts, they can be combined and put together in many ways. There are no specific directions, and the usage is determined by the children (Gull, 2020h). This chart lists simple machines that might be found on schoolyards, posed as a design challenge, or brought in for exploration. Use your discretion in choosing materials, and remember to adhere to your school's policies. Some spaces may be temporarily used for observation or exploration with proper safety precautions. For example, students might follow directions to make spoon catapults with rubber bands, plastic spoons, and craft sticks and then use the finished catapult for exploration of loose parts.

LEVERS	INCLINED PLANES	WEDGES
Seesaw	Ladders	Butter knife
Fork	Step stools	Chisel
Catapult	Ramps	Shovel
Yard rake	Marble runs	Hand tools
Handmade teeter-totter	Stairs	Scissors
Scissors	Driveway	Nail
Hoe	Door wedge	Screw
Tongs	Triangle	Stick
Spatula	Hollow blocks	Claw hammer
Baseball bat	Wood planks	Fork
Clippers	Slide	Veggie peeler
Launcher	Dump truck	Ax
Tweezers	Gutters	
Garden shovels	Stormwater drain	
	Roller coaster	
	ADA-accessible ramp*	
	Hill	
	Skate park	
	Sink	

WHEELS AND AXLES	SCREWS	PULLEYS
Variety of carts	Drill bit	Flagpole
Bicycle wheels	Hand drill	Sail and mast
Rolling pins	Stool with screw	Basket and rope
Spools with sticks	Lid from a jar	Pulley wheel
Toy cars	Screws	Fort with portcullis or drawbridge
Windmill	Rigamajig	
Bicycle	Nuts/bolts	Clothesline
Fan	Apple peeler/slicer/corer	Block and tackle
Trundle wheel	Grain grinder	Climbing
Wagon	Door lock	
Eggbeater	Spinning tops	
Doorknob		
Coasters with wheels		
Trucks		
Wheelbarrow		

*Note: An unused ramp can serve as an interesting space for exploration. Of course, you don't want to interfere with anyone who needs to use the ramp.

If using pulleys, you might set up invitations to extend the exploration. For example, try the following:

- **Use heavy items**—Explore pulling heavy items up and down with the pulley. Put rocks in socks and tie them off, use tree cookies, or weights. How does using a simple machine change the work of moving things?

- **Try stuffed animals**—Invite students to bring their plushies in and give them a ride in the pulley. Do they like it fast or slow? How might the stuffies feel on their ride?

- **Make the colors fly**—Have ribbons and ribbon streamers available to allow children to make the colors fly. How might they attach colors with the rope and pulley to allow colors to fly? What else might they use?

- **Add a handheld scale**—Scales can help see the relevant force used to move an item. Measure the weight of the item with the scale. Experiment with pulley designs to see which option is the easiest to move the heavy item.

(adapted from Gull, 2020k)

After giving students some time to explore, consider giving them an open-ended challenge, such as the following:

- Create a Rube Goldberg or chain-reaction machine.

- Make a simple machines scavenger hunt.

- Build a contraption that can lift something.

- Build something to send a bucket or basket from one place to another.

- Make something that can move items across the classroom.

- Use the engineering design process to solve a problem with simple machines:

- Think.

- Create.

- Share.

You could also create challenges based on stories and books you have in your classroom (Gull, 2020k).

SUGGESTED BOOKS ON SIMPLE MACHINES

Use this list as a springboard for creating your own list of science books that are appropriate for your grade level. Add to your list as you find other books that are rich with scientific vocabulary, beautiful illustrations, and loose parts.

Adler, David. 2016. *Simple Machines: Wheels, Levers, and Pulleys.* New York: Holiday House.	In this picture book, the author explains simple machines used in everyday life. Invite the children to experiment with many different loose parts in relation to wheels, levers, and pulleys.
Douglas, Lloyd. 2002. *What Is a Pulley?* New York: Scholastic.	This book has photographs and simple text that introduce children to the fundamentals of the mechanics that drive simple machines. Challenge the children to find ways to use pulleys around the classroom and at home.
Smith, Sian. 2012. *Ramps and Wedges.* Portsmouth, NH: Heinemann.	This book explains the scientific principles of ramps and wedges. Encourage the children to explore and experiment with creating and using ramps and wedges.
Wells, Robert. 1996. *How Do You Lift a Lion?* Park Ridge, IL: Albert Whitman and Co.	This book introduces scientific vocabulary such as *gravity* and explains how ramps and other simple machines can help objects travel. Challenge the children to create and use pulleys, levers, and wheels.

Investigating Chemical Interactions

Children love mixing things together to cause a reaction. Suzanne remembers doing a volcano experiment. The children were so excited but a little scared at the same time. When they saw that it was a "cool" experiment, they wanted to do it again and again!

While the classic volcano experiment is very engaging, it can become a loose-parts invitation if you let the children investigate the ingredients. Carla gave each child a tray or baking sheet with a lip, a squirt bottle of vinegar, food coloring, various containers of different shapes, spoons, and a small container of baking soda. She found that the color and material experimentation was much higher than it would have been if she had done a demonstration or the students had followed an exact recipe. In many science situations, allowing students to come up with their own ways to explore the materials (within safety parameters) in addition to the official experiment can allow them to connect more deeply to the material, build their curiosity, and make connections they might not do otherwise. Provide children with loose-part ingredients and then have them go through the steps of the scientific method:

- Observe
- Formulate questions
- Develop a hypothesis
- Test the hypothesis
- Record the results
- Share the results

Oobleck Exploration

What about mixing up ingredients to create oobleck, which is neither a liquid nor a solid?

Materials

Water

Corn starch

Food coloring (optional)

Containers

Measuring cups

Measuring spoons

What to Do

Instead of giving the children a recipe, simply give them the materials needed and let them experiment. Ask them to observe what happens when they mix the materials, formulate questions about what they observe, develop a hypothesis and test it, and then record and share the results.

Crystals Exploration

Consider letting students make their own crystals.

Materials

Hot water

Epsom salt

Measuring cups

Measuring spoons

Containers

What to Do

Give each child the materials needed and let them explore what happens when they mix Epsom salt and water. Of course, consider safety and your students' abilities to refrain from eating the Epsom salt. Yuck! Ask them to observe what happens when they mix the materials, formulate questions about what they observe, develop a hypothesis and test it, and then record and share the results.

Slime is another good one to try. You can find ingredient lists online. *Super Science Concoctions* by Jill Hauser (1997) is an excellent book to use and share with young children. It is filled with fifty different science experiments using various materials and supplies to create a science lab.

Cooking can also be a great way to explore chemical reactions with students and can be tasty as well. Children enjoy making ice cream by hand using crushed ice and salt in a coffee can and a plastic milk jug. Students can change the variables of ice and salt ratios using a loose-parts mindset and make predictions of what they think will happen to their ice cream.

How about making butter? Learners are in awe when they mix the ingredients for butter and they keep on shaking it until it turns from liquid to solid. There are so many recipes for children to discover chemical reactions.

SUGGESTED BOOKS ON CHEMICAL REACTIONS

Use this list as a springboard for creating your own list of science books that are appropriate for your grade level. Add to your list as you find other books that are rich with scientific vocabulary, beautiful illustrations, and loose parts.

Allegra, Mike. 2019. *Scampers Thinks Like a Scientist*. Nevada City, CA: Dawn Publications.	This is a good introduction to the scientific method as the children read about a mouse who experiments in the garden. Encourage the children to think like scientists by observing and solving a problem using materials and loose parts, such as garden vegetables, rag dolls, sticks, string, instruments, flags, a catapult, a rock, paint, paintbrushes, and glitter.
Dahl, Roald. 1981. *George's Marvelous Medicine*. New York: Puffin.	George tries to make medicine to help make his grandma nicer. Invite the children to create potions and lotions with loose parts, such as soaps, sprinkles, seasonings, food coloring, and kitchen tools. (Remind them not to drink their potions!)
Weakland, Mark. 2017. *Kaboom! Wile E. Coyote Experiments with Chemical Reactions*. North Mankato, MN: Capstone.	Encourage the students to experiment with different potions and liquids, observing the chemical reactions.

Studying Animals, Nature, and Plants

Animals

Young children love learning about animals, nature, and plants. Based on NGSS for kindergartners, children need to develop understanding of what plants and animals (including humans) need to survive and the relationship between their needs and where they live (K-LS1-1). Focusing on local animals and place-based education can be powerful in the early childhood classroom as children get to know their natural environment. Farm animals are a common thematic unit explored in the early childhood years to gain knowledge on the relationship between farmers, animals, and plants for survival. Children can peruse picture books and early readers about farm animals and then use loose parts, such as paint, cotton balls, yarn, pompoms, clothespins, stickers, and chenille stems, to create their own versions of farm animals. Students can even dress up as farmers using clothes found in the dress-up area of the classroom.

Many wild animals build homes or places to raise their young, and children often enjoy learning about different types of eggs and nests. Carla taught her students about the variety of nests that animals construct and then took the class outside to create their own nests with found natural materials. Later, after they had read a book about a young beaver building a dam with sticks, the students built and created with sticks, recycled tin cans, blocks, boxes, and other loose parts.

Creating native-plant habitats in our outdoor spaces can also be helpful as it attracts local animals for observation and provides more loose parts variables within our environments. As a safety note, students should only observe animals in the outdoors from a distance. Consider adding some of the following options to your outdoor space:

- A bird feeding station
- A pollinator garden
- Bug hotels
- Native plants and shrubs in the landscape
- A brush pile for animals

To explore one option in more depth, children can use a variety of loose parts to create bug hotels. These creations can be made in a variety of shapes to provide shelter for the bugs.

Students can construct bug hotels out of many different natural materials, such as wood, dry leaves, bark, pipes, twigs, flowerpots, soil, moss, and old roof tiles. The bugs will love scurrying in and out of their creations. Students can observe the bugs with magnifying glasses, like real scientists! *Bug Hotel* by Libby Walden is a great book to spark construction ideas.

Additionally, the children could re-create the local habitat in miniature for small-world play using a large tub or base, toy animals of the area, and representative details, such as rocks, trees, small plants, and so on. Carla came up with the following list of options for including animal play in various settings:

- Puppets
- Costumes and open-ended accessories, such as scarves, boas, and so on
- Stuffed animals
- Games, such as Hide and Seek
- Toy animals
- Stick animals
- Wooden or fabric animals
- Felt animal play sets
- Magnetic animals
- Laminated pictures of animals
- Animal action cards
- Animal-related arts and crafts
- Books and field guides
- Animal-related puzzles and pattern-block activities
- Tools such as nets, magnifiers, containers, observation jars, and so on (Gull, 2015)

When these materials are available as options or special activities in the classroom, they can be included with other loose parts for children to use to explore and role-play about animals. For example, stuffed animals might be used with pulleys; spontaneous Hide-and-Seek games may ensue. Children may sort laminated pictures of animals or use them with playdough and other loose parts to create scenes. Students can consult field guides to learn about new birds that visit the classroom feeder. Costumes and other dramatic-play items allow students to become any animal they can imagine and take on the role of that animal. Children might use common classroom and outdoor loose parts to illustrate scientific processes such as the life cycle of a frog or butterfly.

Nature

Nature provides so many opportunities to use loose parts in the science content area. Let the children explore outside the classroom. Provide each child with a clipboard, paper, and pencil, and go on a nature walk around your school grounds. Look at the sky, clouds, trees, plants, water, ground, rocks, sticks, grass, mud, insects, and more. The children can record their observations by writing and drawing pictures. The students can also create their own nature pictures with loose parts gathered inside or outside the classroom. For example, children could find a rock and to paint it to resemble an insect or spider. As Carla describes in a blog post (2018g), artists such as Chelsey Bahe, Patrick Dougherty, and Andy Goldsworthy use natural materials with artistic elements to create nature play scenes, whimsical stick creations, and just-for-the-moment nature art.

Children could go on a nature scavenger hunt to look for specific loose-parts items—what a fun way to explore the space!

Materials

Paper

Baskets or paper bags

What to Do

Write a scavenger list of natural loose parts for the children to find, such as five rocks, three leaves, six sticks, and so on. Children could even make their own loose-parts scavenger hunts.

Give each child a basket or paper bag and a copy of the scavenger list, and invite them to go on a scavenger hunt outside.

When they've collected the items, invite them to make a creation out of them. You could divide the outdoor space into different areas or zones and set up stations with specific loose-part invitations. The loose parts may be unique for each area, such as rocks, dishes, spoons, pinecones, water, mud, and herbs in a mud kitchen outside (Gull, 2017a).

Plants

Based on NGSS for second graders, students need to develop an understanding of what plants need to grow (2-LS2-1). Children love to grow plants from seeds. Children can experiment with planting seeds and letting them grow in different conditions, such as near a sunny classroom window or in a dark closet, with different amounts of water, or with or without soil. Again, the children can use the scientific method by observing, dictating or writing questions, creating hypotheses, experimenting, observing, and recording and sharing their results and conclusions.

Collecting seeds on a nature walk is a great way to integrate loose parts in the science content area. Upon returning to class, the students can count their seeds, pods, leaves, sticks, and other natural items; sort and classify the materials; and record their findings in a science journal. Seeds can also make great loose parts for individual creations, but be aware of any student allergies.

Using plants to enhance your outside environment and loose-parts options can also benefit students. If you decide to add plants to your outdoor classroom, Gull (2016) offers the following advice.

"In the spring, at the end of the day, you should smell like dirt."
—Margaret Atwood, *Bluebeard's Egg*

- **Assess what you already have.** Your site may already have great attributes; for example, are there significant trees growing within the space? Is there a natural path already in your play area? Sketch out a map of the unique features to work with. Think about your water source as you look at the area.

- **Find plants that would be good for your soil or area.** You might consider getting a soil test through your local extension office. Additionally, you may want to know your hardiness zone. Look at how much sun and shade the area receives, as that may affect what will grow there. Explore textures as you plan. Think of the various textures that would appeal to children, such as soft, feathery, bumpy, spiky, pointy, and so on.

- **Go native!** Native plants require less maintenance in the long run, are well suited for your area, and provide food for the native insects and animals. Contact local native-plant groups for help in selecting and finding native plants. Often, big box stores and most chain gardening centers do not carry native plants. Look for smaller nurseries, and call around to see what they might offer. For help understanding why to plant native plants, read Doug Tallamy's (2009) book *Bringing Nature Home*. As we considered our site, we were able to bring experts out to look at the soil and sun and give suggestions for appropriate plants.

- **Consider safe edibles.** You might try planting a garden to have food to harvest. Some outdoor classrooms have planted mini orchards to add to the rich learning experience. Additionally, consider wild edibles that will continue to produce safe food with minimal effort. Depending on your area, you might plant black raspberries, mulberries, or other edible plants. Avoid planting overly toxic plants in an outdoor classroom meant to be explored by children. Teach the children explicitly about which plants to avoid. Try to clear out plants that might pose a hazard in an outdoor classroom, such as poison ivy, or plants that produce toxic berries, such as holly.

- **Feed the animals.** Think about animals that might benefit from your garden and plantings. Consider planting a pollinator garden. Once again, go native!

- **Make it fun!** Consider making a pizza garden with tomatoes, bell peppers, onions, basil, oregano, and parsley; a sensory garden with plants that have appealing aromas, have interesting textures, or make distinct sounds; or a salsa garden with cilantro, onions, peppers, and tomatoes.

- **Plant extras to use in nature art and other projects.** Plants can be great loose parts for children's play. Purposely choose additional plants with the intent of nature play, considering projects such as natural weaving, art projects, and nature pounding. Also, ask local gardens, neighbors, and florists for garden scraps that might be used for projects. Think of pinecones, seedpods, sunflowers, sweet gum balls, buckeyes, and more for loose-parts play. Add herbs near a mud kitchen to invite children to include these in their soupy creations.

- **Add whimsy!** Speaking of sunflowers, consider making a sunflower or willow fort for a whimsical touch. Make a beanpole tent. Add a fairy garden or recycled art to enhance your space. Add a fountain with water.

- **Create a maintenance plan.** Hopefully, the plants will not need much work once they are established, but they will need some weeding, watering, and seasonal refreshing from time to time. Many schools have issues over the summer with maintaining a garden. Consider having parent volunteers, a local garden club, and/or a (paid) teacher water and do other needed tasks.

- **Add a rain barrel.** You can make your own rain barrel with plans found online. In our area, our soil and water conservation district will help fund a rain barrel and/or a rain garden if we attend a class. The water can be used to water the plants or for mud play.

- **Look for inexpensive sources for seeds and plants.** Look for organizations that offer free or low-cost plants and seeds, such as a seed library in a local library, community-supported agriculture groups, or gardeners who want to share plants they have divided or thinned. Some gardening and environmental groups have annual plant exchanges where you can find free or low-cost plants. Additional places to look might be on Freecycle or Craigslist; on the website of the city forester, your local soil and water conservation district, tree alliances, or the local agricultural extension office; ads in local free newspapers; and the pages of garage-sale groups on Facebook. Additionally, if you make a large order, the price per plant will be less expensive.

- **Apply for a grant!** There are lots of gardening- and pollinator-based grants available for school gardens, offered by companies and organizations such as Captain Planet, Jamba Juice, the Scotts Miracle-Gro Foundation, and the David Rockefeller Pollinator Education Initiative.

- **Make a map of the plants in your outdoor classroom.** Label select plants along the path, involving children in the process. Have the children make their own maps as well. Gather information sheets on the plants in a resource binder for extended learning for both the educators and the children.

SUGGESTED BOOKS ON ANIMALS, NATURE, AND PLANTS

Use this list as a springboard for creating your own list of science books that are appropriate for your grade level. Add to your list as you find other books that are rich with scientific vocabulary, beautiful illustrations, and loose parts.

Anderson, Constance. 2017. *A Stick Until . . .* Cambridge, MA: Star Bright.	This book takes the reader through the life of a stick, exploring its uses with animals and humans. Provide sticks, water, and leaves, and invite the children to demonstrate their uses. Let them document through photography or drawing and then dictate the uses they have discovered and their reasoning.
Brandenburg McLellan, Gretchen. 2018. *I'm Done!* New York: Holiday House.	This book follows a beaver as he perseveres to build the perfect dam. Provide a variety of loose parts, and invite the children to build a dam or lodge.
Carle, Eric. 2009. *The Tiny Seed*. New York: Little Simon.	The story describes how a seed travels and grows. Provide a variety of seeds for the children to plant. Encourage them to observe the plants as they grow.
Ehlert, Lois. 2003. *Planting a Rainbow*. San Diego, CA: Red Wagon Books.	This book highlights the rainbow of colors that grows from many different seeds and bulbs. Invite the children to plant a variety of seeds and bulbs to create a garden rainbow.
Jenkins, Martin. 2017. *Bird Builds a Nest*. Somerville, MA: Candlewick.	This book tells the story of a bird that builds her nest, including simple descriptions of forces such as gravity, heavy, light, pushing, and pulling. Provide a variety of materials and encourage the children to create nests.

Exploring Wind

Do you enjoy having the wind blow through your hair? Do you like riding in the car with the windows open? What about riding down the street on a scooter and feeling the wind against your face? Wind is a fun element to explore! Take your class outside and have the children just stand on the playground without moving. Ask them what they feel on their faces and bodies. Perhaps bring towels or blankets outside, and invite the children to sit on them and stare at the clouds. When the children see the clouds moving, use this as an opportunity to discuss wind. Students can draw and write what they are observing in their science journals.

Think about having the children create a kite, wind chime, or a pinwheel from loose parts. Hang these up or hold them and observe when and how fast they move. Student-made parachutes and kites, straws, folded paper fans, wind socks, and PVC tubes are all great loose parts to use when experimenting with wind.

Children can gather many different materials and use a hair dryer to discover wind velocity. They can put the dryer on different speeds and observe which objects move with the wind force. This exploration can transform into a loose STEM challenge for any topic or holiday.

Flying Jingle Bells

Materials

Tape

Paper cones

String

Jingle bells

Small plastic cups

Coffee filters

Feathers, balloons, and other lightweight objects

What to Do

Provide a variety of materials and challenge the children to find ways to make jingle bells "fly." For example, Carla uses a clear wind tunnel with a fan at the base from KodoKids. She has also used a hair dryer on the cool setting or a fan.

SUGGESTED BOOKS ON EXPLORING WIND

Use this list as a springboard for creating your own list of science books that are appropriate for your grade level. Add to your list as you find other books that are rich with scientific vocabulary, beautiful illustrations, and loose parts.

Dorros, Arthur. 2000. *Feel the Wind*. New York: HarperCollins.	This is a nonfiction book that explores the wind, what causes it, and how it can affect weather. On a windy day, go outside and feel the wind. Invite the children to experiment with various items in the wind.
Hutchins, Pat. 1993. *The Wind Blew*. New York: Aladdin.	This is a story about how the wind blows and moves everyday items. Provide loose parts, such as scarves, umbrellas, balloons, hats, kites, shirts, handkerchiefs, paper, flags, and newspapers, and a hair dryer, and invite the children to experiment with the items and wind.
Konola, Hanna. 2018. *A Year with the Wind*. Layton, UT: Gibbs Smith.	This book shows how the wind pushes and pulls many different objects. Invite the children to explore different objects, such as kits, sailboats, and leaves, and observe how wind helps them travel.

Loose parts are a perfect addition to the science curriculum and compliments NGSS for K–3 learning! Using loose parts provides children with opportunities for hands-on science experimentation and inspiring experiences that will be etched in their minds for a long time.

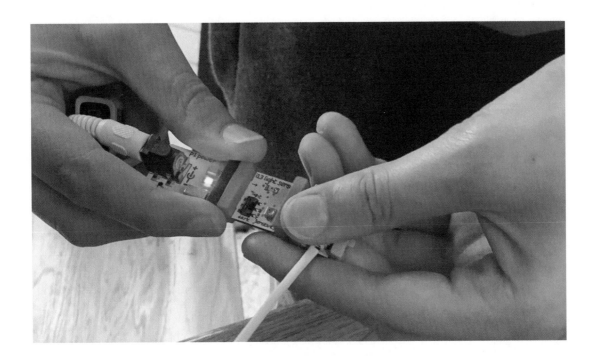

· CHAPTER 10 ·
Technology

Loose parts are an important part of open-ended play and exploration. In their study of the ways educators perceive loose-parts play, Rebecca Spencer and colleagues (2019) state, "Loose parts enable children to take risks; loose parts spark creativity and imagination; loose parts contribute to problem-solving abilities; loose parts cultivate independence; confidence; and loose parts build relationships and leadership."

In the area of technology, a loose-parts mindset supports an inquiry-based and active learning environment. When you infuse the classroom with loose parts, children can experiment with and create codes, robots, electrical circuits, Lego structures, animation, and much more. These explorations will support them in becoming digitally literate.

The International Society for Technology in Education (ISTE) Standards (2021) list the components of digital literacy, including the following.

Digitally literate students are:

- empowered learners,
- digital citizens,
- knowledge constructors,
- innovative designers,
- computational thinkers,
- creative communicators, and
- global collaborators.

Digitally literate students understand:

- basic operations;
- word processing;
- multimedia and presentation tools;
- acceptable use, copyright, and plagiarism;
- research;
- gathering information;
- communication and collaboration; and
- innovation.

Discovering Light and Reflection

In addition to the scientific connections, light can be an interesting way to explore technology. While technology is often viewed as high-tech applications, projectors, flashlights, and other light sources are also technology. Gather a variety of sources of light and reflection, as well as plenty of translucent and opaque items, for students to explore. For groups of children, consider using a room with the overhead lights turned off. Hang sheets or umbrellas to use for projection, and allow students to have individual light sources to explore. Understanding the properties of light and reflection works best by having time and materials to experiment with light as a loose part.

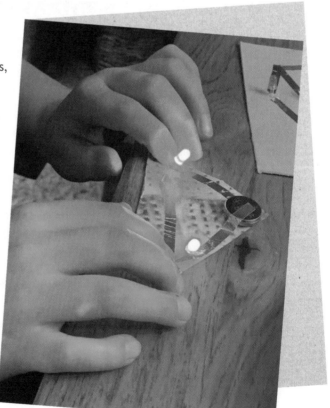

Light Sources

- Overhead projector
- Light table
- Projector with computer images
- Light-up pegboards, such as Lite Brite
- Light pad or panel
- Light box or tracing panel
- Light jars or lanterns
- Battery-operated candles
- Flashlights
- UV/black-light flashlights
- Sunlight
- Light wands
- Small lamps with flexible stands

Reflectors

- 12" x 12" acrylic mirrors
- Handheld mirrors
- Domed mirrors
- Mirror book
- Mirrored table
- Shiny tinker trays with nuts, bolts, washers, and paper clips
- Foil
- CDs
- Mylar
- Candy wrappers

(adapted from Gull, 2018d)

Loose Parts

- Plastic colored cubes
- Magna-Tiles or PicassoTiles
- Magformers
- Glass pebbles
- Mosaic tiles
- Translucent plastic glasses
- Translucent plastic swizzle sticks
- Acrylic table scatter:
  - **Leaves**
  - **Hearts**
  - **Pumpkins**
  - **Acorns**
  - **Gems**
- Printed transparencies
- Translucent dividers
- Tissue paper
- Slides
- Sliced agate rocks
- Clear geoboards
- Sternhalma (sometimes called "Chinese checkers") checkerboard
- Color-mixing paddles
- Clear colored cups
- Icicles
- Plastic colored test tubes
- Ping-Pong balls
- Translucent shapes
- Translucent counting chips

- Sequins
- Blokus and game pieces
- Translucent letters and numbers
- Natural items
  - **Leaves**
  - **Sticks**
  - **Sea sponges**
  - **Pinecones**
  - **Flowers**
- Doilies (paper or thread)
- Dry-erase markers
- Colored water in bottles
- Large clear tubing
- Clear containers, such as recycled fruit cups
- Clear egg containers
- Translucent building blocks
- X-ray films
- Marbles
- Petri dishes
- Tulle or other gauzy fabrics
- Feathers, feather boa
- Insects in resin
- Paint in ziplock bags
- Translucent bracelets
- Sections of beads
- Translucent pattern blocks
- Old costume jewelry

Carla shares additional ideas or considerations with light play in her blog post "Lights and Reflection as a Loose Part" (Gull, 2018d). She suggests providing a clear tray with a lip and filling it with sand, salt, marbles, or water beads on top of the light table. You might also consider adding seasonal items, such as leaves in autumn, paper snowflakes in winter, hearts for Valentine's Day, flowers in springtime, and so on. Add mirrors in a corner on the wall by a light table for additional reflectivity. And experiment with shadow play!

In the Loose Parts Play Facebook group, Chris Binder suggests using a clear tray of sand on the light table for writing or hiding gems. The children might use their fingers, a candy cane, stick, or feather for mark-making. They can also draw squiggly patterns, their names, a shape, or whatever they like, keeping the sand in the tray. She uses sand or salt, sometimes scented with maple in the fall, peppermint in December, or lavender when the class needs a calming effect (Gull, 2018d).

Make connections to art. Study *Starry Night* by Vincent van Gogh in conjunction with play. Project the art on the wall to immerse the children in the setting. Provide tinted glass pebbles, tiles, beads, and other transparent and opaque loose parts in blue, gold, yellow, white, and black on the light table for children to use to re-create their own starry night.

SUGGESTED BOOKS ON EXPLORING LIGHT AND REFLECTION

Use this list as a springboard for creating your own list of books that are appropriate for your grade level. Add to your list as you find other books that are rich with vocabulary, beautiful illustrations, and loose parts.

Boyd, Lizi. 2014. *Flashlight*. San Francisco: Chronicle Books.	This wordless picture book is set in a camping adventure. A child finds bats, mice, an owl, and more animals at night. In the classroom, provide dark spaces, plants, toy animals and insects, and flashlights. Encourage families to go on a flashlight hike at night.
Holeman, Joseph. 2018. *Into the Shadows*. Scotts Valley, CA: CreateSpace.	The story is illustrated in silhouettes, featuring a new story about facing fears on each page. Outside, let the children explore land features, shaded spaces, trees, sticks, and vines. Make a compiled class book of simple silhouette stories that the children create.
Lee, Suzy. 2010. *Shadow*. San Francisco: Chronicle Books.	This wordless picture book's unique illustrations show the imagination of a girl while she plays with found items in the attic. Provide light, shadow, a ladder, tools, a bicycle, a vacuum, a broom, and other items from the book for the children to explore. Use light sources and a variety of items for shadow play, imagining stories for the shadows cast.
Rosinsky, Natalie. 2002. *Light, Shadows, Mirrors, and Rainbows*. Bloomington, MN: Picture Window Books.	This nonfiction book explores reflections, rainbows, and shadows. Provide light, shadows, water, rainbows, flashlights, a projector, shapes, mirrors, and so on for the children to explore. Encourage them to investigate shadows at different times of the day outside and use flashlights indoors to make shadows and shadow creatures. Spray water or make bubbles for rainbows.

Understanding Electricity

Electricity offers many options as a loose part. After learning the basics of circuits and safety as a class, students can move beyond a step-by-step experiment or teacher demonstration and explore electrical concepts. Younger children may explore static electricity to see how various elements react to it. In one of Carla's classes, an older student lit up twenty-three LEDs with one button battery, and another taped a button battery and red LED to his nose and pretended to be Rudolph the Red-Nosed Reindeer. Other students have explored in ways we might not have noticed if we had limited the loose parts to just copper tape cards (Gull, 2020c).

While you might give a direct instruction lesson on how to complete a circuit, also give time for students to experiment and explore with the concepts. If you give only step-by-step instructions, students lose out on the opportunity to exercise their imaginations and ingenuity. Start with a simple challenge to get started with the concept, and then give students the freedom to try it in their own ways.

"Electricity is just organized lightning."

—**George Carlin, comedian**

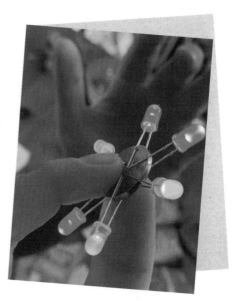

Consider having children leave loose parts for electricity exploration at school, or ask for a one-dollar donation if students want to take these materials home. Alternatively, seek grant funding or community donations for your supplies. For safety reasons, be sure to let parents know if you will be sending home something containing button batteries. You may have old electricity sets at the school that could be refreshed for electricity exploration.

Loose Parts for Electricity Exploration

- Alligator clips
- Wire
- Conductive copper tape
- Button batteries
- Battery holders
- Wire stripper/cutter
- Screwdrivers in a variety of sizes
- Needle-nose pliers
- Electronic components kit (fan, light, wires, and so on)
- Switches
- LEDs
- Lightbulbs
- Bulb holders
- Buzzer

Commercial Electricity Sets

- Snap Circuits
- Little Bits
- Circuit Blocks
- Electric building block sets
- Arduinos
- Raspberry Pi

(adapted from Gull, 2020c)

Parallel circuit	an arrangement of a circuit that splits the current into two or more paths
Series circuit	an arrangement of a circuit that allows the whole current to pass through each part without branching
Voltage	the amount of energy moving between two points on a circuit, with one point having more energy than the other
Capacitor	a device used to store electrical energy
Resistor	a device used in an electric circuit for protection, operation, or current control
Short circuit	a connection of comparatively low resistance between points on a circuit where the resistance is normally much greater; this results in excessive current flowing through a circuit; also called a *short*
Battery strength	the power capacity stored in a battery

(adapted from Merriam-Webster Dictionary, https://www.merriam-webster.com/)

In any of these applications, additional loose parts, such as cardboard, paper, markers, and other design supplies, may help extend the opportunities and allow student voice and choice in their end products. You might mount various circuit components on blocks, using alligator-clip wires to easily connect the various components. Applications may include light-up cards, ornaments, and so on. Practice and try out circuits on your own as the educator, having your own playtime before introducing electricity to students (Gull, 2020c).

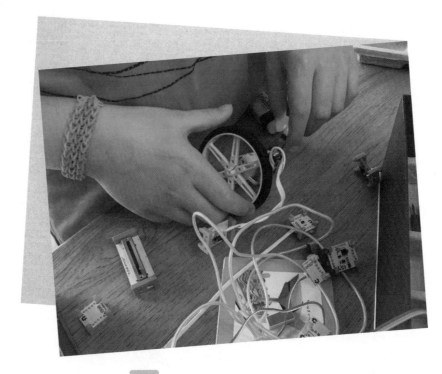

Practical Considerations

Try to anticipate and mitigate any logistical concerns you know students might have. For example, limit the amount of copper tape available as it is expensive, or have students sketch their designs before giving them materials. Consider having experienced volunteers to assist with trickier parts. Simple issues can derail an exploration. For example, flipping button batteries over can be helpful if a circuit isn't working right, being mindful of the plus and negative sides of the battery.

Consider repurposing other electronic components from tinkering tables. Cut any wires as long as possible, and save them for use with other projects. In one situation, Carla worked with a group of students to take apart a blow dryer. The fan became a great component to use as part of a study on the book *Rosie Revere, Engineer* and helping her fly. The fan was wired into other electronic components such as batteries. The children then added Ping-Pong balls, feathers, and other lightweight items that might easily float. *Making and Tinkering with STEM* by Cate Heroman (2017) outlines many good starting points for educators to explore STEM concepts and stories (Gull, 2020c).

Tips for using electricity in open-ended ways with students:

- Cut off any plugs or cords of repurposed electronics for use with other explorations.

- Work in small groups or centers to have enough supplies for the students.

- Use helpers or volunteers who are used to working with tools and/or this type of material.

- Ask for donations and look for things at garage sales and thrift stores.

- Make sure to have a variety of tools to address the students' needs.

- Scaffold to help activate prior knowledge and build skills. (Gull, 2020c)

Safety Considerations

Review safety considerations with students, such as not plugging anything into wall sockets without permission, being aware of an electric short, and not mixing electricity with water. Have students ask first before using materials outside of the approved resources in this section of exploration. Students should report to the teacher if there are any injuries or issues.

Be aware of lead or other harmful substances. Have students wear gloves and/or wash hands after taking apart old appliances or using repurposed parts. Of course, don't lick the items!

Regularly review materials used for safety concerns. Discard materials that are too worn out, sharp, or will no longer work.

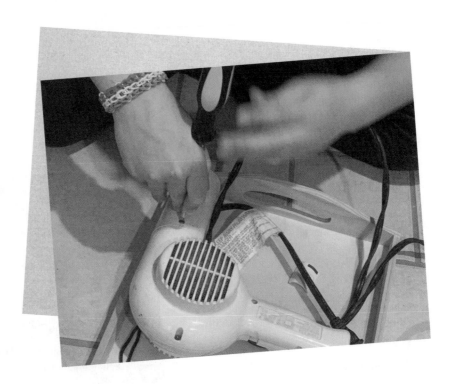

Creating Squishy Circuits

Squishy circuits are one application of electricity as a loose part. Create the circuits using conductive playdough, such as the regular playdough you have in your classroom, and insulating playdough.

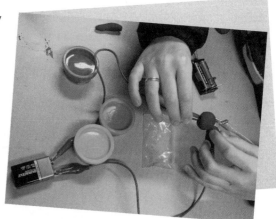

Materials

Playdough (any brand)

2 cups distilled water

¾ cup sugar

2 cup all-purpose flour

4 tsp. cream of tartar

2 Tbsp. vegetable oil

Food coloring

Electronic components, such as LED lights, alligator clips, battery holder, wires, motors, and batteries

What to Do

Use any commercially available playdough as the conductive dough.

To make the insulating dough, combine the water, sugar, flour, cream of tartar, and vegetable oil.

(Commercial kits are also available.)

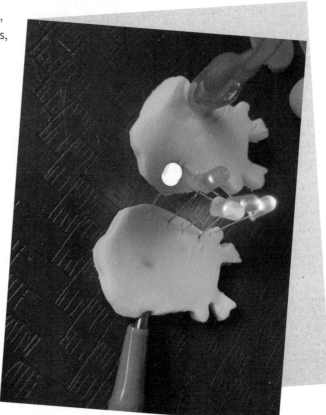

To make the squishy circuits, students will want to have two separate balls of regular playdough, separated by the insulating playdough in between. Use one or multiple LED lights between with one wire in each of the playdough balls. Connect the wires from the battery packs (with batteries) to the dough balls (not directly to the LED light), experimenting with the direction

126

of the LED wires to complete the circuit. Students can create their own options, simply exploring electronic components and/or adding artistic designs with colored dough that can be illuminated. They might build a playdough house, car, animal, or whatever they may want to make with glowing eyes, windows, or headlights. Students might also use the motor as part of the circuit to make fans or sculptures that move.

Carla also likes to use an energy ball or stick that lights up and makes noises when the circuit is complete. What is unique about it is that the current can go through bodies, so the children's bodies become part of the circuit. The circuit may start with students holding hands in a circle and using an arm as a switch to turn the circuit on and off. Children find other applications of this when given time to experiment with the circuit (Gull, 2020c).

Exploring Green Screens

Green screens are a flexible technology option that can be used across content areas to illustrate learning with cool effects. Taking a picture or video in front of a green screen allows the user to replace the green background with a different setting. There are many other fun and interesting tricks to tinker with as well, such as putting a Lego minifigure on a green skewer with green playdough, so the figure seemingly flies (Goodwin, n.d.b).

To use green screens in the classroom, start with a green screen, an app, and an idea. Slowly introduce the concept of green screens with examples, and allow the children to play around with the technology. Students can explore in small groups and eventually work toward paired or individual projects. Allow for mistakes, as well as student choice and voice, as children get used to this technology (Goodwin, n.d.b).

To get started, Carla gathered a bin of anything green she could find, downloaded applicable apps to a few devices, and kept a portable green screen up in her setting. She played with the variables, and then she shared green screen examples and ideas with students before giving them free rein to experiment. This green screen concept can be used for any subject matter (or combinations) as a tool of expression and content, such as retelling a story, giving a report on a historical figure imposed on a background from that time era, or explaining a life cycle of an insect.

Loose Parts for Use with Green Screens

- Green cardboard trifold
- Green felt
- Wall painted green
- Green plastic tablecloth
- Green Lego baseplates
- Pop-up green screen
- Green screen backdrop
- Green fabric
- Green bulletin board paper
- Green folder
- Green fabric storage cube
- Pizza box painted green
- Green Astrobrights paper
- Playdough
- Chair
- Bottle
- Colored water in a clear bottle
- Plastic egg
- Stretchy putty
- Skewer painted green
- Green gloves for hands
- Green fabric or felt for disappearing body parts
- Color-changing cups
- Cookie cutters
- Slinkies
- Plastic cups
- Masks
- Craft sticks
- Straws

Apps and Tech to Consider

- Green Screen by Doink
- iMovie
- WeVideo (works with Chromebooks)
- Kinemaster
- Pic Collage EDU
- Easy Stop Motion Studio
- Theme Poem
- eCamm Live
- Parrot Teleprompter
- iPad
- Chromebook
- Wireless microphone
- Tripods
- iPad or device holders

(adapted from Goodwin n.d.a, n.d.b.)

Using Stop-Motion Animation

Stop-motion animation is a technique that allows students to create a scene with small figures and items; it's another option for self-expression using a technology tool. Students position a figure in a scenario, take a photo, move the figure a little bit and take another photo, and then repeat and repeat. The end result of the stacked photos is the appearance that the figure is moving. The characters, backgrounds, settings, and objects in the scenario are all variables and can be composed of loose parts. Students can use this approach to tell their own stories or share content and knowledge in their own way. With stop-motion animation, students are engaged, motivated, and have choice and voice in the learning process. Many educators use the Stop Motion app on iPads with small loose parts, such as Lego minifigures and blocks, Scrabble tiles, foil, sticky notes, cutouts, playdough, puppets, scenery pieces, dry-erase boards and markers, small toy cars and animals, toothpicks, cotton swabs, and so on. Use the tablet, with an app loaded, on a tripod or case to set up the scene for recording. This can also be combined with green screens. Consider lighting, and set up near a window for natural light or use an external light on a tripod for lighting.

Stop-motion animation is especially useful for showing a progression or process, such as life cycles, food webs, moon phases, place value, fractions, spelling practice, timelines, and historical reenactments. Loose parts can easily be used to show the construction of any of the above with a new rock or other loose part being added or slightly moved for the next frame. Stephanie Hatten (2014), a district technology specialist, suggests the following process to use stop-motion animation with students:

- Pick a technology or app for stop-motion animation.

- Practice using the program.

- Share stop-motion animation samples with students.

- Set up basic parameters for student projects, such as a time limit or topic.

- Encourage the students to work together in groups.

- Allow students to use simple materials, manipulatives, or loose parts to illustrate the process.

- Secure the camera.

- Practice the sequence with small movements.

- Share with an audience, such as on a classroom blog.

- Repeat the process!

Investigating Coding

Coding gives students the skills to create whatever they want in the digital realm, with the digital elements and coding serving as the loose parts or variables. As they follow their own interests, students become motivated to be producers rather than just consumers (Common Sense Education, 2017). Coding can begin with simple games such as Simon Says to let the children get used to following step-by-step instructions before you introduce the technology.

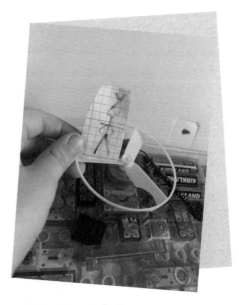

Code.org, Scratch, CodeMonkey, and Made with Code are four websites to help students get used to coding. Common Sense Education (2017) offers the following tips to include coding in the classroom:

- Learn along with your students.

- Help students become experts with a student-led knowledge base.

- Let students' own interests drive their learning.

SUGGESTED BOOKS ON CODING

Use this list as a springboard for creating your own list of technology books that are appropriate for your grade level. Add to your list as you find other books that are rich with vocabulary, beautiful illustrations, and loose parts.

Antony, Steve. 2018. *Unplugged.* New York: Scholastic.	Blip the robot lives connected to a computer, listening to music, playing games, and (virtually) visiting faraway places. When the power goes out, Blip accidentally trips over a wire to the outdoors. She becomes friends with the animals and enjoys real-life nature, building a fort, playing on a seesaw, and more. Take computer activities off-screen and outside! Build a fort. Use popular computer games in real-life activities.

SUGGESTED BOOKS ON CODING

Funk, Josh. 2018. *How to Code a Sandcastle.* New York: Viking.	Pearl has diligently been working on a sandcastle, but it keeps being ruined by puppies and frisbees. Pearl and her robotic friend, Pascal, decide to use code to build the sandcastle, creating small steps to solve the problem and introducing the reader to basics of coding. Coding has applications to any big problem: break down a big problem into smaller steps to solve. Then sequence the steps to complete an action. The terms *sequence* (code written in a specific order), *loop* (repeat something in the code), and *if-then-else* (conditional that tells you what to do, similar to true-and-false questions) are illustrated in the book and defined in more detail at the back. Encourage the children to work in pairs to apply their own code by completing a movement in the classroom with the terminology, such as moving from one spot to another. The pairs can then play around with their own nondigital "code" to complete simple classroom tasks to prepare for the logic sequencing needed in other digital coding projects such as Scratch, Minecraft Education, Micro:bit, Sphero, and other devices that use the same digital terminology. Tutorials and simulators using block coding are available within the programs.
Karanja, Caroline. 2018. *Gabi's If/Then Garden.* North Mankato, MN: Capstone.	Using computer coding if/then commands, Gabi and her friend take care of a garden. The girls use coding to enjoy their work in the garden and play. They often ask, "What if?" and "I wonder." Create your own if/then game. Try simple coding on the computer or with a robot. Apply coding to play. Try "What if?" and "I wonder" in a new situation. Garden in real life. Use loose parts such as soil, seeds, water, sunlight, if/then statements, vegetables, animals, shovels, music, art supplies, books, and sounds.
Liukas, Linda. 2015. *Hello Ruby: Adventures in Coding.* New York: Feiwel and Friends.	Ruby has a large imagination and perseveres in puzzle solving. She makes friends with the animals and robots in her world as she uses concepts of basic coding, exploration, and creativity. This book includes suggestions for activities, such as hosting a gem hunt, creating a map for problem solving, building a raft challenge, and much more.
McCloskey, Shanda. 2018. *Doll-E 1.0.* New York: Little, Brown Books for Young Readers.	Charlotte tinkers, imagines, and knows how to work with computers. When her mother gives her a doll, her dog quickly rips it apart. Charlotte fixes and programs the doll with an upgrade. Use toys, a Micro:bit, and electronic spare parts to create an upgraded toy. Code the Micro:bit to play tones or light up, and embed it into the toy. Lessons and options for using the Micro:bit can be found at: https://microbit.org/lessons/

Designing and Using Robotics in the Classroom

Robotics can be an engaging, open-ended option that has the potential to teach coding as well. Students build skills in logic, systems thinking, problem solving, collaboration, and teamwork through robotics play and interdisciplinary STEM learning (Common Sense Education, 2019). There are a variety of robotics options to use in early childhood classrooms, such as Bee-Bots, Ozobots, Dot and Dash Robots, Blue-Bot, Root Coding, and RoboCode (Common Sense Education, 2019; Griffiths, 2019). After choosing a robotics platform, playing around with technology as the educator, and introducing robots (including classroom management) to students, the children can use the technology tool to solve problems. Technology becomes another variable to build creativity and imagination. For classroom management, consider numbering each robotic set, using a designated cart or cabinet for storage, exploring the technology yourself, rotating through team roles, and planning in time for cleanup at the end of each session (Lego Education, 2017).

Lego Education WeDo 2.0 is a developmentally appropriate brick-building robotic system for early elementary classrooms, offering students the opportunity not only to build their own creations but also to program how the creation is used. While expensive, STEM grants and fundraising are available to help cover costs. Additionally, one set could be used as a station that students rotate to or select rather than having a full classroom set. The school could also have one mobile classroom set available for checkout for all classes. Lego Education (2020) suggests DonorsChoose.org for community funding; writing grants (and includes a grant writing guide on its website); and using Individual with Disabilities Education Act and Perkins funding as well as Title I, II, III, and IV sources to help offset costs. The core set comes with materials and technology for two students, along with a curriculum pack. In addition to the WeDo proprietary set, each group using the materials will need a computer or tablet. Students are encouraged to question and explore their understanding and can solve real-life problems with a hands-on approach.

The WeDo system works with a variety of subjects and connects with standards using an "explore, create, and share" process. During the explore stage, students connect and discuss. During the create phase, students build, program, and modify. During the share phase, students document and present. Guided projects can help students get acquainted with the materials, the design process, and programming. Open projects are also available to allow students to have more control over the experience while having design library support (Lego Education, 2017).

Lego WeDo is built around the six engineering habits of mind:

- Systems thinking
- Creativity
- Optimism
- Collaboration
- Communication
- Ethical considerations (Lego Education, 2017)

Additionally, WeDo 2.0 projects develop eight science and engineering practices:

- Ask questions and solve problems.
- Use models.
- Design prototypes.
- Investigate.
- Analyze and interpret data.
- Use computational thinking.
- Engage in argument from evidence.
- Obtain, evaluate, and communicate information (Lego Education, 2017).

Exploring these habits and practices can benefit any loose-parts interaction.

Encouraging Open-Ended Technology Options

Some technology is inherently open ended and can be used in many ways. Simple technology, such as word-processing programs, slides, recording options, and so on allow the variables within the program to be used for whatever topic or application that is desired by the student and teacher.

GarageBand is a sound engineering program that allows experimentation with sound and music. Minecraft and Roblox are two popular applications that allow children to use resources within the program to build and create whatever they may want within the application. Capitalize on students' natural interests and build STEAM curriculum that utilizes open-ended options.

In one group, Carla worked with the children to formulate Minecraft IRL (In Real Life). In collaborating with the students—who were also the experts—the group brainstormed options. Her group created Minecraft-inspired zones for their outdoor classroom, such as a crafting table, a potions area, a cartography table, and so on. They created a cart with basic supplies needed for their adventures, such as map-making supplies, potion experiments, cardboard builds, chain reactions, creating a blueprint of a house, simple machines, water exploration, archery, and so on. To inspire play connected to Minecraft during outdoor free time, they color-coded the activities in the outdoor classroom zones and made slips that students could draw to select their activities (Gull, 2020i).

She suggests the following tips for doing this type of project:

- Note the children's interest.

- Have children show and/or explain their interest.

- Facilitate brainstorming for extension or IRL options.

- Group and categorize the ideas.

- Make the ideas visual.

- Do it! PLAY!

- Celebrate and document! (Gull, 2020i)

Technology has the open-ended power apply in a variety of circumstances and can be used as a tool to meet many classroom standards. How we structure interactions with technology can really allow students to use this tool for imagination and creativity. Technology itself can become a loose part.

· **CHAPTER 11** ·
Reading and Literacy

The bumper sticker that says, "If you can read this, thank a teacher" is so true. Providing a strong literacy foundation is of primary importance to the early childhood education teacher and using loose-parts supports an active learning environment. Children love to hear a delightful story and then use puppets and dress-up items to act it out. Smith-Gilman (2018) explains, "Children have opportunities to create their own stories, ponder, and use open-ended materials to transform them into imaginative constructions or tales." In a literacy-rich environment, baskets of books surround the elementary-age child. Teachers use labels to reinforce letter recognition and help the children learn to read important words. McClure et al. (2017) advise: "The environment should be an intentionally created, aesthetically beautiful space that continually demonstrates a negotiation of the tensions between flexibility and static, richness/complexity and clarity/simplicity, the unexpected and the expected, and children's desires and educators' abilities to listen and respond." A loose-parts environment adds a dimension to the classroom that ultimately enriches the opportunity for choice, creativity, and individualization.

135

The Common Core State Standards Initiative (National Governors Association Center for Best Practices and Council of Chief State School Officers, 2010) includes reading, writing, speaking, and listening benchmarks for early elementary children. Teachers are to support children's learning of reading skills, such as asking questions, recounting stories, describing characters, understanding rhyme, recognizing point of view, using text features and reading for information, comparing and contrasting, understanding the main idea, drawing conclusions, phonemic awareness, recognizing similarities and differences, and understanding concepts of print.

In the area of writing, students increase their knowledge of syntax, vocabulary, and writing organization. In the areas of speaking and listening, students engage in conversations with peers and adults, read aloud, and speak audibly.

Loose parts can play an integral role in developing these skills. As noted in chapter 10, many open-ended technology options can provide a space for students to practice literacy and communication skills in a loose-parts digital environment. In this chapter, you will find ways to meet early literacy standards by using loose parts and open-ended technology.

Storytelling with Loose Parts

A variety of loose parts materials can help children bring stories to life. For example, story baskets filled with rich children's books, puppets, felt pieces, and other loose parts are a great way to support children's abilities to tell, retell, and understand stories. Simply fill a basket, box, plastic shoebox, or any container with a children's book, puppets, rocks, felt pieces, and other loose-parts props that relate to the book (Ball, 2013). Then, children can re-create the story using the loose parts in the basket or make up a new story.

If You Give a Mouse a Cookie Story Basket

Materials

If You Give a Mouse a Cookie by Laura Numeroff

Felt

Glue

Milk carton

Straw

Napkin

Unbreakable mirror

Child-safe scissors

What to Do

If You Give a Mouse a Cookie by Laura Numeroff is an engaging book to use. In the story basket for this book, include felt and other materials for the students to create their own mouse. Also include props for retelling the story, such as a milk carton, straw, napkin, mirror, and so on. Additionally, the items in the basket could be to support oral language and vocabulary development and storytelling skills.

Inspired by the book *Idea Jar* by Adam Lehrhaupt and Deb Pilutti (2018), idea jars are excellent springboards for writing in the early childhood years and beyond!

Story Idea Jar

Materials

Large, clear plastic jar

Paper

Marker

Scissors

Objects, such as plastic animals, people, rocks, trees, and other small loose parts

What to Do

Cut paper into strips. On each strip, write a word. Put the strips into the jar.

A student reaches into the idea jar and pulls out two slips of paper. The student writes the words on a larger sheet of paper. For example, a child pulls out the words *cat* and *tree*. She then writes these words on a larger piece of paper.

The student then thinks about ways these words are related and how they can weave a story. The student draws a picture and writes the story. In our example, the student might write and draw a story about a cat who climbs a tree and meets a bird.

Another possibility is to include actual objects in the jar for storytelling, such as plastic animals, people, rocks, trees, and other small loose parts.

Storymaking

Authors Mary Compton and Robin Thompson (2018) offer ideas for using loose parts in their book *StoryMaking*. The stages of the storymaker cycle include imagine, play, make, and share. Loose parts are an integral component of the play and make stages. Options for storymaking makerspaces include but are not limited to blocks, sculpting, housekeeping/dramatic play, drawing and painting, collage, and weaving.

During the imagine phase, students plan and think of possibilities focusing on how materials might be used. The teacher is the "guide on the side" and is instrumental at this phase. Teachers ask important open-ended questions, such as "What do you think?" or "How can these materials be used to create that?" Building vocabulary, developing oral language, sparking imagination, and inspiring creativity are the goals at this stage. During the play phase, students explore and use loose parts to experiment and create use critical thinking. Then, the pupils make their ideas. During the last stage, share, the students can set up museums, write stories or books about their project, or think of other ways to share their work.

Stonework Play

Rocks can be a loose-parts vehicle to express a story that can then be written down. In her article "International Stonework Play Day," Diana Suskind (2019) suggests a wonderful, open-ended, kinesthetic way to create a meaningful, descriptive story.

In the gathering step, students find the rocks they will use for their project. Then, in the constructing step, learners spend time creating their ideas with the stones. Rendering is the next phase, during which students spend time illustrating their stone arrangements. In the narrating step, the students write the stories about their stone creations. Last, in the sharing step, students display both the stonework and the story with an audience (Suskind, 2019).

A memorable book to connect rocks and literacy is *Roxaboxen* by Alice McLerran. In this book, the neighborhood children create a town using stones, pebbles, rocks, boxes, and any other found materials. This book contains complex storytelling and sparks imagination. Gull (2017c) suggests other noteworthy rock books to spark children's imaginations and support their growing literacy skills:

Baylor, Byrd. 1985. *Everybody Needs a Rock.* New York: Aladdin.

Christian, Peggy. 2000. *If You Find a Rock.* New York: Harcourt.

Goldsworthy, Andy. 2011. *Stone.* Revised ed. New York: Thames and Hudson.

Griffin, Molly Beth. 2014. *Rhoda's Rock Hunt.* St. Paul, MN: Minnesota Historical Society Press.

Iselin, Josie. 2007. *Heart Stones.* New York: Harry N. Abrams.

Lionni, Leo. 1995. *On My Beach There Are Many Pebbles.* New York: HarperCollins.

McGuirk, Leslie. 2011. *If Rocks Could Sing: A Discovered Alphabet.* New York: Tricycle Press.

Pouyet, Marc. 2009. *Natural: Simple Land Art through the Seasons.* London, UK: Frances Lincoln Children's Books.

Pouyet, Marc. 2013. *Land Art in Town: Simple Inspiration through the Seasons.* London, UK: Frances Lincoln Children's Books.

Rosinsky, Natalie. *Rocks: Hard, Soft, Smooth, and Rough.* Mankato, MN: Picture Window Books.

Salas, Laura Purdie. 2015. *A Rock Can Be . . .* Minneapolis, MN: Millbrook Press.

Stuve-Bodeen, Stephanie. 1998. *Elizabeti's Doll.* New York: Lee and Low.

Sharing Loose Parts–Inspired Books

Books are a wonderful, motivating introduction to a lesson! There are so many engaging cross-curricular books to spark student interest, motivate, and engage. For example, you could use *The Button Box* by Margaret Reid to teach color words.

Materials

The Button Box by Margarette Reid

Box or container

Buttons in a variety of colors

Index cards

Markers

What to Do

Fill a container with a variety of colorful buttons. On index cards write color words, one word per card.

Read the book to the students.

Invite the students to empty the container and explore the buttons.

Eventually, the students can sort the buttons by color. Spread out the color-word index cards on the floor. Invite the children to sort the buttons by placing them on or near the card with the button's color written on it.

When they complete the activity, they can return the buttons to the container and place it and the color-word cards on a shelf for the children to use later during their explorations.

There are so many books for storytelling and creating that you can use to help teach literacy skills. Consider using loose parts–inspired books as read alouds, for children to read to themselves, for shared reading, as springboards for creation, as an invitation or extension of learning, as options for retelling a story, as inspiration for small-world play options, and for role playing. The following is a short list of books that could be springboards for loose parts–inspired literacy lessons. This list is just the beginning!

SUGGESTED LOOSE-PARTS BOOKS TO SUPPORT LITERACY SKILLS

Use this list as a springboard for creating your own list of loose parts-inspired books that are appropriate for your grade level. Add to your list as you find other books that are rich with vocabulary, beautiful illustrations, and loose parts.

Anderson, Constance. 2017. *A Stick Until . . .* Cambridge, MA: Star Bright Books.	This book takes the reader through the life of a stick, exploring its uses with animals and humans. With sticks, water, and leaves, children can demonstrate the uses of these items. Invite them to document their explorations through photography or drawing and then to dictate their uses and reasoning.
BooydeGraaf, Wendy. 2016. *Salad Pie*. Portland, OR: Ripple Grove.	Maggie is enjoying her time alone in the park making "salad pie" until Herbert shows up. He tries to add to her salad pie, but she doesn't want his help. He persists, saving her and the salad at the bottom of the slide. Outside, set up a mud kitchen, and encourage the children to "cook" using natural loose parts. Inside, discuss sharing and including others, make and eat salads, and learn about vegetables.
Castella, Krystina, and Brian Boyl. 2005. *Discovering Nature's Alphabet*. Berkeley, CA: Heyday Books.	This is a beautiful picture book of letters found in nature. Go for a walk with the students. Take pictures with a camera, and then encourage them to write about what they found.
Christian, Peggy. 2000. *If You Find a Rock*. New York: Harcourt.	The book takes the reader on a journey through various kinds of rocks, but not the scientific kinds—the practical kinds, the ones for memory, kicking, worrying, and so on. Provide or go outside to find assorted rocks. Invite the children to make their own rock book using photography, drawing, and writing.
Ehlert, Lois. 2005. *Leaf Man*. New York: Harcourt.	During autumn, Leaf Man travels to many locations in which leaves of all kinds create animals and landscapes. Go out in nature and encourage the children to gather materials for loose parts. Create "leaf men" and other characters outside. Invite the children share their creations and to make collaborative stories about the creations.

SUGGESTED LOOSE-PARTS BOOKS TO SUPPORT LITERACY SKILLS

Ferry, Beth. 2015. *Stick and Stone*. New York: Houghton Mifflin Harcourt.	Stick and Stone stick up for each other and become friends. Give children a stick, a stone, a pinecone, and water to act out the story. Encourage children to go outside and collect items to create their own stories.
Gilman, Phoebe. 1988. *Jillian Jiggs*. New York: Scholastic.	Jillian loves to create and tinker! She uses boxes to make robots until she needs to clean her room, when she creates pirates, dragons, trees, chickens in a cage, and so much more. Provide pots, pans, kitchen utensils, dress-up clothes, paper, cardboard boxes, magnets, blankets, tubes, and yarn. Invite the children to create costumes to tell stories. They could write stories based on their play. Help them work on a system to clean up after they play.
Gilman, Phoebe. 1992. *Something from Nothing*. New York: Scholastic.	This Jewish folktale about a young boy, his beloved blanket, and his grandfather, who shows how to repurpose items to make something from nothing. Provide fabric, scissors, paper, pebbles, glue (tacky), sequins, buttons, pencils, markers, crayons, fabric paint, and old clothing. Encourage the children to use the materials to make creations. Invite the children's families to share family stories.
Heder, Thyra. 2013. *Fraidyzoo*. New York: Abrams Books for Young Readers.	A family creates zoo animals out of many different household items. Provide loose parts such as tongs, cardboard, plastic bags, sticky notes, ropes, cardboard tubes, blankets, boxes, plastic bottles, umbrellas, and newspapers. Encourage the children to create a zoo and then write about it. They can use cardboard to make dramatic-play costumes.

Hutchins, Hazel, and Gail Herbert. 2008. *Mattland*. Toronto, ON: Annick Press.	Matt has moved many times and is unhappy about the family's latest move. He's about to break a stick in anger when he realizes the stick feels good in his hand. He begins drawing in the dirt, gradually creating a river, a lake, and a town: Mattland. Other children help him save the town from a rainstorm, and he finds new friends. Provide loose parts such as sticks, mud, rocks, scrap wood, tin, seeds, craft sticks, shingles, pinecones, berry containers, pine needles, keys, pennies, pebbles, tile, string, and water. Encourage the children to build their own land. Talk about the challenges of moving, the need to include others, and what you might see at construction zones.
Hutchins, Pat. 1987. *Changes, Changes*. New York: Aladdin.	This is a wordless book in which two characters build a house, a fire truck, a boat, and more. Provide block people figures, colorful blocks, red tangrams, gray or white wool or cotton, blue fabric, and yellow sand, and encourage the children to make different scenes from the book or to create their own, then use the scenes for creating stories.
Jocelyn, Marthe. 2004. *Hannah's Collections*. Toronto, ON: Tundra Books.	Hannah loves to collect treasures and almost has a museum of collections in her room. She must choose just one collection to share with her class. She uses items from her collections to make a sculpture—the first in her new collection! Provide loose parts such as buttons, craft sticks, seashells, feathers, leaves, barrettes, stuffed toys, and jewelry. Invite the children to sort, arrange, and categorize by color, size, shape, and type. Encourage them to count the items in a collection and then to count backward. They can create their own collections or make sculptures out of found objects. Invite them to bring a collection from home to class to share. They can make sorting boxes for collections too.

Lechner, John. 2009. *The Clever Stick*. Somerville, MA: Candlewick.	A stick wants to talk and express itself but has no voice until a happy accident gives him one. Outdoors, provide or encourage the children to find sticks, leaves, sand, pebbles, rocks, water, and rakes. Encourage them to smooth the sand or mud and write or draw.
Piven, Hanoch. 2002. *The Perfect Purple Feather*. New York: Little, Brown Books for Young Readers.	Follow the perfect feather along its journey. Encourage the children to extend the story by writing or dictating. Provide loose parts such as feathers, scissors, forks, bulbs, springs, buttons, cones, nails, combs, metal, and computer parts. Invite the children to create.
Portis, Antoinette. 2006. *Not a Box*. New York: HarperCollins.	When Rabbit is asked why it is sitting in a box, Rabbit insists that it's NOT a box, but a race car, a mountain, a house on fire, a robot, a pirate ship, and much more. Provide assorted boxes of all sizes, and invite the children to see what they can create. Follow the pattern in the book to make a class book about the children's creations.
Portis, Antoinette. 2007. *Not a Stick*. New York: HarperCollins.	When Pig is warned to be careful with a stick, Pig insists that it's NOT a stick, but a sword, a fishing rod, a horse, and much more. Provide assorted sticks of all sizes and a variety of pretend-play props, and invite the children to see what they can create. Make a class book about the children's creations.
Reid, Margarette. 1990. *The Button Box*. New York: Dutton Juvenile.	A young boy explores his grandmother's button box, swirling them and choosing which ones he likes best. He counts them, sorts them, pretends they are jewels, imagines what they came from, creates rainbows, and makes observations. Explore the activities in the book. Listen to the children's stories about grandma's buttons. Encourage the children to imagine a visit to grandma's home. Provide a variety of buttons, and invite the students to sort them, create collages, or do other explorations with these materials. Encourage them to write about the project they create.

SUGGESTED LOOSE-PARTS BOOKS TO SUPPORT LITERACY SKILLS

Stuve-Bodeen, Stephanie. 1998. *Elizabeti's Doll*. New York: Lee and Low.	Elizabeti has a new baby brother but no doll of her own. She finds a rock just the right size and names it Eva. When the baby has a bath, so does Eva. Elizabeti loses her "baby" while she is doing her chores, but they are reunited as she cooks over the stone fire pit. Provide rocks, cloth, and paint, and encourage the children to make rock dolls and then to write their creations.
Thompson, Clare. n.d. *Junk DNA*. Chester, England, UK: C. P. Thompson Creations. (Available on Etsy.com.)	Follow the journey of a pile of junk in this wordless picture book. As it shifts and moves, a few pieces land perfectly to create a being. The creature uses more metal scraps to build a house and then another being. They create vehicles, more people, and shelter. Provide a variety of metal loose parts, such as keys, screws, springs, bottle caps, wrenches, locks, gears, hinges, and so on. Invite the children to create with the materials, perhaps making a character and story and their own wordless picture book.
Yolen, Jane. 2016. *What to Do with a Box*. Mankato, MN: Creative Editions.	This book explores how a boy uses his imagination to do various things with a box. Gather materials, such as books, keys, dolls, stuffed animals, tea sets, paint and paintbrushes, crayons and markers, a fan, helmets and goggles, a suitcase, and boxes. Invite the children to experiment with using a box to create.

(adapted from Gull, 2018c)

Learning Words, Concepts, and Ideas

"Reading is the undeniable foundation for success in society. The children of the twenty-first century will face many challenges that will require them to use reading and writing in different forms" (Levenson Goldstein, 2007). Tompkins (2017) states, "Teaching reading and writing effectively is a great responsibility." Many parents have an a-ha moment when they are driving in the car and their child sitting in the backseat says, "Mommy, look! That says Target!" or asks, "Daddy, can we stop at that McDonald's?" They may be proudly thinking, "My child can read!" However, as educators we know that the child is recognizing environmental print. Children are like sponges and want to learn to read; it is essential to surround them with classroom materials that foster literacy.

Provide a variety of loose parts for children to use during classroom literacy time. In their book *Guided Reading: Responsive Teaching across the Grades*, Irene Fountas and Gay Pinnell (1996) encourage a classroom environment that is print rich. Levenson Goldstein (2007) also describes how to create a classroom that includes spaces for a book corner, a writing center, a library, among others. The classroom can have a reading corner that includes a diverse selection of books ranging from fiction big books, picture books, board books, rhyming books, early emergent readers, and chapter books to nonfiction books on animals, history, science, math, and engineering. An elementary classroom should be filled with hundreds of books, including many books that demonstrate the power of loose parts and literacy.

Think about your classroom environment. Do you provide specific areas such as a reading corner, writing center, dramatic-play area, block area, or a makerspace? Here is a list of supplies and loose parts you could use to equip your classroom zones for literacy, critical thinking, problem solving, and engagement. Please be sure to add other areas and items that will encourage learning, critical thinking, problem solving, and conversations.

Loose Parts and Supplies to Support Writing

- Colored pencils
- Crayons
- Fine-tipped markers
- Playdough
- Stamps
- Paint
- Paintbrushes
- Variety of paper—construction, lined, cardboard
- Sand and salt trays
- Dry-erase boards and markers

Loose Parts and Supplies to Support Literacy

- Baskets or tubs of books organized by reading level, theme, author, or topic
- Phonics baskets or tubs
- Clipboards
- Pencils
- Markers
- Headset/CD player/tablet
- Green screen
- Stop-animation supplies
- Videomaking and literacy software
- Individual whiteboards and markers
- Alphabet cookie cutters
- Playdough
- Letter tiles or cards
- Word-family tiles or cards
- Sandpaper letters
- Letter stamps
- Plastic and/or magnetic alphabet letters
- Puppets
- Costumes
- Tree cookies with letters
- Rocks with letters

Miscellaneous Loose Parts

- Small plastic toys
- Costumes
- Beanbag chairs
- Pillows
- Blocks
- Buttons
- Wooden cubes
- Cookie sheets
- Muffin tins
- Divided trays and bowls
- Squirt bottles
- Clothespins
- Craft sticks
- Variety of tapes
- Hole punch
- Scissors
- Stapler
- Magazines
- Wallpaper
- Fabric pieces
- Scarves

Early literacy skills are made up of many different components that create a balanced literacy program:

- Concepts of print
- Phonemic awareness
- Decoding and word attack (sight words)
- Systematic explicit phonics
- Spelling
- Comprehension (Levenson Goldstein, 2007)

In this section, we describe language arts skills along with ways to use loose parts to foster proficiency in early elementary reading/language arts skills. To start, instruct the students how to complete each of the following listed activities. Then, you can include these activities in a systematic fashion on a weekly choice chart.

Concepts of Print

Knowledge of the concepts of print is the first step toward literacy. As young children gain reading-readiness skills, they learn the parts of a book, correct book orientation, left-to-right directionality, how to move their eyes from the end of a line of text to the beginning of the next line (called *return sweep*), and letter/word concepts. Many loose-parts materials, such as magnetic letters, alphabet tiles, and foam letters, can support children in developing letter recognition. In addition, these materials can also be used to reinforce other reading skills in the areas of phonics, sight-word recognition, and spelling. Although not necessary, you can organize the materials in tubs, shoeboxes, or baskets. Students can freely manipulate and create their own letter sorts and letter explorations. The following activities will promote mastery of concepts of print.

Letter Sorting

Materials

Tub or box

Letter tiles

Magnetic letters

Letter cards

What to Do

Children can sort the tiles, magnetic letters, and cards by letter, by uppercase letters, by lowercase letters, and into sets of consonants and vowels. This is an example of sorting letters and placing under the correct alphabet letter. Children can also place loose-parts objects under the appropriate beginning letter.

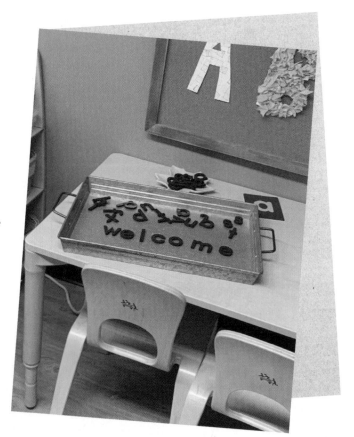

Alphabet Graphs

Materials

Alphabet cards

Children's name cards

Pocket chart

What to Do

When children come to class, they can take their name card and place it under the letter that is at the beginning of their name. Children can also place loose-parts objects under the appropriate beginning letter.

Painting Letters

Materials

Rocks

Leaves

Scrap tile

Wood pieces

Sticks

Paint

What to Do

Children can use paint on a variety of surfaces to make letters. Also, they could glue objects to a paper and paint the beginning letter of the object.

Letter-Hunt Collage

Materials

Magazines

Newspapers

Scissors

Construction paper

Glue

What to Do

Provide magazines or newspapers, and encourage the children to find a specific letter, such as the first letter in their names.

They can cut out the letters and create a collage, adding images or drawings as they wish.

Phonemic Awareness

Phonemic awareness is one of the best predictors in learning to read. Researchers Keith Stanovich, Anne Cunningham, and Barbara Cramer (1984) conclude, "The relative predictive accuracy of the phonological tasks was equal to or better than more global measures of cognitive skills such as an intelligence test and a reading readiness test." Researchers Hallie Yopp and Ruth Yopp (2000) explain, "Phonemic awareness is the awareness that the speech stream consists of a sequence of sounds, specifically phonemes, the smallest unit of sound that makes a difference in communication." They also state, "It is widely acknowledged that phonemic awareness is important in learning to read."

The skills that comprise phonemic awareness are the following:

- Rhyming
- Blending
- Sound substitution
- Sound deletion
- Segmentation

It is important that students "play around with sounds" to discover these phonemic-awareness skills. By the way, sound is a loose part! Sing songs and say chants, such as rhyming songs, nursery rhymes, tongue twisters, and clapping/rhythm games. Teachers can first instruct the students in each of the following activities. Then, during literacy time, the students can have a choice.

Hink/Pink

Materials

Index cards

Marker

What to Do

On one side of an index card, write a rhyming pair of one-syllable words, such as "fat cat." On the other side of the card, write a clue, such as "overweight feline." You can make several of these cards using rhyming words such as "third bird," "one bun," "top pop," and many more.

Challenge the children to listen to each clue and then say the rhyming pair.

Children can think of other rhyming pairs and clues, and then illustrate and create a book.

Word Finds

Materials

Clipboards

Paper

Pencils

What to Do

Provide clipboards, paper, and pencils. Invite the children to walk around the classroom or outdoors finding objects that have a particular sound, such as words that start with /m/ or words that end with /ot/, and draw pictures of the items.

Hinky/Pinky

Materials

Index cards

Marker

What to Do

On one side of an index card, write a
rhyming pair of two-syllable words,
such as "better sweater." On the
other side of the card, write a clue,
such as "improved cardigan."

You can make several of these cards
using rhyming words such as "funny bunny," "double trouble," and
many more.

Challenge the children to listen to the clue and then say the rhyming pair.

Children can think of other rhyming pairs and clues, and then illustrate and create a book.

Elkonin Boxes

Materials

Paper

Marker

Ruler

Small loose parts, such as pebbles or shells

Images, such as a cat, dish, stop sign, pen, and so on

What to Do

Draw four squares in a row on a piece of paper to make Elkonin boxes (or you can print ones
found online). Make copies for the children to use, and provide small loose parts.

Show a student a picture. Encourage her to slide a loose part from box to box to indicate the
number of sounds she hears when she names the object in the picture. For example, if the
picture showed a cat, the child would slide the pebble into three boxes and say each sound:
/c/a/t/. If the illustration were of a stop sign, the student would slide the pebble into four boxes
and say "/s/t/o/p/." If the picture showed a dish, the child would slide the pebble into three
boxes: /d/i/sh/.

SUGGESTED BOOKS TO SUPPORT PHONEMIC AWARENESS

Use this list as a springboard for creating your own list of books that are appropriate for your grade level. Add to your list as you find other books that are rich with vocabulary, beautiful illustrations, and fun sounds.

Ahlberg, Janet, and Allan Ahlberg. 1999. *Each Peach Pear Plum*. New York: Viking Books for Young Readers.

Brown, Margaret Wise. 1967. *Goodnight Moon*. New York: Harper and Row.

Carlstrom, Nancy White. 1996. *Jessie Bear, What Will You Wear?* New York: Little Simon.

Cole, Joanna. 1989. *Anna Banana: 101 Jump-Rope Rhymes*. New York: HarperCollins.

Cole, Joanna, and Stephanie Calmenson. 1993. *Six Sick Sheep: 101 Tongue Twisters*. New York: William Morrow and Company.

Gelman, Rita Golden. 1993. *More Spaghetti, I Say!* New York: Scholastic.

Guarino, Deborah. 1997. *Is Your Mama a Llama?* New York: Scholastic.

Hoberman, Mary Ann. 2003. *I Know an Old Lady Who Swallowed a Fly*. New York: LB Kids.

Raffi. 1999. *Down by the Bay*. New York: Knopf Books for Young Readers.

Sendak, Maurice. 1962/1990. *Alligators All Around: An Alphabet*. New York: HarperCollins.

Shaw, Nancy. 2016. *Sheep in a Jeep*. New York: HMH Books for Young Readers.

Slepian, Jan, and Ann Seidler. 2001. *The Hungry Thing*. New York: Scholastic.

Yektai, Niki. 1987. *Bears in Pairs*. New York: Simon and Schuster.

Decoding and Word Attack (Sight Words)

Dolch and Fry are lists of common sight words (high-frequency words). JoAnne Vacca and colleagues (2003) describe the Fry High Frequency word list: "The first 100 instant words on this list make up half of all written material, and the 300 words make up 65 percent of all written text." Sight words are those that cannot be phonetically broken apart or "sounded out." Learners just need to look at those words and read the whole word with automaticity.

You can create games (or let students create them) to help the children learn sight words. For example, make games such as Memory, Go Fish with sight-word cards, Sight-Word Bingo, and a word search with sight words. In addition, the following activities to support sight-word learning can become a part of children's options during literacy time.

Sight-Word Hop

Materials

Sidewalk chalk

What to Do

Outside, write sight words on the blacktop, patio, or sidewalk.

Invite the children to run, jump, or hop to each word you call out.

Sight-Word Detectives

Materials

Clipboards

Paper

Pencils

What to Do

Take the children on a walk around the classroom, school, or neighborhood.

Encourage them to write down sight words they find.

Sight-Word Search

Materials

Old newspapers or child-friendly magazines

Highlighter pens

What to Do

Invite the children to search for sight words and highlight them.

Rainbow Sight Words

Materials

Crayons

Paper

What to Do

Write or type sight words on different pieces of paper.

Invite the children to draw a line around a sight word with a crayon. Then they can use another color to draw another line around the word, then another color and another color, and so on.

Sight-Word Word Shapes

Materials

Crayons

Paper

What to Do

Write or type sight words on different pieces of paper.

Invite the children to trace the shape of each word with a crayon. Then they can use another color to outline the word shape, then another color, and another color, and so on.

Sight-Word Poetry

Materials

Poems

Paper

What to Do

Select poems to show and read with the children.

Show a poem to the children and ask them to help you count how many times they see a specific sight word.

Systematic Explicit Phonics

Phonics are another important piece of reading instruction. The phonics lessons should be systematic and explicit in nature. In his article "Learning and Using Phonics in Beginning Reading," John Shefelbine (1995) states that "the program should be systematic and thorough enough to enable most students to become independent and fluent readers." Playing around with sounds as loose parts allows students to develop phonics skills. Guide the students to understand how to complete each of these activities, which then can become a part of their literacy choice time.

Word Sorts

Materials

Index cards

Construction paper

Writing utensils

What to Do

Use index cards or construction paper to make word-family cards, such as *pig, rig, jig, twig,* and *bin, win, pin, tin.* You can make these cards, or ask students to make them. The student or groups of students then sort the cards into the correct *–ig* and *–in* word families. Loose parts objects that reflect the word family can also be used.

Word-Family Books

Materials

Paper

Stapler

Pencils

Markers

Crayons

What to Do

Fold pieces of paper in half and staple along the fold to create booklets. Place these and the writing materials in the literacy area.

Invite the students to create their own word-family books by writing a word from a certain word family on each page and then illustrating the pages. For example, a student could write *–ig* words such as *pig, big, rig,* and *fig,* and illustrate them.

Onsets

Materials

Index cards

Letter tiles

Magnetic alphabet letters

What to Do

Students or teachers can use index cards to make word-family cards, such as words ending in *–et.* Students can use single letter cards, magnetic letters, or letter tiles to substitute the onset (first letter) plus the rime (*–et*) to create words.

157

Word Wheels

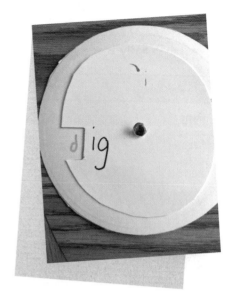

Materials

Paper plates

Brads

Scissors

Markers or crayons

What to Do

Give each student two paper plates. Ask the students to cut a small circle out of one of the plates and write the rime or word family, such as –*at*, on that small circle.

Use the brad to fasten the small circle to the middle of the larger plate.

On the larger plate, the students write onsets, such as *C*, *H*, and *B*.

Students can rotate the outer plate and read the words created to a friend or to an adult.

Spelling

Early childhood education students learn sound-symbol relationships to effectively communicate using written language. In her book *Literacy for the 21st Century*, Gail Tompkins (2017) states, "Children's early spellings reflect what they know about phoneme-grapheme relationships, phonics rules, and spelling patterns." The following activities use loose parts to promote spelling proficiency. Show the students how to do each of the activities, which can be choices during literacy time. Create a choice board of activities the children can choose from.

Magic Slates

Materials

Magic slate boards

Magic slate board stylus or fingernail

Index cards

Marker

What to Do

Create sight-word cards by writing sight words on index cards. Using the sight-word cards, students can practice writing the sight words on the magic slate boards.

Sand or Salt Tray

Materials

Sand or salt

Cookie tray with lip

Styrofoam trays

Mark-making instruments, such as fingers, sticks, old pencils, and craft sticks

What to Do

Pour sand or salt into a tray. Encourage students to copy their sight words using their fingers, sticks, pencils, or craft sticks.

Dry-Erase Letters

Materials

Dry-erase boards

Dry-erase markers

Erasers

What to Do

Provide dry-erase boards and markers, and encourage the children to practice letter formation, spelling words, and sight words. The students can also practice substituting the onset letter with the word family (rime) by writing the word family on the dry-erase board, writing the onset letter, and then erasing it to write the next onset letter.

Stick Spelling

Materials

Sticks

Pencil

Paper

What to Do

Students can use craft sticks or any other sticks from nature to create their spelling words. Then, the student can copy the words onto a piece of paper.

Lemon Juice Writing

Materials

Lemon juice

Water

Small cups

Cotton swabs

Paper

What to Do

Children touch the cotton swab into the lemon juice and then dot the paper to spell out their spelling words. They can then hold the paper up to a light source to reveal their secret disappearing words.

Bright Spelling

Materials

Light-up pegboard with colored pegs

What to Do

Provide a light-up pegboards with colored pegs, such as Lite Brite. Invite the children to spell out words with the colored pegs.

Spelling-Word Snack

Materials

Alphabet cookies or cereal

What to Do

Invite children to spell words with alphabet cookies or cereal. Then they can eat their (spelling) words!

Comprehension

Understanding print is a complicated process that involves the reader, the text, and the purpose. Readers bring background knowledge and experience to the text and read it with a purpose in mind. Word usage and how the author organizes the print affect comprehension. Comprehension is the ability to interact with words and ideas on the page to understand what the writer has to say.

Students can demonstrate comprehension of a book by completing one of the projects listed below. However, first teachers should provide initial instruction so students can successfully complete the project on their own. Then, when given the choice, the students will know how to independently create the project to represent their free-reading book. An environment rich in loose parts, a writing station, makerspaces, and other classroom options allow student choice and voice in showing reading comprehension in a variety of ways. These options could be made into a choice board to help students think of potential possibilities.

Activities using loose parts that promote comprehension mastery include the following:

- Make a gameboard based on a book.

- Create a postcard.

- Craft a T-shirt.

- Make puppets/masks and act out a story.

- Design bumper stickers.

- Craft a diorama.

- Participate in a reader's theater.

- Create a mural.

- Dramatize a story.

- Design a book jacket.

- Create brochures/pamphlets about a book.

- Draw a cartoon/comic strip.

- Create a storyboard.

- Make a model/mural.

- Complete a comprehension cube.

- Retell a story with a story basket.

For example, to make a gameboard based on a book, students can create a gameboard with a path from beginning to end. The student can make cards that each player picks and answers, based on the book. The cards could ask,

- "Who are two characters in the book?" Move two spaces.

- "Where does the story take place? Move three spaces.

- "What was the problem in the story?" Move one space.

- Whoever gets to the finish space first is the winner.

Students could choose a book and create puppets or masks reflecting the characters in the story. Loose parts are great for making puppets! They could then act out or retell the story.

To make a bumper sticker, the student could read a story, such as "Three Billy Goats Gruff." The student could draw the three billy goats, the bridge, and the meadow and write the title and author.

For the book jacket, the student could fold (with the teacher's help or already prefolded) paper to create a book jacket. The student would write the title, the author, and a picture of their favorite part of the story.

To create a cartoon/comic strip, the student could draw sequential pictures of the story in a comic strip form, including the words of the characters.

For a comprehension cube, on each side of a cube printout (prefolded by the teacher and glued by the student when done), the student answers the required questions by drawing and writing. For example:

- Title of book
- Author
- Favorite part
- Problem
- Solution
- Ending

Teachers can always include other ideas stemming from concepts taught in class.

Literacy is woven into every content area. There are countless rich, motivating, and inspirational activities using loose parts that can serve as springboards to teaching literacy. The suggestions shared in this chapter serve as a beginning to plant a seed for you to create more powerful and meaningful literacy connections.

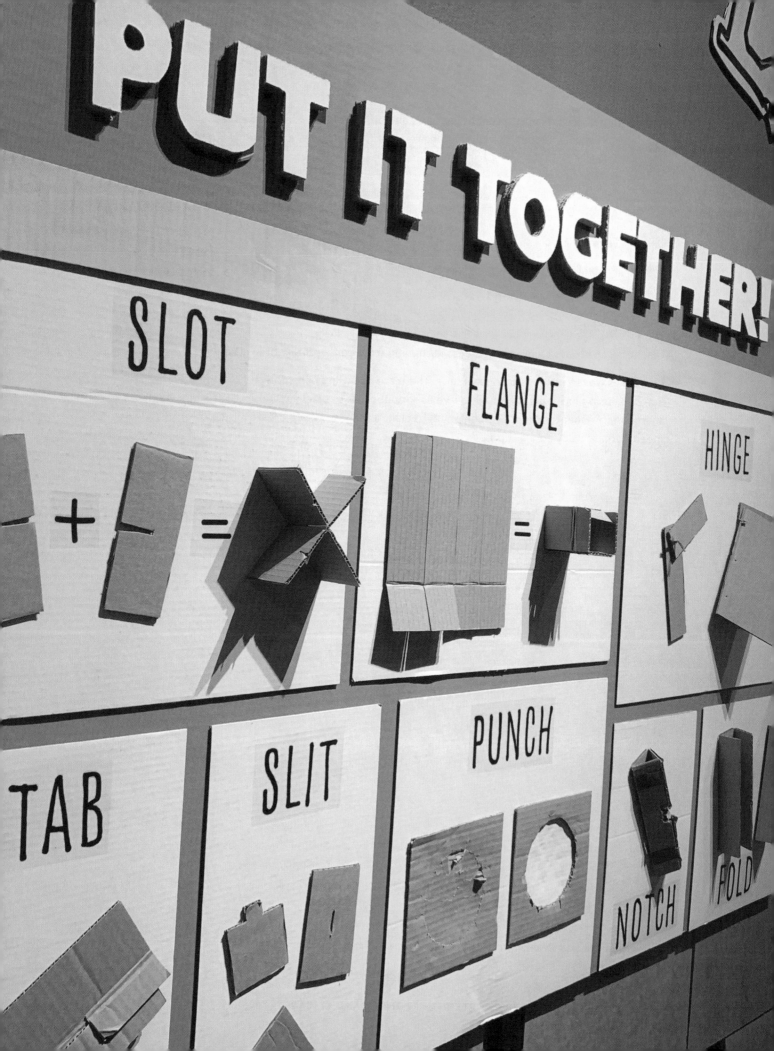

CHAPTER 12

Engineering

Children delight in creating different structures from blocks, building sets, balls and ramps, and tinkering. "Tinkering is a mindset—a playful way to approach and solve problems through direct experience, experimentation, and discovery. Engineering extracts principles from direct experience. It builds a bridge between intuition and the formal aspects of science by being able to better explain, measure, and predict the world around us" (Martinez and Stager, 2013). Embracing a loose-parts mindset is beneficial for dynamic student learning in engineering, which is included in the Next Generation Science Standards (n.d.), highlighting foundational skills and attitudes such as the following:

- Asking questions

- Developing and using models

- Analyzing and interpreting data

- Understanding the relationship between structure and function

Engineering combines math and science to improve lives and solve problems.

In this chapter, we introduce the engineering design process and offer activities to support building and creating with architecture and with block sets, tinkering, using balls and ramps, building chain reactions, and understanding biomimicry.

SUGGESTED BOOKS ON ENGINEERING

Introducing engineering through books connects students to interesting characters who use materials in ingenious ways. Use this list as a springboard for creating your own list of books that are appropriate for your grade level. Add to your list as you find other books that are rich with engineering vocabulary, beautiful illustrations, and loose parts.

Aronson, Sarah. 2019. *Just Like Rube Goldberg: The Incredible True Story of the Man behind the Machines.* New York: Beach Lane Books.

Rube Goldberg began drawing early in life and studied engineering as his father wanted him to. But he dreamed of drawing comics for the newspaper, so he developed an alter ego that made complicated things that didn't follow physical laws. On purpose, he solved problems in his comics in ridiculous ways without ever making the inventions himself. This book can inspire students to devise their own contraptions! Provide loose parts such as boots, pipes, horns, yarn, rope, weights, bowling balls, buckets, and so on. Encourage students to develop chain reactions, including chain reactions that accomplish a goal that you define. For fun, play the game Mousetrap, which is patterned from one of Goldberg's sketches.

Beaty, Andrea. 2007. *Iggy Peck, Architect.* New York: Abrams Books for Young Readers.

Iggy is an expert builder at an early age, building a diaper tower and a dirt sphinx at age two. He builds arches, churches, towers, and castles. His teacher doesn't like architecture until Iggy saves the day by helping the class build a bridge. Encourage students to follow Iggy's building acumen by providing them with loose parts, such as cloth diapers, Lego blocks, wooden blocks, dirt, clay, chalk, shoestrings, branches, and sticks. Invite the children to learn about buildings and to try various approaches to building bridges, sculptures, towers, and so on.

Beaty, Andrea. 2013. *Rosie Revere, Engineer*. New York: Abrams Books for Young Readers.	Rosie is a secret inventor, keeping ideas to herself for fear of being laughed at. Her aunt tells her that ideas first need to fail, so Rosie keeps designing and building. Provide students with loose parts such as parts of a fan, string, old machine parts, old toys, nuts and bolts, a broom, wire, belts, unbreakable mirrors, and logs so they can build their own inventions. Challenge the children to sketch an invention, design it, and select materials to build it. Photograph the invention, and let the inventor dictate or write what the invention does and how someone would use it.
Dodds, Dayle Ann. 2004. *Henry's Amazing Machine*. New York: Farrar, Straus, and Giroux.	Henry makes an amazing machine by the time he is six, covering his bedroom and then his bathroom! He keeps building, eventually expanding outside. Henry's parents are incredibly patient, until they have had enough. Henry's creation becomes part of the local carnival, bringing the community together. Provide loose parts such as levers, rods, gears, wheels, balls, arrows, bowling pins, water, bubbles, silverware, mailboxes, pipes, dice, bowls, tools, and pool balls, and invite the children to make their own amazing machines. For a challenge, encourage them to create carnival games.
Gall, Chris. 2013. *Awesome Dawson*. New York: Little, Brown.	Dawson's motto is "Everything can be used again!" Dawson invents a robot to do his chores, but it gets out of control. He still uses his inventions to help with chores but in a more realistic way. Provide students with loose parts such as old vacuum cleaners, brooms, old toys, water hoses, tools, trashcan lids, radiators, hockey sticks, water bottles, forks, tires, motor parts, wood, bike wheels, springs, and gloves. Encourage the children to combine two or more different toys to make a new toy or to develop an invention to do a chore.

Hale, Christy. 2012. *Dreaming Up: A Celebration of Building*. New York: Lee and Low.	This celebration of building alternates pictures of children building with a variety of materials and pictures of famous buildings that feature interesting architecture. Creative text arrangements and profiles of the architects add to the appeal. Provide loose parts, such as stacking cups, stacking rings, soil, water, sunlight, air, mud, blankets, chairs, cardboard boxes and tubes, blocks, sand, shells, sea glass, Lego bricks, playing cards, toothpicks, sticks, pinecones, snow, craft sticks, and cushions. Encourage the students to study a specific architecture style and re-create a classic building with loose parts. For more inspiration, bring in blueprints and building plans. Allow the children plenty of time to build.
Howes, Katey. 2019. *Be a Maker*. Minneapolis, MN: Carolrhoda Books.	Follow explorers to see what they can make in a day—a tower, a universe, a sound, a telescope, a blueprint, a friend, a snack, a plan, a gift, a difference, and a playground. What will you make? Provide cardboard, playing cards, toys, blocks, beads, dominoes, pots and pans, books, tubes, paper, paints, soil, wood, and so on. Invite the children to draw blueprints for an invention, make a map, create sounds with pots and pans, plan a service project, make an open-ended snack, or create whatever they can imagine.
Lovell, Patty. 2012. *Have Fun, Molly Lou Melon!* New York: G. P. Putnam's Sons.	Molly tries making her own toys, such as an outdoor dollhouse in the trees, a cardboard racer, shapes in the clouds, and more. A new girl with more traditional toys moves into the neighborhood, but Molly Lou Melon rubs off on her until the neighbor starts making her own toys as well. Provide loose parts, such as twigs, leaves, flowers, tape, dominoes, tin cans, acorn caps, cicada exoskeletons, electric mixers, cardboard boxes, and so on. Invite the children to make toys, create a tree-root palace, build a car with boxes, use tin cans and string to chat with a friend, or make a gift for someone.

SUGGESTED BOOKS ON ENGINEERING

Rack, Michael. 2007. *Edward Built a Rocketship*. London, UK: Meadowside Children's Books	Edward wants to explore space, so he makes a plan. He gathers odds and ends and tinkers to create his rocket ship. His mother kisses him goodbye as Edward's rocket ship blasts off into the space of his imagination. Provide funnels, tools, buckets, boxes, garbage cans, fishbowls, sheets, rope, and other loose parts for the children to use. Encourage them to decide on a place to visit and create a mode of transportation to travel there. Enjoy the journey!
Schermbrucker, Reviva. 1992. *Charlie's House*. New York: Viking Juvenile.	After seeing his own house built, a young boy in humble circumstances builds an even better house and a car made of mud and scraps. His imagination takes him on a ride in the car. Provide scrap metal, mud, sticks, cardboard, boxes, nails, tins cans, bottle caps, water, cartons, plastic bags, clay, plastic bottles, wool, craft sticks, and other loose parts. Encourage the students to construct a building, such as one's own house, a dream house, a local building, or famous architecture. Learn about and display pictures of diverse types of houses. Consider hosting a fundraiser to benefit people who need housing.
Spires, Ashley. 2014. *The Most Magnificent Thing*. Toronto, ON: Kids Can Press.	A girl decides to build a "magnificent thing," yet runs into challenges and eventually quits. After she goes on a walk with her dog, she returns to her project and achieves success. Provide sticks, paper, old appliances, boxes, hangers, tools, wooden planks, balls, and other loose parts. Invite the children to sketch and plan their own inventions and then create prototypes.
Ward, Helen. 2003. *The Tin Forest*. New York: Puffin.	A man lives surrounded by metal. He dreams of living in a forest and makes plants out of the tin that surrounds him. He turns the metal into flowers, birds, and branches—a forest made of garbage and tin! Soon real animals and plants also fill the space. Provide metal scraps, pipes, wires, appliances, and other loose parts. Encourage the students to make a metal creation, use foil to sculpt a flower, or plant a rain garden.

Williams, Curtis Mark. 2018. *Addy-Matic and the Toasterrific!* Scotts Valley, CA: CreateSpace.

A girl attempts to create an automatic system for making toast using principles from a chain-reaction machine. The book shows how simple machines work and how to face a problem and carry out a plan in creative ways. Provide a toaster, planks, books, string, chairs, a broom, a toy mouse, nails, a fan, a frying pan, a bucket, a wheel, a seesaw, a pulley, rope, balloons, and other loose parts. Invite the children to create a chain-reaction machine for a simple task chosen by the student.

Yamada, Kobi. 2014. *What Do You Do with an Idea?* London, UK: Compendium.

This award-winning book with universal appeal explores how we get and share ideas, how we wrestle with the opposition of others, and how we can protect and feed our own unique ideas. The idea itself is the loose part or variable. Invite the children to use the engineering design process to develop ideas. Discuss with them their feelings about sharing ideas. Explore ideas that have changed the world.

Understanding the Engineering Design Process

The engineering design process is cyclical and can be simple or more complex. A simple version may include the steps think, create, and share (Hand, n.d.). A more complex version may include the following steps:

- **Ask:** What is the problem?

- **Imagine:** What are the possibilities?

- **Plan:** What will your solution look like?

- **Create:** Build your plan.

- **Experiment:** Test your solution

- **Improve:** How can you make it better?

- **Share:** Share your results (Hand, n.d.).

This process can be applied in many situations as students solve real-life problems using loose parts. Loose parts are the "stuff" used for the engineering design process, as students imagine, plan, create, experiment, and improve their designs. Many classrooms use this model as the basis of their exploration and problem solving.

Building and Creating with Architecture

Architecture affords many opportunities to experiment and manipulate materials. To investigate building, consider the following:

- Watch a short documentary on architecture.

- View and discuss homes and unique buildings around the world.

- Investigate animal homes, and then challenge children to make their own.

- Try an architecture challenge, such as building the tallest tower.

- Create a bridge that supports a certain amount of weight.

- Host an egg-drop challenge: create protection to keep an egg from breaking when dropped.

- Have a Three Little Pigs day, during which the students test various types of constructions.

- Build a fort.

- Learn about bricklaying.

- Create plans or blueprints for building.

- Design an amusement park.

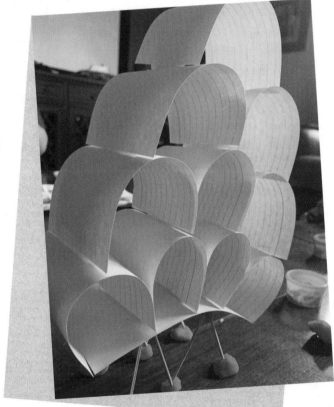

Architecture can be a springboard for cross-curricular connections, such as measurement, artistic elements, historical movements, and culture, which can be woven into the exploration. While we include suggested materials and tools, as Shigeru Ban, an architect who created a paper-tube school, said, "Anything can be building structure material" (quoted in Hale, 2012).

Building Materials		Tools
Tape	Snow	Measuring tape
Toothpicks	Sticks	Chalk line
Lincoln Logs	Sheets	Plummet
Keva planks	Lego bricks	Paper and pencil
Variety of blocks	Chairs	Blueprints
Playdough	Scrap wood	Levels
Toothpicks	Cushions	Hammer
Bricks	Cardboard	Saw
Mud	Craft sticks	Screwdriver
		Drill
		Rulers
		Carpenter squares
		Nails and screws

Building is also inherently place based, using the location and materials available to create at that moment. Having a rich space with access to many options for building can be ideal to problem solve and understand the properties of the materials.

Building and Creating with Block Sets

Consider bringing a block area back to your early elementary classroom. Well-known architect Frank Lloyd Wright attributed many hours of playing with blocks with building his understanding of mathematical and building concepts, stating, "The maple-wood blocks . . . are in my fingers to this day" (quoted in Hale, 2012). No matter the material, building provides students opportunities to create and imagine. R. Buckminster Fuller, creator of the geodesic dome, said, "[Children] spontaneously experiment and experience . . . They select, combine, and test, seeking to find order in their experiences" (quoted in Hale, 2012). Blocks sets may include Lego bricks, Wedgits, Keva planks, Rigamajig, and Imagination Playground's Big Blue Block sets. Having building sets available allows construction to happen when needed on a small or large scale.

Tinkering

Building and creating with recycled and other materials can be very empowering to students. Tinker carts and makerspaces are excellent options for tinkering in the classroom. Tinker carts (usually mobile) and makerspaces (typically in one space) are a collection of materials, tools, and connectors to inspire creativity and engineering. Trina Deboree (2018) states, "A Makerspace is a place where students can gather to create, invent, tinker, explore and discover using a variety of tools and materials. In a nutshell, it is an astonishing place to think and learn!" She mentions how applicable makerspaces are across curriculums with endless options.

Educators might designate an area or tray where children can take apart old appliances. Ask for donations from families or watch for low-cost options at garage sales or thrift shops. (*Safety note:* Be sure to cut the electrical cords off before taking appliances apart.)

"To invent you need a good imagination and a pile of junk."
—**Thomas Edison**

Consider the following materials for your tinker cart or makerspace.

Consumable Materials

Craft sticks

Pompoms

Chenille stems

Recyclables

Paper—graph, color, textures, copy paper

Cotton balls

Foil squares

Coffee filters

Googly eyes

Straws

Dowels

Clothespins

Feathers

Ping-Pong balls

Rubber bands

Bubble wrap

Sun-print paper

Packaging

Wrapping

PVC pipe and connectors

Toothpicks

Marker caps

Bottle caps/lids

Mesh netting

Golf tees

Light sticks

Cardboard box corner inserts

Stickers

Bells

Writing utensils

Cardboard

Playdough

Magnets

Sticky foam

Paper water cones

(adapted from Gull, 2020l)

Connectors

Tape—masking, metal, duct, copper, packing, painting, washi, cellophane, double-sided

Glue—rubber cement, paste, classroom glue

Bungee cords

Wire

Glue sticks

Elastic

Paper clips

Brads

String

Yarn

Fishing line

Tools

Low-temperature glue guns

Makedo cardboard system

Wood burner

Wood angled cutter/miter box

PVC cutter

Tin snipper

Tape measures

Paintbrushes

Cardboard cutters, such as Klever Kutters or Makedo tools

Slingshot

Screwdrivers

Allen wrenches

Saw

Hammer

Mallet

Rulers

Scissors

Staple gun

Stapler

Chalk

Paint

Pliers

Wire cutters

Hand drills

In general, students might have free rein to imagine and try things out, with some limitations. The class might also start with an engineering challenge with limited materials. In a classroom setting, we suggest the following:

- Put out "just enough" supplies as students learn to self-regulate. You can always bring out more as needed.

- Categorize supplies and add labels to show where things go.

- Use recycled materials for storage.

- Consider setting a "cost" for supplies, and challenge students keep their projects within the set budget.

Using Ramps and Balls

Carla shared in a podcast episode (Gull, 2020h) that inclined planes are part of our daily lives. We see them in the form of a roof, a slide, ADA-accessible ramps, roller coasters, bathtubs, roadways, and skate parks. Ramp exploration can be practical in students' lives, engaging their interest, meeting content standards, and building twenty-first-century skills.

While we are including this in the engineering section, many of the suggestions in the book are multidisciplinary. For example, ramps and inclined planes specifically address the following subject areas:

- **Science**—force, motion, gravity, cause and effect, chain reactions

- **Technology**—simple machines

- **Engineering**—solution-driven design, construction strategies, connect systems

- **Math**—angles, measurement, comparison

(Kodo Kids, 2019)

Additionally, you could bring literacy into the mix as students reflect and write about their experiences. Students also build twenty-first-century skills as they engage in creativity, communication, critical thinking, and collaboration. About ramp play, one educator remarked that her teaching goal "is not necessarily to have the students reach the right answer but to have them practice scientific processes and communicate their thinking" (PBS and WGBH Educational Foundation, n.d.).

Building communication skills is a natural extension of ramp investigations as children develop specific vocabulary and communicate ideas. Vocabulary words related to ramp explorations include the following:

General Vocabulary	Positional Words	Directional Words
Ramp	Higher	Up
Inclined plane	Lower	Forward
Slope	Next to	Backward
Plane	Between	Sideways
Gravity	On top of	Through
Force	Under or underneath	Over
Push	Beside	
Pull	Behind	
Incline	In front of	
Pathway	Below	
Track	Above	
Sphere		
Fast		
Slow		
Object		
Speed		

(adapted from Iowa Regents' Center for Early Developmental Education, n.d., 2021)

Shelley Counsell and colleagues (2016) offer these suggestions as you implement ramp play in the classroom. Spend time playing and experimenting before using ramps and materials with the students. Provide sufficient space for exploration. Consider how to reconfigure or use additional space in the classroom, moving around desks and furniture as needed. To alleviate space issues, tape off an area to show boundaries between groups. Leave plenty of time to explore. Time is essential. Don't make this a one-day experience; keep coming back for additional iterations of this concept, and consider having regularly scheduled classroom time (such as Friday afternoons) for ramp exploration. Be patient with the students' experimenting and exploration; allow them to solve problems. To get started with inclined planes in the classroom (or outdoors), gather materials to give the students options for building ramps.

Ramp/Inclined Plane Options

Wooden planks

Cove molding—1 ¾" wide, flat on back, 1-, 2-, 3-, and 4-foot lengths

Gutters

Drainage tubes

PVC pipes

Cardboard "corners"

Tubes—cardboard, plastic

Toy car tracks

Marble sets/runs

Sand

River rocks

Rubber tracks

Foam insulation

Cushions—wedges and flat

Wedge hollow blocks

Tables

The inside of a tire

Slide

Magnetic wall ramp set

Aluminum foil

Wooden trim

Flat surfaces—baking trays, large books, cardboard

Options for Building Height

Stumps or logs

Tree cookies

Dry sponges

Stands

Cardboard boxes

Mini sandbags

2" x 4"s

Crates

Chairs

Stage

Shelf

Stairs

(adapted from Gull, 2020h)

Allow students time to explore materials and think about how they might combine them. Likewise, provide a variety of things that roll, don't roll, or might roll differently, such as the following.

Things that Roll

Balls—Ping-Pong, tennis, football, golf, soccer, basketball, baseball, beach, cotton ball, pool balls, pompoms, bouncy, wooden, foam balls, balls with texture

Noisy balls—melodic balls, bells

Natural objects—acorns, hickory nuts, water droplets, mud, sweet gum balls, rocks, sand, pea gravel, small tree cookies

School supplies—pencils, crayons, balls of clay

Toys—small cars, marbles, toy wheels

Wool balls

Balls of yarn

Spools

Balls of foil

Things that Don't Roll

Square or rectangular blocks

Paper

Shells

Paper clips

Small dolls

Things that Roll Differently

Egg-shaped objects

Cone-shaped objects

Tops

Jacks

Craft sticks

Jingle bells

Flat glass gems

Buttons

Coins

(adapted from Gull, 2020h; Iowa Regents' Center for Early Developmental Education, n.d.)

The role of the educator in ramp play includes modeling play and experimenting; providing materials, space, and time; asking questions; and evaluating learning. Remember that ramps and pathways are an open-ended activity, "which provides opportunities for both the instructor and the children to think, create, make mistakes, fix mistakes, and create again. The key to the instruction is 'facilitate.' Be a good facilitator" (Iowa Regents' Center for Early Developmental Education, 2021).

The Iowa Regents' Center for Early Developmental Education (n.d.) offers the following suggestions of questions to ask students about their explorations:

Attention-focusing questions	• Where did you notice . . . ? • What have you noticed . . . ? • Why did you decide . . . ? • What did you do first?
Measuring and counting questions	• How far did the marble travel when . . . ? • How far did the marble fly off . . . ? • How high do you need to elevate to . . . ?
Comparison questions	• How do these objects move differently? • Which marble/ball travels the farthest? • Is there a difference when . . . ? • Which goes faster? • Which supports make a sturdier base? • Which type of surface allows . . . ?
Action questions	• What do you think you could do to . . . ? • What happens if . . . ? • What happens if you add (or take away) . . . ? • Can you do that again? • What if you tried . . . ? • Show me how you did that. • Can you try that again?
Questions to pose problems	• How can you. . . . ? • Can you make the marble . . . ? • Are there other ways you can . . . ? • What can you do to make . . . ?
Reasoning questions	• I wonder why . . . • Why do you think . . . ? • I wonder if it would work if you . . .

As students experiment with ramps, you may wish to consider additional explorations such as the following. These are all starts and should not be considered an all-inclusive list or limit how the children might investigate inclined planes.

- Add paint on the ramps before sending objects down, or spread out a long piece of paper over a wide ramp and dip items in paint before sending them down the ramp.

- Consider texture, size, weight, material, and so on. For example, compare how a heavy pool ball rolls in relation to a lightweight Ping-Pong ball. Choose a variety of things that roll of different sizes, textures (bumpy, with holes, from nature), weights, and materials (wood, plastic, metal, natural) to see how these variables affect the journey down the ramp.

- Cut compostable straws into smaller pieces to roll down the ramp.

- Provide spray/squirt bottles. Some children add water to their ramp explorations by squirting water along the track while their object is rolling down.

- Provide buckets or bins to catch the rolling item at the end of the ramp run. This could be used as a target and/or as a safety feature to stop flying cars or balls.

- Cover ramps with textured materials, such as cloth, sandpaper, and so on. Try a variety of materials in turn to cover the ramp, or place one material on each of a series of ramps to investigate how different textures might affect how balls roll down the ramps. Does one slow down or accelerate the ball?

- Invite the children to make balls. They could use aluminum foil, clay, or mud and roll the balls made from these materials down the ramps.

- Add melodic balls or jingle bells to the options to roll down the ramp. Consider adding a musical option as part of the series of ramps, such as a tambourine at the end where the ball makes music when it finishes the course. (adapted from Gull, 2020h)

Building Chain Reactions

Chain reactions, often referred to as Rube Goldberg machines after his crazy contraption drawings, are an engaging way to experience simple machines and how they can be combined to get things done. Consider the following loose parts for potential chain-reaction options.

- Large craft sticks
- Keva planks
- Balls
- 3-ounce plastic portion cups
- Paper cups
- Index cards

- Dominoes
- Magnets
- Blocks
- 1-inch wooden cubes
- Tin cans (smooth edge)
- Shoeboxes

- Paper-towel tubes
- Tape
- Marbles
- Recycled materials
- Anything else within reason, such as stacked books, rulers, and so on

(adapted from Gull, 2020j)

To get students started with chain reactions, Clay Swartz (n.d.) offers the following tips:

- Start at the end.
- Make a plan.
- Gather your materials.
- Work on it piece by piece.

Some educators start with giving a challenge for one trick and gradually expand the requirements as students build skills.

Understanding Biomimicry

Biomimicry is a neat intersection between science and engineering. We often look toward nature to find solutions to problems in our lives or to be inspired for innovation. For example, nature has inspired many inventions, such as gecko feet inspiring sticky notes, hitchhiker burdock seeds inspiring Velcro tape, shark-skin studies helping decrease the drag time of swimsuits, an elephant's trunk inspiring a robotic arm, and kingfisher birds inspiring the shape of bullet trains (Aranca, 2017; O'Connell, 2018).

Loose parts are great for experimenting with biomimicry. Students can use the engineering design process along with nature as an inspiration for improving and creating designs. For example, after studying how seeds travel, Carla's students created their own windborne seeds to apply this principle. With supplies of feathers, cotton balls, ribbons, sticky notes, cotton swabs, and other consumables, students created and tested their designs in a wind tunnel. The children revised their designs to try again, learning about nature, design, and flight in the process. Challenge students to study how spiderlings travel and see what might inspire their engineering creativity.

Engineering can be a powerful tool for exploring and experimenting in the elementary classroom. Engineering options encourage students to solve problems, test ideas, make improvements, and build persistence.

CHAPTER 13

Art

Early childhood classrooms and art specialty classrooms should be filled with many different media. A materials-rich classroom encourages creativity and inquiry. In their article for *Arts Education Policy Review*, Marissa McClure et al. (2017) state, "We support the creation of environments for young children that encourage boundary crossings of materials and ideas in ways that support children's inquiry and learning but do not result in chaos."

The National Core Arts Standards (2015) include dance, media arts, music, theater, and visual arts. Within each of these areas, students create their own art, perform, respond as an audience member, and personally connect. This chapter explores ways to incorporate loose parts in the arts, including in music and motion, sounds, sculptures, and nature art. In addition, we describe ways to integrate art into the curriculum content areas.

> *"Loose parts theory is about remembering that the best play comes from things that allow children to play in many different ways and on many different levels."*
> —**Margaret Sear, "Why Loose Parts?"**

183

The arts help develop a loose-parts mindset in many ways, such as developing imagination, creativity, and collaboration (Sousa and Pilecki, 2013). Adding the arts helps develop more divergent thinking, with no one correct answer but many possibilities. As educators, we must look beyond and value students' unique questions and answers (Maslyk, 2016). Including the arts in STEM moves beyond decoration to embracing a wide variety of artistic applications in the learning process. Sousa and Pilecki (2013) suggest that the arts encourage cognitive growth, engage the brain, enhance long-term memory, advance creativity, and minimize stress. The arts bring a sensory, experiential aspect to learning that can be integrated throughout content areas. Additionally, students can express their own personality in artistic representations, avoiding cookie-cutter craft projects. "Art has the role of helping children become like themselves instead of more like everyone else" (Clemens, 1991). Perspective shifts through an artistic lens may also allow students to approach content matter in unique ways (Maslyk, 2016). Embracing and expanding the making movement can be an effortless way to allow the arts to be an essential component in the classroom.

Exploring Process Art

Just as Nicholson (1971) focuses on the process over the product regarding loose parts and play, process art aligns with these same principles. MaryAnn Kohl, an author in the process art movement, notes the connection:

> When children explore art, they are testing possibilities and working through challenges, much like a scientist who experiments and finds solutions. Process art allows children to make their own assessments, while also teaching them that a problem may have more than one answer. Instead of following specific rules or directions, the child's brain becomes engaged in the discovery of "how" and "why" (Kohl, personal communication, May 11, 2020).

Process art allows students to express themselves and share their voices. They get to experiment and discover on their own. Process art can be integrated in all areas and has no specific directions. It doesn't include a sample finished product, so children create with no expectation of a right or wrong way. The focus on experimenting and exploring materials, techniques, and tools promotes relaxation and can have a calming effect. As students engage in process art, they will do so with their own unique and original approaches and choices of materials and outcomes (Bongiorno, 2014).

When implementing art focusing on the process, remember the following tips:

- Consider art as similar to free play; provide many material options and allow children to lead.

- Art should be a joyful experience—allow children to create and use resources.

- Allow ample time for experimenting.

- Make it a "yes" environment.

- Use music as part of the experience.

- Allow students' ownership of art (Bongiorno, 2014).

Artist Study

Consider letting the students do an artist study, in which they look at a particular artwork or an artist's style and re-create it in their own way with their own choice of materials. Some classes have done an artist study using loose parts to create their own masterpieces. In the COVID-19 period, when education quickly moved online, many people and digital classrooms re-created art masterpieces with easily accessible household items, sharing the products on social media (Waldorf and Stephan, 2020). The creativity was amazing. Educators

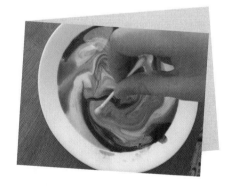

also shared choice options and electronic choice boards for students to complete assignments digitally, allowing for student choice and voice in art and other curriculum areas. Thankfully, we don't have to wait for a pandemic to get creative with what we have readily available.

SUGGESTED BOOKS ON PROCESS ART

Many books support a process-based arts approach with a loose-parts mindset. These can be great read-aloud books or for classroom display. Use this list as a springboard for creating your own list of books that are appropriate for your grade level. Add to your list as you find other books that are rich with vocabulary, beautiful illustrations, and loose parts.

Ehlert, Lois. 2009. *Boo to You!* New York: Beach Lane Books.	The mice realize the cat will cause trouble for their harvest party. They decorate pumpkins, gourds, and masks, and then they frighten the unwelcome cat with a scary pumpkin face. This book has great harvest pictures for inspiration. Provide students with loose parts, such as pumpkin seeds, felt, twine, craft sticks, textured paper, seedpods, gourds, string, burlap, buckeyes, straw, pinecones, acorns, and dried flowers. Invite the children to arrange loose parts to create stories or self-portraits. They can dictate the stories of their designs.
Ehlert, Lois. 2014. *The Scraps Book: Notes from a Colorful Life*. New York: Beach Lane Books.	This book inspires readers to create. Ehlert shares her personal experiences in creating books and encourages readers to be inspired to create. Provide scraps—paper, pieces of nature (for example, crab apples), soda-can tabs, scanned fruits, strings, zippers, leaves, metal, dolls—and invite the students to create. Consider going on a scrap hunt to look for more loose parts. Encourage the children to plan, create, and redesign until they are satisfied with their creations.
Hall, Michael. 2011. *Perfect Square*. New York: Greenwillow.	A perfect square is changed and manipulated through scissor cuts, holes, tearing, shredding, snipping, and crumpling. These bits and pieces turn into a mountain, river, bridge, park, garden, and fountain. Provide paper, scissors, and hole punches, and invite the children to explore and create.

Moon, Nicola. 1995. *Lucy's Picture*. London, UK: Watts Publishing.	Lucy wants to do her art differently, because she would like to share it with her blind grandfather. She incorporates textured objects for a picture her grandfather can "see" with his hands. Provide loose parts, such as velvet, feathers, twigs, and more. Invite the children to make a texture collage or to create artwork based on other senses beyond the visual.
Piven, Hanoch. 2013. *Let's Make Faces*. New York: Atheneum Books for Young Readers.	Everyday objects, such as buttons, bolts, and bananas, can be arranged in a variety of ways to make faces. Provide keys, balloons, small toys, nuts and bolts, buttons, tools, natural items, letter tiles, and so on, and encourage the children to explore what they can make.
Robinson, Nikki Slade. 2018. *Anywhere Artist*. Boston, MA: Clarion.	A child creates art in various locations using found and everyday objects and elements. Provide sticks, stones, leaves, shells, sand, seaweed, driftwood, shadows, rain (puddles), mud, clouds, and so on. Invite the students to create what they see outdoors.
Saltzberg, Barney. 2010. *Beautiful Oops!* New York: Workman.	An accidental tear, a spill, a drip of paint, a fold, holes, a strain, a smudge, or scraps of paper—all can become something beautiful. Provide materials, such as paint, markers, crayons, pencils, and paper, and encourage the students to create holes, smudges, spills, and stains. Then they can embrace their mistakes and transform "oops" into art!
VanDerwater, Amy Ludwig. 2018. *With My Hands: Poems about Making Things*. New York: Clarion.	This collection of poems celebrates making things with our hands, with an emphasis on the maker movement, the characteristics of a maker, and following our own ideas. Create an art makerspace in the classroom. Provide wood, cardboard, paper, paint, clay, plastic, string, elastic, scraps, photographs, boxes, ice, stone, and fabrics, and encourage the children to make. They can then write poems about their loose-parts creations.

Integrating Arts in the Content Areas

By giving students choices with work, we also give them options to express themselves creatively and to demonstrate their learning. Arts naturally integrate into the process and final presentation, for example, when a student shows a math equation with natural objects, loose parts, or art materials; represents a habitat in small-world play or collage; explores a historical period through clothing, food, music, and shelter representations and presentations; or reports on a book by creating a diorama, a book jacket, or a dramatic representation.

The list could truly be endless, with parameters on what information should be included but with many options for how to show it. This moves us away from cookie-cutter projects and allows students to use their ingenuity in sharing information.

Makerspaces for Process Art

A classroom area for process art or makerspace materials for creating is a great option for bringing more art into the classroom. Art classrooms have long been the makerspace of the school. One first-grade class has a permanent maker corner, stuffed with recycled materials, yarn, paper, and other materials. There, students are free to create and bring home whatever they want. This concept can also be a temporary station. Anything can happen in arts makerspaces. Consider the following options:

- Textiles and fiber arts

- Knitting, crocheting, and sewing

- Cardboard art

- Origami and paper crafts

- Electronic options, such as green screens, art apps, or wearable media

Stock the art makerspace with materials such as yarn, wool fiber, hooks, plastic needles, looms, buttons, sewing machines, thread, fabric, craft sticks, paint, felt, cardboard, pompoms, tape, wallpaper, foam pieces, toothpicks, glue, a variety of papers and scraps, markers, colored pencils, and crayons.

Light Painting: Science and Technology

Patrick Rochon is an artist who creates through light painting, a technique using photography and light. In their interview with him, Jordan Peterson and Austin Craig (2017) learned how to get started with light painting. Rochon finds and makes his own light "tools," using modified flashlights, light sabers, light wands, and gels and filters to experiment with light. He captures the trace of light and body movement through prolonged-exposure camera techniques (Peterson and Craig, 2017). Rochon suggests the following items and tips:

- Start with a digital single-lens reflex (DSLR) camera that can allow prolonged exposure, or use a smartphone app, such as Pablo, Slow Shutter, Light Paint, or Holography.

- Experiment with multiple light sources—flashlights, toys, glow sticks, or anything that makes light. Get creative! Try three-dimensional tools to add shapes and textures.

- Wear dark clothes to help you blend into darkness.

- Turn off the lights. A dark room or outside space away from lights is ideal.

- Set the camera for an open shutter of several seconds of prolonged exposure, then start the camera (a remote works well if you want to be involved in the image).

- Make movement with the light.

- Review your light art on the camera screen.

- Let go! Experiment with new ways of moving and different colors and types of light (Peterson and Craig, 2017).

Carla shared a version of the following exploration on her blog Inside Outside Michiana (Gull, 2017b).

Materials

DSLR camera or smartphone with an app such as Pablo, Slow Shutter, Light Paint, or Holography

Light sources

Dark room

What to Do

In the classroom, use a dark room and work in groups while other students are working on projects.

Explore the variables of light, darkness, movement, and tools. Experiment, play, discover, learn, and have fun.

Building Sculptures: Oral Language and Literacy

Found and natural objects can be used for a variety of purposes, including building sculptures. Consider having baskets or bins of items available for use during art, storytelling, or free time. In any of these options, student choice and voice should be front and center.

Materials

Cardboard

Embellishments, such as yarn, chenille stems, mesh, fabric, puzzle pieces, old jewelry, metal pieces, recycled lids, paper scraps, and spools

Foil

Magnets

Blocks

Natural items, such as sticks, seeds, seedpods, rocks, clay or mud, and leaves

Rolled paper

Recyclables

Packaging

What to Do

Choose some materials to start with, encouraging the children to explore them as starting points. Add materials over time.

The children can make sculptures in a variety of ways. Let them have time to understand how the materials work and to experiment with how they might combine some elements.

Building Faces: Social-Emotional Skills

Like sculptures, faces can be made from a variety of materials in many ways. You could connect building faces to social-emotional standards.

Materials

Face Base	Eyes/Noses	Mouths	Embellishments
Playdough	Buttons	Ribbons	Yarn
Cork circle	Washers	Balloons	Chenille stems
Wooden base	Found plant material	Train tracks	Mesh
Chalk circle	Fake flowers	Spoons	Fabric
Open picture frame	Rocks	Seedpods	Puzzle pieces
Tree with clay	Wooden circles	Craft sticks	Old jewelry
Mud	Letters	Shells	Metal pieces
Cardboard	Glass pebbles	Sticks	Leaves
Head printout	Corks	Feathers	Recycled lids
Mirror	Beads	Old keys	Paper scraps
Light table			Spools
Lids			

What to Do

The materials listed are a great starting point, but anything could be incorporated. Students love finding and repurposing items to use to create.

They can make faces outside with natural items or inside with natural and found objects. The book *Let's Make Faces* by Hanoch Piven is a great starting point if needed.

Assembling Nature Art: Science and Technology

Environmental art, land art, ephemeral art, and nature art are all ways to use elements from the outdoors to create. Choosing natural items allows student voice and choice in their creations.

Richard Shilling and Julia Brooklyn offer a step-by-step method for land art with children.

1. Spend time exploring nature, making forts, looking for insects or tadpoles, and finding materials in nature. When they find something interesting that has potential for land art, go to step 2.

2. Collect materials. Look around in the unique spot for materials that could be used, collecting sticks and leaves in the woods, dandelions and daisies in the park or garden, or whatever they may find as they open their eyes to loose parts in the space.

3. Find a place to make a sculpture. Invite the students to investigate the location for a special place that catches their eye to use the natural pieces they have collected.

4. Decide what to make. Encourage the children to let their imaginations run wild. There are no rules; however, they might want to make a face, spiral, circle, or other element of art.

5. Use the collected materials and create! Take a picture of the sculpture and share it with classmates.

6. Encourage them to think about what they learned. Reflect on the colors, shapes, and textures they have explored. Note the trees, plants, animals, and insects in the space. Consider the experience (Shilling and Brooklyn, n.d.).

Many artists create their work from natural materials. For example, Patrick Dougherty makes large stick sculptures using volunteer efforts around the world. He uses fast-growing sticks found in the local area, harvested fresh. The sticks are woven together to build whimsical outdoor sculptures that last about two years. You can see his work at www.stickwork.net.

Andy Goldsworthy experiments with principles of art outdoors, using snow, ice, cattails, leaves, and thorns for his creations. Photography captures these ephemeral pieces of art. Chelsey Bahe creates art out of natural elements found along a trail at a nature center in Minnesota. She shares her work on social media as Take 'Em Outside. She has created owls made of acorn caps and leaves; frogs made of maple seeds; and play scenes made of sticks, bark, and nature bits.

Marc Pouyet uses natural materials in urban settings to remind us that nature can be in any of our settings. He combines natural elements with city life to help the audience take notice of nature in their spaces. He also does nature art through the seasons. You can see examples of his work on is blog at https://www.marc-pouyet.net/.

Richard Shilling from Land Art for Kids shares instructions and many examples for creating land art. In an interview with Jean Van't Hul (2010), he mentions, "Land art for me begins with seeing the world and nature through child's eyes, I am grateful that it is something I have never lost. Making natural sculptures allows me to indulge a little longer in that child's world. Whether you are proficient or just dabbling, an adult or a child, making a sculpture or just kicking through fallen leaves, it is all the same to me. It's all about being outside experiencing all nature has to offer."

Nick Neddo (2020), the author of *The Organic Artist for Kids*, shares ways to experiment and create one's own art materials from the natur al elements around them. He creates art from berries, fungi, plants, vines, and more, and empowers students to create their own art materials.

Students can study any of these artists, look at examples, and be inspired to create their own art outdoors. Consider combining nature art with digital devices to capture art electronically.

Frames can be a clever way to have a "canvas" for creating art. You can often find frames without the glass at garage sales or resale shops. If you find one with the glass in it, just remove the backing and glass. The students can use these to "frame" nature, as a base for creation, and for collaborative work. Frames can be transformed to create looms for natural weaving, as Carla shares in this adapted blog post (Gull, 2013).

Wooden Stick Loom

Materials

Sticks, both straight and Y shaped

Yarn or twine

What to Do

Lash four sticks together with yarn or twine to make a rectangular wooden loom, or create a loom from three sticks in a triangle shape.

Use a Y-shaped stick for another effect. One educator wrapped her yarns around her square both horizontally and vertically, creating boxes that could easily have things tucked in. It was chunkier than some options and allowed the colors of nature to pop!

Cardboard Loom

Materials

Cardboard

Scissors or safe box cutter, such as Klever Kutter or Makedo tools

Yarn or rubber bands

Paint (optional)

Yarn, ribbon, twine

What to Do

Cut the cardboard into a square or rectangular shape. These could be painted beforehand, if desired. Cut slits on opposite sides for the yarn.

Thread the yarn (or rubber bands) through the slits, and tie the ends in the back.

Invite the children to weave to their hearts' content. A cardboard base is a little sturdier and easier to find than sticks. These could also be used when studying spiders and weaving.

Chicken-Wire Loom

Old picture frames

Chicken wire

Wire clippers (adult use only)

Duct tape

Work gloves

Safety goggles

Yarn, ribbon, twine

What to Do

Cut the chicken wire to an inch larger than the size of the opening in a frame. (Be careful—the cut wire ends can be sharp. Wear gloves to protect your hands and goggles to protect your eyes.)

Duct-tape the chicken wire to the back of the picture frame, covering the sharp wire points.

Make as many looms as needed.

Invite the children to work together to weave their creations. The added texture of the wire is a powerful addition to the mix.

Grapevine Looms

Materials

Grapevine wreaths

Yarn, ribbon, twine

What to Do

Wrap yarn or twine back and forth across the opening in the wreath, and knot it to secure it in place.

Encourage the children to weave on the loom. They can incorporate many natural elements into the final product.

Large Outdoor Loom

Materials

Large branches or reclaimed wood

Two 4" x 4" wooden posts

Wire

Wire cutters (adult use only)

Saw (adult use only)

Work gloves

Safety goggles

Hammer

Nails

Post-hole digger

Cement

Eye-head lag screws

L brackets or corner braces (optional)

Twine

What to Do

Find a good spot for a permanent outdoor loom. Decide how wide the loom can be, based on the length of your branches. Dig a hole for each 4" x 4" post with the post-hole digger. Place each post in a hole, and set in cement if desired. Refill the hole, as needed.

Screw branches horizontally from top to bottom between the posts, at a comfortable height for the children to reach.

Wire the branches or nail the wood pieces together. For extra strength, consider connecting the wood corners with L brackets (also called corner braces).

Screw in eye-head lag screws at intervals along the interior of the loom.

To make the base for weaving, loop twine through the eye heads and across the loom opening. Knot the twine ends to secure it in place. Alternately, wrap twine around the top and bottom branches for the weft.

These looms are large and usually stay in one place. The large scale makes them perfect for adding to over time or seasonally. This is a great collaborative way to have a loom, with a group working on it together or having people add to it over different days. Invite the children to describe how they view the changes over time.

195

Tree-Stump or Tree-Cookie Looms

Materials

Tree stump or tree cookies

Nails

Hammers

Yarn

What to Do

Pound nails into the wood. (Let the students help!)

Weave yarn back and forth around the nails as a base for weaving.

Invite the students to use natural materials to weave through the yarn.

Mat Weaving

Mats can be woven from a variety of materials, such as cattail or palm fronds or other natural materials.

Materials

Grasses	Seedpods	Ribbon
Sticks	Herbs	String
Bark	Cattail	Cassette tape
Flowers	Palm fronds	Recycled cloth cut in strips
Stems	Vines	Rubber bands
Leaves	Yarn	
Seeds	Twine	

What to Do

Gather "weeds" and other items in an overgrown area or grassy area. Try picking invasive species and grass, and avoid picking protected species. Talk with students about which plants are okay to pick or find on the ground and which are not. The rules may be different, depending on where you are located.

You might bring nature into the classroom (a little messy) or let the students weave outside. Invite the children to lay out some materials as their base and to weave other materials into the mat. The over-and-under motion of weaving, the various textures, and attention to detail are perfect for sharing expression and creativity! It is a sensory-filled activity.

Listening for Sounds

Sound is a great variable, and allowing sound exploration can yield memorable results.

One way to explore sound is through making a sound map.

Materials

Paper

Pencil

Clipboards

What to Do

Go outside with students and ask each student to find their own space. Encourage them to take time to be silent and listen to the sound around them.

Invite them to use paper and pencil to make a map of the sounds they notice.

Later, invite them to share and debrief with the group.

Offer opportunities for the children to experiment with sound in a variety of ways. Carla has taken groups of students outside and invited them to explore sound with spoons, wooden mallets, sticks, and other items. How do students explore sound in your space?

The students can also explore sound with a variety of containers (glass, metal, wood); water; and utensils, such as sticks, metal or wooden spoons, whisks, and so on. Watching the vibrations of the sound through the water is fascinating as children discover this.

"Nature's music is never over; her silences are pauses, not conclusions."

—**Mary Webb, author**

SUGGESTED BOOKS ON SOUND EXPLORATION

Use this list as a springboard for creating your own list of books that are appropriate for your grade level. Add to your list as you find other books that are rich with vocabulary, beautiful illustrations, and loose parts.

Gershator, Phillis. 2007. *Listen, Listen.* Cambridge, MA: Barefoot Books.	Follow the sounds of the season. The simple rhyming text focuses on sounds in a village as children splash in water, pick apples and corn, and crunch through the snow, and as flower bulbs pop in the spring. Invite the students to explore water, snow, ice, flowers, fruit, vegetables, and leaves, paying particular attention to the sounds these loose parts make. Listen to seasonal sounds in your outdoor space.
Pinkney, Brian. 1997. *Max Found Two Sticks.* New York: Aladdin.	A boy in an urban setting finds two sticks. He taps the rhythms he hears around him, such as the rustle of pigeons, the drip drop of rain, the groans of the subway, and church bells in the distance. Provide sticks, water, bottles, and so on. Invite the children to experiment with sounds in your environment. Encourage them to make musical instruments out of recycled materials.
Showers, Paul. 1961/1991. *The Listening Walk.* New York: HarperCollins.	A father and daughter take a quiet walk and experience the many sounds in their neighborhood. Go outdoors with the students and explore the sounds in your environment. Listen for wind, dogs barking, car noises, and so on as you take a sound walk. Make a sound map of the noises.

Making Music and Motion: Dramatic Play

Loose parts can be a fantastic way to support dramatic play. Consider having a dramatic-play area inside or outside the classroom; for example, provide a stage where children can perform. They might act out a story, create their own storylines, perform music, or play around with sound variables. Basic props and materials can enhance these areas.

Music/Sound

Hand instruments, such as bells, maracas, and so on

Sticks

Metal pieces

Wood cookies

Pots and pans

Drums

Homemade instruments

Seedpods

Spoons

Recycled musical instruments

Wooden bowls and spoons

Wind chimes

Water

Sensory bottles

Movement

Scarves

Ribbon wands/sticks

Hand kites

Old sheer curtains

Large pieces of outdoor fabric

Drama

Fabric pieces

Feather boas

Hats

Vests

Aprons

Skirts

Play props

Baskets

Metal bins

Cans

Wooden boxes

Additionally, provide loose parts that children can use to create their own instruments or sound experiments. These could be set up in a makerspace or in a station in the classroom.

Cardboard boxes

Cardboard tubes

Rubber bands

Metal pieces

Tape

Recycled plastic containers/ bottles

Small rocks

Rice/beans

Plastic eggs

Wooden blocks

Balloons

Tin cans

Sticks

Lids

Chopsticks

Bottle caps

Wire

Bells

Metal containers

Craft sticks

Wooden spoons

Beads

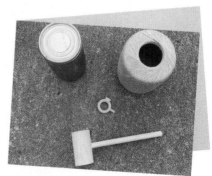

Apps such as Garage Band allow students to easily explore electronic sounds. Combining sensors with light, movement, and sound allow for great experimentation with cause and effect and sound.

Art and related disciplines can enhance our lives in many ways. Look for ways to infuse art into other subject areas for a whole experience. Michelle Obama reminded us, "Every day, through engagement in the arts, our children learn to open their imagination, to dream just a little bigger, and to strive every day to reach those dreams" (Zakarin, 2013).

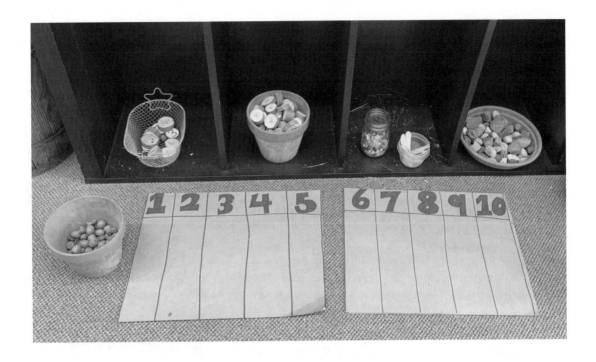

CHAPTER 14

Math

Math is often a subject that causes anxiety and confusion; however, math is a great subject for integrating loose parts. Learning happens best when students can relate it to real life. On her website Fantastic Fun and Learning, Michelle Lipp (2021) states, "An environment rich in loose parts invites children to develop math skills led by their own curiosity." In her article "Why Loose Parts?" Margaret Sear (2016) reminds us, "Environments that include loose parts are infinitely more stimulating and engaging than static ones." What fun for a child to be able to count and sort the rocks she finds on the playground! Imagine the boost to a child's confidence when she uses problem-solving skills to divide sticks among her friends so they can build a castle.

According to the Common Core State Standards Initiative (National Governors Association Center for Best Practices and Council of Chief State School Officers, 2010), students in early childhood grades experience mathematics in five different strands:

- Counting and cardinality

- Operations and algebraic thinking

- Number and operations in base ten

- Measurement and data

- Geometry

This chapter explores many ways to use loose parts to create an actively engaged mathematics classroom environment. Building with blocks, creating shapes, and working with manipulatives are just some of the ways to incorporate loose parts into the math content area. Math is everywhere! Children can count leaves, rocks, flower petals, or silverware. Students can place objects in order by size. Learners can sort hair ties by color, size, or shape. Toy cars can be counted and arrays created. In her blog post on loose parts, math, and nature, Carla Gull (2020g) writes, "The world is alive with mathematical learning opportunities. Nature is full of patterns, cycles, shapes, and numeric opportunities. Take a walk outside with a mathematical lens to discover possibilities."

There are so many items that can further mathematical thinking. For example, digital tools can support play. Depending on the technology you use and have available, digital devices have cameras you can use to document and record information, timers, stopwatches, tally apps, and other basic math tools. Consider adding some of the following tools to extend children's play and exploration in mathematics.

- **Number and operations:** Add arrays, such as egg cartons, ice-cube trays, muffin tins, tic-tac-toe boards or checkerboards, and sorting trays, to encourage children to organize items in rows and columns. Also add number lines, dominoes, yard dice, calendar numbers, sticks, milk or applesauce lids, ten frames, dice, fabric, and a hundreds chart.

- **Geometry and spatial reasoning:** Add frames, two- and three-dimensional shapes (both found and from a set), attribute blocks, tangrams, and unbreakable mirrors.

- **Measurement:** Add both standard and nonstandard measuring tools, such as rulers, yardsticks, ribbons, yarn, rope, thermometers, measuring tapes, sand timers, digital timers, scales, a trundle wheel, balances, and sticks and ropes in standards sizes (feet, two feet, yard, meter).

- **Patterns and algebraic reasoning:** Add pattern blocks and game pieces.

- **Displaying and analyzing data:** Add a garden lattice and tally sheets.

- **General items:** Add chalk, wooden planks, milk crates, light-colored fabric squares, recyclables, sticks, rocks, acorns, sweet gum balls, driftwood, pine needles, mark-making tools, and paper. (Gull, 2020g)

SUGGESTED BOOKS TO SUPPORT MATH LEARNING

Use this list as a springboard for creating your own list of books that are appropriate for your grade level. Add to your list as you find other books that are rich with mathematics vocabulary, beautiful illustrations, and loose parts.

Anno, Mitsumasa. 1977. *Anno's Counting Book*. Springfield, OH: Crowell-Collier.	This is a delightful book that reinforces one-to-one correspondence, sets of objects, number sequence, and mathematical relationships. Provide students with a variety of loose parts found in the classrooms and ask them to place a specified number of objects on their mats.
Crews, Donald. 1994. *Ten Black Dots*. New York: Mulberry Books.	This is a great book for counting. In this book, black dots are used to create pictures. Provide dot stickers, and encourage the students to create their own pictures. Make a class book of their work.
Jocelyn, Marthe. 2004. *Hannah's Collections*. Toronto, ON: Tundra Books.	Hannah loves to collect objects and has many collections. She is asked to bring her favorite one to school, but she can't choose just one. She creates a way to share all her collections. Invite the students to create collections of their favorite items, such as buttons, craft sticks, shells, feathers, leaves, barrettes, stuffed animals, figurines, jewelry, keys, clothespins, books, or paper clips. They can sort by size, shape, or color. Then they could design a creation to display the collection.
Kroll, Virginia. 2005. *Equal Shmequal: A Math Adventure*. Watertown, MA: Charlesbridge.	Mouse wants to ensure that the teams are equal and figures out how to divide equally by weight. Provide balance scales and assorted objects. Invite the children to experiment with weight and balance. If your school has one, encourage them to get on a teeter-totter and experiment with weighing and balancing themselves.

Mariconda, Barbara. 2008. *Sort It Out!* Mount Pleasant, SC: Arbordale.	Pack Rat keeps all kinds of stuff, sorting them this way and that way. His collection begins shrinking, and he finds that his sister has been taking things for her own purpose. Provide items for the children to sort, such as toy turtles, lockets, marbles, books, acorns, plastic needles, toy eggs, umbrellas, brushes, threads, kettles, pinecones, yarn, and clovers. Encourage them to write labels for their collections. They can graph the items by living and nonliving.
Martin, Bill, Michael Sampson, and Lois Ehlert. 2013. *Chicka Chicka 123*. New York: Simon and Schuster.	This colorful book demonstrates counting by ones to twenty, then counting by tens to one hundred. All the while, the zero wonders if there will be room in the tree. Zero ends up being the hero! Some indoor and outdoor loose objects can be used to count, and then groups of ten can be used to get to one hundred.
Pinczes, Elinor. 1993. *One Hundred Hungry Ants*. New York: HMH Books for Young Readers.	This is a fun book to read on the hundredth day of school. Ants go marching in different arrays, introducing children to counting by twos, fives, and tens. Provide egg cartons or muffin tins; graph paper; and an assortment of objects that can be grouped into twos, fives, and tens. The children can design their own arrays.
Sidman, Joyce. 2011. *Swirl by Swirl: Spirals in Nature*. New York: Houghton Mifflin Books for Children.	This book reveals the beauty and usefulness of spirals found in nature. Invite the children to investigate shells, tree stumps, flowers, leaves, and other items that have swirls. Go on a spiral hunt outdoors. Invite the children to draw spirals.

Manipulatives

Manipulatives are assorted concrete items that early childhood teachers use to introduce and help children practice concepts. Manipulatives can be almost anything that can be counted, measured, added together, or manipulated to reinforce a math idea, such as the following:

Paper money

Buttons

Blocks

Cuisenaire rods

Tangrams

Geoboards

Pattern blocks

Algebra tiles

Base-ten blocks

Unifix cubes

Snapcubes

Multicolored links

Wooden cubes

Counters, such as plastic bugs, cars, dinosaurs, animals, and teddy bears

Assorted tiles

Counting chips

Foam counters

These materials offer students tactile and visual models for exploring mathematical relationships. Well-known mathematics educator Marilyn Burns considers manipulatives essential when teaching math. According to Hand2Mind (n.d.), Marilyn Burns "finds that manipulatives help make math concepts accessible to almost all learners, while at the same time offering ample opportunities to challenge students who catch on quickly to the concepts being taught."

You can purchase commercially made manipulatives, make your own, or help the students make their own. Joseph Furner and Nancy Worrell (2017) advise using manipulatives instead of worksheets. They explain that it is particularly important to use manipulatives when first introducing a mathematical concept.

Counting and Cardinality

Students in the early grades learn number names and how to count numbers in sequence. They count objects and compare numbers. Using loose parts is a perfect way to teach these standards. On the playground, you can ask the children to count the number of pinecones or leaves and then write the number with chalk.

Who Has the Most?

Materials

Common classroom items

Number cards, plastic numbers, or pencil and paper

What to Do

Invite each child to look for a specific common classroom item, such as chalk, markers, counting bears, or blocks. Ask them to collect the items they find.

Have the children bring their collections back to the table or carpet, and count the number of objects they found.

Ask them to write or put a number card or plastic number next to their collection to show how many items they have.

When students have their number, ask, "Who has the most?" Let them discuss who does and explain how they know.

Next ask, "Who has the fewest?" Let them discuss who does and explain how they know.

Operations and Algebraic Thinking

Solving number equations come to life with loose parts! Loose parts are easy to use when working with number operations such as addition and subtraction: "If I have two rocks and you have three rocks, how many do we have all together?" Loose parts serve as visual examples, and students can figure out the number problems with ease by manipulating the objects. Some activities for using loose parts in algebraic thinking might include the following.

Scoop and Add

Small loose parts, such as pompoms

Plastic cups

Paper

Pencils, crayons, or markers

What to Do

Invite the children to scoop pompoms into two plastic cups.

Encourage them to count the number in each cup, and then write a number equation to show how many there are all together.

Adding Plate

Materials

Paper plates

Marker

Paper

Pencils, crayons, or markers

Small loose parts, such as buttons

What to Do

On each paper plate, draw a line through the center, dividing the plate in half. On one of the halves, draw a line through the center to divide that space into two quarters.

Encourage the students to use the plate as a base to add together loose parts. For example, they can put some buttons in one of the smaller portions and more buttons in the other smaller portion. As they move the loose parts to the large portion, they can find how many loose parts there are in all.

Then they can write a number sentence to show how many buttons (or other loose parts) they have in all.

Number and Operations in Base Ten

Children have a better understanding of place value when they use loose parts to visually represent the concept. Students can create sets of objects in tens, place a string around each group, and then count by tens to discover the number of objects. Younger children gain a strong foundation of the numbers eleven to nineteen when they use loose parts to identify the number of objects by using a ten-frame plus the number of objects left over. Consider these additional starts.

Tens and Ones Chart

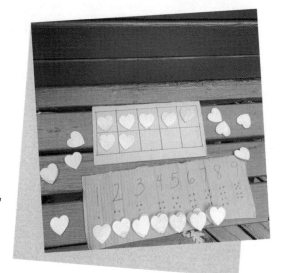

Materials

Tens and ones chart

Small loose parts, such as pebbles

Paper

Pencils, crayons, or markers

What to Do

Provide a tens and ones chart and small loose parts, such as pebbles.

Encourage the children to make a set of ten items in the tens column plus any number in the ones column and then write the number.

Number Flaps

Materials

Construction paper

Ruler

Scissors

Marker

Hundreds chart

Small loose parts, such as washers

On a piece of construction paper, draw a 3-inch square. Inside the square, draw a grid of nine 1-inch squares.

Cut out and remove the center square.

On the top center square, write "10 fewer." On the bottom center square, write "10 more." On the right center square, write "1 more." On the left center square, write "1 fewer."

Cut along the vertical lines of the top center and bottom center squares to create two flaps.

Cut along the horizontal lines of the right and left center squares to create two flaps.

The children can use the number flaps with a hundreds chart. They simply position the open square over any number on the chart, and then use their loose parts to find one or ten more and one or ten fewer than the number in the window.

Hundreds, Tens, and Ones

Materials

Playdough

Bamboo skewers

Buttons or stringing beads

Paper

Pencils, crayons, or markers

What to Do

Invite the students to make three balls of playdough. In each ball, they can stick one skewer so it stands vertically. One stick will represent hundreds, one will represent tens, and the other will represent ones.

Challenge the students to stack buttons or beads on the sticks to represent numbers and then write the numbers in hundreds, tens, and ones. *Safety note:* If the skewers have sharp points, cut those off.

Measurement and Data

When first learning measurement, students typically use nonstandard measures, such as yarn or paper clips. Loose parts are so natural to use! Students can measure an object and write that it is, for example, five shoe lengths long. Later, children transfer to traditional units of measurement with a ruler or yardstick.

Within this math standard, children learn how to use graphs to interpret data. For example, students can place an object on a floor graph to vote for their favorite color. You can use tape, chalk, a garden lattice, pocket charts, sticks, large plastic hoops, and chart paper, along with loose parts, for class-created graphs.

Telling time is also one of the components of this standard. Students can use personal-sized clocks to manipulate and discover how the hands of the clock move to tell us the time. Then, using loose parts, learners can create their own clock.

Loose-Parts Clock

Materials

Round place mat, cork mat, or tree cookie

Toothpicks or craft sticks

Numerals 1–12

Small loose parts, such as buttons, bottle caps, seeds, shells, or beads

What to Do

Set out the materials on a table.

Invite the students to practice showing time on a clock face by building their own.

Challenge them to show specific times, such as lunchtime or time to go home, on the clock face.

Geometry

Unit blocks and shapes such as tangrams, pattern blocks, geoboards, and GeoBlocks are perfect loose parts to incorporate into a geometry unit. Additionally, students can search for shapes in nature and use sticks to create geometric shapes.

Building with Blocks

Blocks offer so many opportunities for learning, growth, and development in the early childhood content areas. In her article "10 Things Children Can Learn from Block Play," Derry Koralek (2015) states, "Every classroom should have a full set of unit blocks." Someone once said that if you have a limited sum of money to purchase materials for a classroom, you should spend the money on unit blocks.

Unit blocks are one type of blocks to use. You can also consider plastic blocks, cardboard blocks, foam blocks, Lego bricks, Bristle blocks, and fabric blocks that students can use to build and create different scenes and objects. Sometimes blocks can transform and become an animal or transportation to expand the play and to increase the students' vocabulary. Understanding of words such as *bigger, smaller, taller, shorter, wider, greater than, less than*, and so on develop naturally during block play as the teacher and pupils interact with each other.

In her article "Cognitive Benefits from Playing with Building Blocks," blogger Ilona Viluma (2020) writes, "When it comes to math, children can learn more about things such as area, size, order, space, shapes, numbers, mapping, patterns, measuring, fractions, operations, estimating, negative space, adding, one to one correspondence, and seriation." Gwen Dewar (2018), in her article "Why Toy Blocks Rock," states that blocks help teach:

- spatial reasoning;
- cognitive flexibility;
- language skills;
- a capacity for creative, divergent thinking;
- social competence; and
- engineering skills.

Students enjoy creating and building structures, creatures, cities, and roads. While they are building, it is important that teachers listen to the vocabulary that they are using. You can be the "guide on the side," modeling the use of words such as *bigger than* and *smaller than* to help children grow a mathematical vocabulary. Then, when they are finished building, the students can draw their creations.

As part of their explorations, ask students to count the number of each shape that they use. You could provide a preprinted page, similar to the one below, in the block area that the children can fill it out.

I used _____triangles.   I used _____rectangles.   I used _____cubes.

I used _____cylinders.   I used _____rainbows.   I used _____arches.

Koralek (2015) also points out the important concepts and skills children can practice and strengthen through block play, including length, measurement, comparison, number, estimation, symmetry, and balance. Children can sort and count blocks. For example, students can count the number of blocks used to build the castle, count the number of blocks to build a house, and then add together to find the total number of blocks used. Another great idea is to use a measuring tape or a yardstick to measure the structure. When the students clean up their structures, they can sort them and place them back on the shelves.

Use this list as a springboard for creating your own list of books that are appropriate for your grade level. Add to your list as you find other books that are rich with mathematics vocabulary, beautiful illustrations, and loose parts.

Adamson, Heather. 2000. *A Day in the Life of a Construction Worker*. North Mankato, MN: Capstone.

Alling, Niki. 2012. *When I Build with Blocks*. Scotts Valley, CA: CreateSpace.

Macken, Joanne Early. 2008. *Building a Skyscraper*. North Mankato, MN: Capstone.

Murphy, Stuart J. 2006. *Jack the Builder*. New York: HarperCollins.

Portis, Antoinette. 2006. *Not a Box*. New York: HarperCollins.

Shulman, Lisa. 2004. *Old MacDonald Had a Woodshop*. New York: Puffin.

Stevenson, Robert Louis. 2005. *Block City*. Columbia, MO: Songbird.

Creating Shapes

Shapes are all around us! In her book *Dreaming Up: A Celebration of Building*, Christy Hale (2012) quotes architect Frank Lloyd Wright, "That early kindergarten experience with the straight line, the flat plane, the square, the triangle, the circle! These primary forms and figures were the secret of all effects . . . which were ever got into the architecture of the world." Bright Hub Education (2008) advises, "Students in the lower elementary grades need opportunities to explore geometry and get geometry help."

Included in teaching geometry, students should be able to have a conversation using the shape's attributes and the correct geometric name. Students can practice manipulating the shapes to "physically and mentally change the position of the objects" (Bright Hub Education, 2008). In addition, students will begin to see relationships among the shapes, such as putting two triangles together makes a square. All this knowledge is the result of playing with and discovering shapes. Students enjoy exploring and manipulating many different commercial materials as they discover shapes:

Tangrams	Attribute blocks	Goobi construction set
Magna-Tiles	Geometiles	Legos
Pattern blocks	Geoboards and rubber bands	GeoStix

SUGGESTED BOOKS FOR USE WITH SHAPES

Use this list as a springboard for creating your own list of books that are appropriate for your grade level. Add to your list as you find other books that are rich with mathematics vocabulary, beautiful illustrations, and loose parts.

Adler, David. 1998. *Shape Up! Fun with Triangles and Other Polygons*. New York: Holiday House.

Baranski, Joan Sullivan. 2000. *Round Is a Pancake*. New York: Dutton Juvenile.

Burns, Marilyn. 2008. *The Greedy Triangle*. New York: Scholastic.

Dodds, Dayle Ann. 1996. *The Shape of Things*. Somerville, MA: Candlewick.

Hall, Michael. 2011. *Perfect Square*. New York: Greenwillow.

Hoban, Tana. 1996. *Shapes, Shapes, Shapes*. New York: Greenwillow.

Hutchins, Pat. 1987. *Changes, Changes*. New York: Aladdin.

Leedy, Loreen. 2013. *Seeing Symmetry*. New York: Holiday House.

Micklethwait, Lucy. *I Spy Shapes in Art*. New York: Greenwillow.

Pallotta, Jerry. 2004. *Icky Bug Shapes*. New York: Scholastic.

Schuette, Sarah. 2002. *Triangles*. North Mankato, MN: Capstone.

Tompert, Ann. *Grandfather Tang's Story: A Tale Told with Tangrams*. Decorah, IA: Dragonfly Books.

Walsh, Ellen Stoll. 2001. *Mouse Shapes*. New York: Houghton Mifflin.

CHAPTER 15

Celebrations with a Loose-Parts Mindset

A loose-parts mindset creates a culture that acknowledges the inspiration and innovation of our students. Celebrations have been found to be especially beneficial for student learning. In her doctoral dissertation, Virginia Farr (2003) asserts, "Teachers are expected to play a major role in the socialization of their students. Crafting strong classroom communities that incorporate celebration is one technique some teachers have developed to enhance a sense of belonging in their classroom" (Farr, 2003). In her book *Creating Your Classroom Community*, Lois Bridges Bird (1995) affirms that celebrations help to define the classroom as a bonded group by creating a shared experience. Ron Berger, Leah Rugen, and Libby Woodfin (2014), authors of *Leaders of Their Own Learning*, assert, "Celebrations of learning feature students as the communicators. They are front and center, articulating their learning, the process of learning, and their strengths and struggles." This point of view aligns with the loose-parts mindset.

There are many ways to celebrate loose parts in our class and school environments, and it is important to adopt these methods that instill fun and creative learning. Adding loose-parts celebrations in our classrooms can create and promote diversity, culture, and appreciation of nature, current events, and history. These class events empower students to share their strengths and successes. Meg Cox (1998), author of *The Heart of a Family* (1998), lists several positive aspects that celebrations accomplish for children:

- Impart a sense of identity
- Provide comfort and security
- Help them navigate change
- Instill values
- Solve problems
- Teach practical skills
- Cultivate knowledge
- Create meaningful memories
- Generate joy

Celebrating with loose parts provides the opportunity to reinforce these positive aspects, the Common Core Standards, and other skills and values important to student success—plus, it's fun! For example, at the end of a thematic unit, such as a study about the farm or insects, the students can present a child-created play, using many loose parts. Or after reading and learning about biographies, the students can create a Biography Bash or a Wax Museum, using loose parts. The learners can dress up as the important person from the book that they read, and when participants stop by the display, the students can inform them with a speech about the famous person.

"For most students to achieve great success in school, those students must be motivated to do well and to believe in themselves" (Lynch, 2018). In addition to our classrooms, our students' success can and should be celebrated with many audiences in many ways. Celebrations of learning can go beyond the school and be shared with local communities. Multiple audiences can motivate and create a purpose to care about the quality and creativity of their work (Berger, Rugen, and Woodfin, 2014).

What audiences can you share student successes with?

- **Fellow classmates and other classrooms:** Present loose-parts creations and other work with a show and tell, team projects, reading buddies, and so on.

- **School:** Create celebrations for lunchtime, playtime, and events in an auditorium.

- **Parents and families:** Share work on family nights or at parent conferences.

- **Online:** Post work on school social media, in blogs, in class videos, on the Seesaw app, and so on.

- **Local newscasts, newspapers, or newsletters:** Send in a special-interest piece to highlight your students and their successes.

- **Museums:** If possible, create gallery displays of the students' work in the classroom, at the school level, at the local library, or in the community.

- **Library:** Hold events to share the children's work at school, local, and city libraries.

- **Fairs:** Share students' work at farmers' markets, local art shows, county fairs, and so on.

- **Community outreach:** Exhibit children's work at fall festivals and holiday events.

Giving students opportunities to share their loose-parts creations can be such a beneficial experience. Preparing presentations for fellow classmates, other classrooms, families, and their local community can expand their learning and critical-thinking skills. Loose parts celebrations create meaningful conversations among families, students, and teachers about standards and achievement (Berger, Rugen, and Woodfin, 2014).

Based on your grade, content, course objectives, and overall teaching style, you can adapt many of these celebrations in your class, school, and community. Celebrating our students' achievements will lead to greater success in school and in life. Encouraging our students to believe in themselves has lasting impact inside and outside of the classroom (Lynch, 2018). We can support, inspire, and celebrate our loose-parts mindsets across all audiences.

"Celebrate what you have accomplished, but raise the bar a little higher each time you succeed."
—**Mia Hamm, Olympian and world-champion soccer player**

217

Celebrations in Your School

There are so many days to celebrate! Schools regularly commemorate special days, such as the first or hundredth day of school, Dr. Seuss Day, educational holidays, and other momentous occasions. Why not make some of these days celebrations of loose-parts learning and creativity in your school?

Any day is a great day for a special event and celebration of learning. With a little imagination, creativity, and organization, you can plan events that strengthen your students, class, school, and community. Celebrations of learning are more than a display of student work and more than a party at the end of the year. These events compel students to reflect on and articulate what they have learned, how they learned, questions they answered, research they conducted, and areas of strength and struggles. They are powerful opportunities to make learning public (Berger, Rugen, and Woodfin, 2014).

In addition to major federal holidays that we recognize and celebrate each year, there are also lots of fun and unique days that are perfect for applying loose parts. The National Day Calendar (https://nationaldaycalendar.com/) provides a breakdown of local, national, and global days that can apply to your learning objectives and use of loose parts. The Daily Bizarre and Unique Calendar (http://www.holidayinsights.com/) also includes a wealth of information on special days that we can celebrate and tie into class content and standards. We have many children-specific days and lots of wonderful nature and wildlife days that are also perfect for celebrating the use of loose parts in our classroom and school.

Many months that have become important to student learning; for example, February is Black History Month and March is Women's History Month. These are great opportunities to create activities that can highlight important contributions to society and instill values, as well as inspire students to succeed in life.

The list of special days, months, and events to celebrate is a mile long. In the following list, we provide a detailed list of calendar days and have included a few "how to" examples for each month that you might not have considered celebrating, but why not?

LOOSE-PARTS LEARNING IN K-3 CLASSROOMS

A Whole School Year of Celebrations

WHAT AND WHEN	IDEAS FOR APPLYING AND CELEBRATING
September	
4: National Wildlife Day	This is a great holiday to inspire students to learn about different species and their environment. One way to recognize and celebrate is to join the local community to clean up the town or spend some time in nature investigating wildlife and natural materials. https://nationaldaycalendar.com/national-wildlife-day-september-4/
6: National Read a Book Day	https://nationaldaycalendar.com/national-read-a-book-day-september-6/
10: National Swap Ideas Day	https://nationaldaycalendar.com/national-swap-ideas-day-september-10/
16: National Play-Doh Day	Playdough and clay can be great loose parts. Make a station with playdough and other loose parts, and showcase students' use and creations. https://nationaldaycalendar.com/national-play-doh-day-september-16th/
Third full week: National Keep Kids Creative Week	https://nationaldaycalendar.com/national-keep-kids-creative-week-third-full-week-in-september/
Last full week: National Fall Foliage Week	https://nationaldaycalendar.com/national-fall-foliage-week-begins-last-sunday-in-september/
October	
All month: National Go on a Field Trip Month	https://nationaldaycalendar.com/national-go-on-a-field-trip-month-october/
5: Global Cardboard Challenge	This special day is dedicated to creating and playing with cardboard and recycled materials. Design a challenge for students to explain and show their cardboard designs. http://cainesarcade.com/dayofplay/
First Monday: World Habitat Day	https://nationaldaycalendar.com/world-habitat-day-first-monday-in-october/
20: International Chefs Day	https://nationaldaycalendar.com/international-chefs-day-october-20/

WHAT AND WHEN	IDEAS FOR APPLYING AND CELEBRATING
25: International Artists Day	This is an opportunity to display paintings, pictures, sculptures, and writings developed in your class with the entire school. https://nationaldaycalendar.com/international-artists-day-october-25/
28: Global Maker Day	https://www.globalmakerday.com/
November	
3: International Stonework Play Day	http://nurtureinnature.com.au/international-stonework-play-day/
7: Outdoor Classroom Day	
8: National STEM Day	https://nationaldaycalendar.com/national-stemsteam-day-november-8/
15: America Recycles Day	In addition to collecting and playing with recyclable materials (which are perfect loose parts), this day helps to raise awareness of how to properly recycle and reuse items. https://nationaldaycalendar.com/america-recycles-day-november-15/
16: National Button Day	Collecting buttons is a celebration that has so many teaching options that can be ideal for all STREAM subjects. https://nationaldaycalendar.com/national-button-day-november-16/
17: National Take a Hike Day	https://nationaldaycalendar.com/national-take-a-hike-day-november-17/
Week of Thanksgiving: National Game and Puzzle Week	https://nationaldaycalendar.com/national-game-and-puzzle-week-week-of-thanksgiving/
23: Fibonacci Day	https://nationaldaycalendar.com/fibonacci-day-november-23/
December	
4: Wear Brown Shoes Day	Believe it or not, this is a recognized day and hobby. Before you wear your brown shoes around school, make them from loose parts!
8: Pretend to Be a Time Traveler Day	The whole idea is to pretend for the day that we are travelers from a different time. Have students create their costumes and world from various materials and share with others. https://nationaldaycalendar.com/pretend-to-be-a-time-traveler-day-december-8/

WHAT AND WHEN	IDEAS FOR APPLYING AND CELEBRATING
January	
6: National Bean Day	Yes, even dried beans can be loose parts and ideal for learning. This day celebrates the bean in all sizes, shapes, and colors. https://nationaldaycalendar.com/national-bean-day-january-6/
9: National Static Electricity Day	Conduct experiments with your students that demonstrate the cause and effect of static electricity. Use loose parts such as wool, glass, or other objects that can be rubbed against one another to create a shocking and hair-raising celebration. https://nationaldaycalendar.com/national-static-electricity-day-january-9/
Last Monday of the month: National Bubble Wrap Appreciation Day	https://nationaldaycalendar.com/bubble-wrap-appreciation-day-last-monday-of-january/
(varies) US Snow Sculpting Week	https://nationaldaycalendar.com/us-snow-sculpting-week-changes-annually/
February	
1: World Read-Aloud Day	Reading aloud builds many foundational skills and introduces vocabulary and concepts in every subject. In addition to reading the word, how about also creating the word using loose parts? Students can use items to explain their meaning or even use small loose parts to spell the word out.
4: Create a Vacuum Day	Although you can have children create their own vacuum cleaner for their families, this day inspires us to learn more about how vacuums are created. Develop a science or engineering project with your students using a suction cup or other rubber objects that can stick to a flat surface. https://nationaldaycalendar.com/national-create-a-vacuum-day-february-4/
5: Global School Play Day	https://www.globalschoolplayday.com/
8: National Kite Flying Day	https://nationaldaycalendar.com/national-kite-flying-day-february-8/
11: National Inventors Day	https://nationaldaycalendar.com/national-inventors-day-february-11/

WHAT AND WHEN	IDEAS FOR APPLYING AND CELEBRATING
11: International Day of Women and Girls in Science	https://nationaldaycalendar.com/international-day-of-women-and-girls-in-science-february-11/
18: National Battery Day	https://nationaldaycalendar.com/national-battery-day-february-18/
23: National Tile Day	https://nationaldaycalendar.com/national-tile-day-february-23/
28: National Floral Design Day	https://nationaldaycalendar.com/national-floral-design-day-february-28/
March	
All month: National Music in Our Schools Month	https://nafme.org/programs/miosm/music-in-our-schools-month-miosm/miosm-activity-ideas/
(varies) National Wildlife Week	https://nationaldaycalendar.com/national-wildlife-week-changes-annually/
2: National Old Stuff Day	Many loose parts are just "old stuff," so why not encourage students to find, use, and share their creations made from used items? This is also a perfect opportunity to collect stuff from students, families, and fellow teachers for future projects and celebrations. https://nationaldaycalendar.com/national-old-day-stuff-march-2/
13: National Jewel Day	https://nationaldaycalendar.com/national-jewel-day-march-13/
22: World Water Day	Water is a wonderful loose part that can be applied in many ways. This day celebrates the importance of fresh water and reminds us that much of the world still faces a global water crisis. https://nationaldaycalendar.com/world-water-day-march-22/

WHAT AND WHEN	IDEAS FOR APPLYING AND CELEBRATING
April	
All month: National Poetry Month	https://nationaldaycalendar.com/national-poetry-month-april/
First Saturday: National Handmade Day	https://nationaldaycalendar.com/national-handmade-day-first-saturday-in-april/
2: International Children's Book Day	Using loose-parts–inspired books, students can learn to read and explore in a fun and engaging way. https://nationaldaycalendar.com/international-childrens-book-day-april-2/
Second full week: National Library Week	https://nationaldaycalendar.com/national-library-week-generally-the-2nd-week-in-april/
10: Encourage a Young Writer Day	https://nationaldaycalendar.com/tag/encourage-a-young-writer-day/
14: Look Up at the Sky Day	https://nationaldaycalendar.com/days-2/look-up-at-the-sky-day-april-14/
22: Earth Day	Use loose parts to increase awareness and celebrate the importance of our planet. https://nationaldaycalendar.com/days-2/national-earth-day-april-22/
Last Saturday: National Sense of Smell Day	https://nationaldaycalendar.com/days-2/national-sense-of-smell-day-last-saturday-in-april/
May	
1: May Day	https://nationaldaycalendar.com/may-day-may-1–2/
6: Global Day of Design	http://ajjuliani.com/everything-you-need-to-know-about-the-global-day-of-design-gdd16/
18: International Museum Day	https://nationaldaycalendar.com/international-museum-day-may-18/
21: Outdoor Classroom Day	https://outdoorclassroomday.com/
30: National Creativity Day	Unleash your imagination and allow your students to be creative and showcase their innovative loose parts creations with multiple audiences. https://nationaldaycalendar.com/national-creativity-day-may-30/

WHAT AND WHEN	IDEAS FOR APPLYING AND CELEBRATING
June	
All month: National Great Outdoors Month	https://nationaldaycalendar.com/national-great-outdoors-month-june/
All month: Nature Play Days	https://www.indianachildrenandnature.org/npd.html
5: World Environment Day	This important day promotes ways to improve our Earth's environment. We can explore outdoors while learning and understanding the importance of conserving forests, saving endangered species, protecting nature, and planting trees. https://nationaldaycalendar.com/world-environment-day-june-5/
8: National Get Outdoors Day	We all know the importance of exploring nature, taking a walk, visiting a park, and numerous other outdoor activities. Take this opportunity to find natural materials outside.
17: Den Day	https://www.stem.org.uk/news-and-views/opinions/get-creative-and-celebrate-den-day-your-school
21: Make Music Day	https://nationaldaycalendar.com/make-music-day-june-21/
24: International Fairy Day	https://www.checkiday.com/6d6de9e18f4a093a6f2693748510f84c/international-fairy-day
29: International Mud Day	https://worldforumfoundation.org/workinggroups/nature/mud-day/
Last week: National Week of Making	https://www.nationofmakers.us/national-week-of-making

WHAT AND WHEN	IDEAS FOR APPLYING AND CELEBRATING
July	
5: National Hawaii Day	This is such a fun day to celebrate! Who doesn't love Hawaii? Have students use sand water, rocks, and flowers to create their perfect island and learn about this fabulous state and culture.
12: National Simplicity Day	What better day of celebration? In a world with cell phones, computers, video games, and many other technologies, taking a moment to recognize the simplicity of loose parts is ideal.
August	
13: International Left-Handers Day	One of our authors, Tricia, is left-handed, so of course we had to include this special day! Typically, at least one student in your class will be left-handed. This is the opportunity to recognize their uniqueness and differences. Invite a student to share how they write with a pencil, throw a rock, paint a picture, or use a tool in a right-handed world. This is a positive learning moment and cause for celebration.
27: Just Because Day	This day was created to celebrate any way you choose. Give students the opportunity to do and make stuff with loose parts . . . just because.

Planning Your Celebrations

Celebrations can take many forms at the classroom level, at the grade level, at the school level, and at a parent/family night. Refer to the event planning sheet on page 241 to help you think through what you will need. A grade-level celebration might consist of setting up stations and rotating throughout the day, allowing plenty of time for free exploration of the materials. A school-wide celebration could involve visiting other classrooms, sharing on the intranet, or having the event outdoors. Think about involving a committee of teachers, specialists, and an administrator to take the event school wide.

An example of a special day that you and your students could celebrate is the Global Cardboard Challenge on October 5. The challenge is based on Caine's Arcade. Young Caine decided to create an arcade out of cardboard boxes at his father's car-parts store. Using loose parts, tape, tickets, calculators, old toys, and small figurines, Caine created games that he hoped would draw neighborhood people to play. His vision came to life when a customer filmed Caine and his work and shared it on social media. The short film went viral, and the community showed up to play his games. This inspired the Global Cardboard Challenge, an event to urge all children to create with cardboard. You can learn more (and see the film) at https://cardboardchallenge.com/.

Boxes are a universal toy with endless opportunities and are many makers' favorite manufactured loose parts, as they can be so many things and can be used in all subject areas. The price point of cardboard is low (free!) and it is readily accessible. Children can easily cut or customize cardboard with markers, fabric, and paint. Having multiples of tools and supplies available can help:

- Low-temp glue gun

- Scissors or cardboard scissors

- Safe box cutter, such as Klever Kutter or Makedo tools

- Tape—duct, packing, masking, painter's

- Measuring devices

Additionally, reusable connectors, such as Makedo, Box Lox, WondrBolt, and 3DuxDesign cardboard connectors and plastic rivets come in handy.

Train volunteers to use and supervise children with the tools as needed. Additionally, students can draw what they would like an adult to cut for them. Have examples of cardboard connectors and techniques, such as slots, tabs and slots, moveable links (with a brad), exposed corrugation, wings, flanges, scored bends, and fringes.

226

Divide and celebrate! Register the event at the Global Cardboard Challenge (https://cardboardchallenge.com/). Download their official playbook, which has tips and ideas, a sample press release, a materials list, tips on getting sponsors, checklists, and design challenges to help the planning and implementing process.

BOOKS TO INSPIRE CREATIVITY WITH CARDBOARD BOXES

Books can be a special part of any celebration. For example, guest readers may come in to share a special book about ways to use cardboard. Here are some of our read-aloud favorites around cardboard and boxes.

Bruss, Deborah. 2011. *Big Box for Ben*. Cambridge, MA: Star Bright Books.	Ben and his dog use their imaginations to transform a box into a car, airplane, boat, elephant, mountain, and doghouse.
Gauch, Patricia Lee. 2012. *Christina Katerina and the Box*. New York: Boyds Mills Press.	Christina Katerina uses the box from a refrigerator delivery to create a palace, clubhouse, race car, and boat.
Heder, Thyra. 2013. *Fraidyzoo*. New York: Abrams Books for Young Readers.	A girl is afraid to go to the zoo, so her family creates zoo animals with cardboard.
Portis, Antoinette. 2006. *Not a Box*. New York: HarperCollins.	A rabbit's box becomes a car, mountain, burning building, robot, boat, and more. When asked, the rabbit always says, "It's not a box!" You can expand on this idea with other common objects.
Rau, Dana Meachen. 2001. *A Box Can Be Many Things*. New York: Scholastic.	A child rescues a discarded box, which then becomes a car, cave, and house. As it wears down, it becomes dramatic-play props.
Smith, Kim. 2020. *Boxitects*. New York: Clarion.	A girl loves making things out of boxes. At Maker School, Meg is the first boxitect until a new girl shares cardboard tips. The girls learn teamwork through a competition. Consider hosting a maker-match to pair children to build together.
Yolen, Jane. 2016. *What to Do with a Box*. Mankato, MN: Creative Editions.	A box can be anything with imagination. It might be a library, a palace, a nook, a sailboat, or a fairy scene. Consider hosting a stuffed-animal tea party. Paint boxes as scenery, create box transportation, and offer dramatic-play items near boxes to inspire play.

Tools and Resources

- List of Loose-Parts Options

- Plant and Grow: Planning for Loose Parts

- Sample Donation Letter

- Spreading the Word—Networking with Others

- Loose-Parts Map/Resource List

- Loose-Parts Inventory

- Benefit-Risk Assessment

- Reflective Page on Evaluating, Sharing, and Collaborating with Loose Parts

- Event Planning Sheet

LIST OF LOOSE-PARTS OPTIONS

General			
Clothespins	Wooden animals	Wooden dowels
Buttons	Pillows	Wooden rings
Fabric samples	Boxes	Variety of paper
Beads	Carpet squares	Cylinders
Office supplies	Crates	Balls
Golf tees	Yarn	Sheets
Googly eyes	String	Large wooden spools
Chenille stems	Ribbon	Foam
Raffia	Produce netting bags	Floor samples
Jewels/gems	Wool balls	Hardie board
Pompoms	Wooden eggs	Clay
Water beads	Wicker mats	Seeds
Felted wool	Scarves	Birdseed
Plexiglas	Bells	Playdough
Wooden spools	Leather scraps	
Plastic animals		

Block Play			
Wooden blocks	Magformers	Tree cookies
Cardboard brick blocks	Magna-Tiles	Tarps
Scrap wood	Gear sets	Lego bricks
Plastic building blocks	Interlocking wood pieces	Bricks
Plank blocks	Boxes	Mini bricks
Wedgits	Natural tree branch blocks	Wood cubes
		Wooden planks

Recyclable Materials			
Bottle caps	Cardboard tubes	Paint swatches
Lids	Thread cones	Large wooden shapes
Canning jar rings	Keys	Packaging materials
Foil	Tennis ball cans	Egg cartons
Cardboard	Film canisters	Cereal boxes
Plastic tubing	Cups	

LIST OF LOOSE-PARTS OPTIONS

Natural Materials

Sticks	Seeds	Sycamore seeds
Buckeyes	Pods	Crystals
Pinecones	Plant materials	Palm fronds
Acorns	Dried flowers	Branches
Large rocks	Eucalyptus	Christmas trees
Feathers	Dried gourds	Sunflower heads
Bark (found only, never pull bark off a tree)	Cork	Wood chips
	Natural sponges	Stumps
Chestnuts	Loofah pieces	Moss
"Glitter" made from crushed petals and leaves	Sand	Boulders
	Dirt	Pine needles
	Leaves	Evergreen branches
Logs	Driftwood	Pussy willows
Shells	Nuts	Grasses
Tree cookies	Milkweed pods	
	Gravel	

Seasonal Materials

Plastic eggs	Table scatter	Pumpkins
Insta-snow	Seasonal erasers	Straw bales
Artificial leaves	Foam or felt stickers	Ice blocks
Seasonal baubles	Garden blooms	Colored ice balls
	Corn stalks	

LIST OF LOOSE-PARTS OPTIONS

Tools and Accessories			
Magnifying glasses	Sprinkle bottles	Magnets
Buckets	Squeeze bottles	Easels
Shovels	Syringes (needles removed)	Stools
Garden tools		Pulleys
Tongs	Spray bottles	Rope
Goggles	Tweezers	Cameras
Hammers	Eye droppers	Paint
Light table	Turkey basters	Chalk
Bolts	Strainers	Crayons
Pots and pans	Sifters	Sieves
Nuts and washers	Brushes	Scissors
Twine	Paintbrushes	Dishes
Tires	Notebooks	Small plungers
Tiles	Funnels	Potato mashers
Wire mats	Rulers	Craft sticks
Scoops	Measuring tapes	Measuring cups
Clipboards	Hoses	Paint sticks
Unbreakable mirrors	Plastic gutters	Ladders
Clocks	Pipes	Sprinklers
	Wheelbarrows	

Containers			
Bins	Deli containers	Utility trays
Tubs	Wooden drawers	Bowls
Wooden drawers	Baskets	Garden tubs
Small/medium/large sorting trays	Grain bins	Flowerpots
	Bags	Troughs

Defined Workspaces			
Frames	Unbreakable mirrors	Natural mats
Large plastic hoops	Trays	Rope
Chalk-drawn shapes	Looms	Net
Cardboard frames	Placemats	

(Gull and Whitmire, 2015a)

Plant and Grow: Planning for Loose Parts

I. Plant

Loose parts goal: Why do I want to do this? Who will benefit? How does it fit into our work and philosophy? Where will the materials be physically used?

Items: What specific items am I looking for? What will be the purpose for the children? What are the safety concerns and risks?

Inventory: What materials do I currently have for this purpose?

Prioritize: What are the most important items to gather first? Why? Which items will have the most impact?

Resources: Where can I source loose parts in my community? People? Places?

Loose parts goal: Why do I want to do this? Who will benefit? How does it fit into our work and philosophy? Where will the materials be physically used?

Finance: What costs are involved for these materials? Can I find free sources? Do I need to develop a budget?

Organize: How do I keep the materials ready for use and store them appropriately?

Maintain: How will I need to manage and refresh this type of material?

Evaluate: What needs to be adjusted, changed, or removed? What is working well?

(adapted from Gull and Whitmire, 2015b)

Sample Donation Letter

Dear Families and Community Members,

Throughout the year, our class will be using many different "loose parts" in many aspects of our curriculum. We would love your help with collecting interesting items to use in our classroom.

Here is a sample of items to collect and send into class. This list a great start, but please expand the ideas to include items that you stumble across. The children will love it!

- Paper-towel tubes
- Bread twist ties
- Bottle caps
- Egg cartons
- Berry containers
- Art supplies—pompoms, wooden shapes, foam shapes

- Beans, seeds
- Tile
- Pieces of wood
- Boxes of all sizes
- Broken appliances (please cut off the cords)

- Gift-wrapping paper
- Old tools—screwdrivers, pliers, tweezers
- Clearance items that you think the students will enjoy
- Just about anything!

Please be sure to clean the containers. When you have collected a large bag full of items, please send the bag to school. We will sort the items and use them throughout the day during science, technology, reading, engineering, art, and mathematics.

Please encourage your family, friends, and community members to save items as well! The students will be using all of these found treasures for learning in the content areas.

Thank you so much!

Spreading the Word—Networking with Others

Needed Items

Potential Organizations/People to Donate

How Will I Contact Them?

Items Received/Additional Notes

LOOSE-PARTS MAP/RESOURCE LIST		
Organization/Contact	Loose Parts Available/Skills	Location

LOOSE-PARTS INVENTORY			
Category	Items	Location Stored	Additional Notes

BENEFIT-RISK ASSESSMENT

Item or Activity:

Benefits:

Risks:

Things to consider:

- Regulations

- Licensing:

- Local factors:

- Other organizations' solutions:

Decisions to mitigate risk:

Actions taken:

Maintenance:

(adapted from Ball, Gill, and Spiegal, 2014)

Reflective Page on Evaluating, Sharing, and Collaborating with Loose Parts

- What did children do with the loose parts?

- What did they discover or rediscover?

- What concepts were involved?

- Did they carry their ideas back into the community and their families?

- Out of all possible materials that could be provided, which ones were the most fun to play with and the most capable of stimulating the cognitive, social, and physical learning processes? (adapted from Nicholson, 1971)

How might you celebrate loose parts with students?

What options do you have for sharing student work?

How might you share loose parts in your community?

What organizations or individuals might you collaborate with to enhance loose parts in your area?

Challenge: Sketch out an action plan for the next ninety days of what you might implement regarding loose parts in your setting.

(Gull, 2020a)

Event Planning Sheet

- Help educators, students, and families to understand the importance of the event. Discuss student expectations for the event day:

  - **What are the plans for the day?**

  - **What supplies are needed or might students bring to school?**

  - **What might other students be doing?**

  - **What are you excited about for the event?**

  - **What are you worried about for the event?**

  - **How will students communicate with the teacher if needed?**

  - **How will materials be shared?**

- Think about the adult volunteers you will need.

  - **Reach out to families and school volunteers for their assistance at the event.**

  - **If volunteers will be handling and supervising the use of tools, make sure they know how to use them.**

  - **Consider how adults will interact with the event, including when they might intervene or when children can handle issues on their own.**

- Plan a schedule for the event.

  - **What blocks of time will be dedicated to the event?**

  - **Where will students be in the school or on the schoolyard? Consider making a map for more complicated events.**

- Gather materials and supplies.

  - **Decide on the necessary materials and supplies.**

  - **Decide whether students will bring anything from home.**

  - **Work out a plan to collect donations and secure supplies.**

  - **Plan how to put materials and supplies they are needed on the day of the event.**

- Announce the event.

  - **Use social media and press releases to let the press and community know about the event.**

  - **Communicate to students and families about the necessary details of the event via email, apps, flyers, posters, and so on.**

  - **Remind families again one day before the event.**

On the Day of the Event

- Go over what is expected for the day and how students will interact with each other and the materials.

- Enjoy the event! Avoid intervening and teaching during this time. Enjoy a day of unstructured play, celebration, and learning for students.

- Document the event through photos to share on the school intranet and social media, if allowed.

- Check in with the students, asking questions such as the following:

  - **How is the day working for you?**

  - **Are you bothered by anything today?**

  - **How are other children interacting with you?**

  - **What new things have you learned?**

  - **What might you change?**

After the Event

- Share photos (if allowed) on social media or the school intranet.

- Recap the event through a blog post.

- With the students, reflect on the event, discussing how it went, what worked well, and what could be changed.

- Follow up with families, and invite their feedback.

- Share event reflections and the impact on students with other educators.

- Have students write and reflect about the event.

(adapted from Global School Play Day Teacher Resources, n.d.)

Assessment Options

- Assessment Form

- Recording Sheet

- Self-Evaluation Form

Assessment Form

The following is an example of a form that can be used to assess students based on standards. This document reflects the Common Core English/Language Arts Standards in the Literature strand. You can alter this document by simply replacing the standards, grade-level goals, and district objectives you need to assess.

Name:_____Date: _____

Grade 1 English/Language Arts Standards: Literature

Type of assessment used:_____

Standards	Loose Parts Used	Project Completed	Notes/ Observations
1.1 Ask and answer questions about key details in a text.			
1.2 Retell stories, including key details, and demonstrate understanding of their central message or lesson.			
1.3 Describe characters, settings, and major events in a story, using key details.			
1.4 Identify words and phrases in stories or poems that suggest feelings or appeal to the senses.			
1.5 Explain major differences between books that tell stories and books that give information, drawing on a wide reading of a range of text types.			
1.6 Identify who is telling the story at various points in a text.			
1.7 Use illustrations and details in a story to describe its characters, setting, or events.			
1.9. Compare and contrast the adventures and experiences of characters in stories.			
1.10 With prompting and support, read prose and poetry of appropriate complexity for grade.			

RECORDING SHEET

Student Name	Loose Parts Used	Schema/ Standard	Quotes	Notes

(Gull, 2020a)

Student Self-Evaluation Form

Name:_____ Date: _____

Today I made_____.

I made it during_____.

Here is my picture:

I used these items:

_____

_____

I feel proud that I

_____

_____

Next time I will

_____

_____

I discovered

_____

_____

References and Recommended Resources and Readings

Alberta Health Services. 2018. "Health and Safety Recommendations for Natural Materials and Loose Parts in Childcare Settings." Edmonton, AB: Alberta Health Services. https://www.albertahealthservices.ca/assets/wf/eph/wf-eph-recommend-natural-materials-childcare.pdf

All Students Can Shine. 2017. "Morning Tubs in the Elementary Classroom." All Students Can Shine. http://www.allstudentscanshine.com/2017/09/morning-tubs-in-elementary-classroom.html

Almon, Joan, ed. 2017. *Playing It Up—With Loose Parts, Playpods, and Adventure Playgrounds.* Annapolis, MD: Alliance for Childhood.

Aranca. 2017. "Technologies Inspired by Nature." Aranca. https://www.aranca.com/knowledge-library/articles/ip-research/technologies-inspired-by-nature

Backwoods Mama. 2018. "Stop Telling Kids to 'Be Careful' and What to Say Instead" Back Woods Mama. https://www.backwoodsmama.com/2018/02/stop-telling-kids-be-careful-and-what-to-say-instead.html

Baker-Jones, Sally L. 2010. *Early Years Schemas.* Sennen, Cornwall, UK: Sennen and Land's End Pre-school. http://www.sennenpreschool.org.uk/uploads/5/4/5/9/5459458/early_years_schema2_copy.pdf

Ball, David, Tim Gill, and Bernard Spiegal. 2014. *Risk-Benefit Assessment Form.* Scotland, UK: Play England, Play Scotland, Play Wales and PlayBoard Northern Ireland. https://playsafetyforum.files.wordpress.com/2015/03/psf-risk-benefit-assessment-form.docx

Ball, Pearl S. 2013. "Enhancing Language Experiences through Storytelling and the Story Basket." *Montessori Life* 25(2): 26–29.

Bamber, Veronica, and Lorraine Stefani. 2015. "Taking Up the Challenge of Evidencing Value in Educational Development: From Theory to Practice." *International Journal for Academic Development* 21(3): 242–254. https://doi.org/10.1080/1360144X.2015.1100112

Berger, Ron, Leah Rugen, and Libby Woodfin. 2014. *Leaders of Their Own Learning: Transforming Schools through Student-Engaged Assessment.* San Francisco: Jossey-Bass.

Bird, Lois Bridges. 1995. *Creating Your Classroom Community.* Portland, ME: Stenhouse.

Bongiorno, Laurel. 2014. "How Process-Focused Art Experiences Support Preschoolers." *Teaching Young Children* 7(3): 18–19.

Bright Hub Education. 2008. "Teach Geometry in Elementary School: Help for Teachers." Bright Hub Education. https://www.brighthubeducation.com/teaching-elementary-school/16636-help-teaching-geometry

Buchanan, Shelly M., Mary A. Harlan, Christine Bruce, and Sylvia Edwards. 2016. "Inquiry-Based Learning Models, Information Literacy, and Student Engagements: A Literature Review." *School Libraries Worldwide* 22(2): 23–39.

Campbell, Chris. 2014. "Problem-Based Learning and Project-Based Learning." *Teacher*, September 16. https://www.teachermagazine.com/au_en/articles/problem-based-learning-and-project-based-learning

Canadian Public Health Association. n.d. "Loose Parts Policy." Canadian Public Health Association. https://www.cpha.ca/sites/default/files/uploads/resources/play/loose-parts-e.pdf

Carr, Victoria, Rhonda D. Brown, Sue Schlembach, and Leslie Kochanowski. 2017. "Nature by Design: Playscape Affordances Support the Use of Executive Function in Preschoolers." *Children, Youth, and Environments* 27(2): 25–46.

Carson, Rachel. 1956. *The Sense of Wonder: A Celebration of Nature for Parents and Children*. New York: Harper and Row.

Casey, Theresa, and Juliet Robertson. 2016. *Loose Parts Play: A Toolkit*. Edinburgh, Scotland, UK: Inspiring Scotland, Play Strategy Group, and Scottish Government. https://www.inspiringscotland.org.uk/wp-content/uploads/2017/03/Loose-Parts-Play-web.pdf

Child and Nature Alliance of Canada. 2017. "When You Want to Say, 'Be Careful.' " Child and Nature Alliance of Canada. https://childnature.ca/when-you-want-to-say-be-careful/

Child Mind Institute. 2020. "Learning and Development Disorders." Child Mind Institute. https://childmind.org/topics/disorders/learning-and-development-disorders/

Clemens, Sydney G. 1991. "Art in the Classroom: Making Every Day Special." *Young Children* 46(2): 4–11.

Common Sense Education. 2017. *Get Started with Coding*. Common Sense Media. https://d1e2bohyu2u2w9.cloudfront.net/education/sites/default/files/tlr-asset/document-coding-tip-sheet-updated-0.pdf

Common Sense Education. 2019. "Best Robotics Apps and Websites for STEM Classrooms." Common Sense Media. https://www.commonsense.org/education/top-picks/best-robotics-apps-and-websites-for-stem-classrooms

Compton, Mary K., and Robin C. Thompson. 2018. *Storymaking: The Maker Movement Approach to Literacy for Early Learners*. St. Paul, MN: Redleaf.

Counsell, Shelley, et al. 2016. *STEM Learning with Young Children: Inquiry Teaching with Ramps and Pathways*. New York: Teachers College Press.

Cox, Meg. 1998. *The Heart of a Family: Searching America for Traditions That Fulfill Us*. New York: Random House.

Deboree, Trina. 2018. "5 Astonishing Reasons Every Classroom Needs a MakerSpace." Trina Deboree Teaching and Learning. https://trinadeboreeteachingandlearning.com/trinadeb oreeteachingandearningblog/2018/2/14/5-astonishing-reasons-every-classroom-needs-a-makerspace

DeCarbo, Christina. 2021. "Brain Bins Promote Creativity and Essential Skills." Miss DeCarbo. https://www.missdecarbo.com/brain-bins-promote-creativity-and-essential-skills/

DeLanghe, Peggy. 2019. "I LOVE When Children Make a Connection between What We Are Learning in the Classroom and Their Exposure to Certain Materials!" September 25, 2019. Facebook. https://www.facebook.com/groups/357260234957716/permalink/389449801738759/

DeLuccia-Reinstein, Rebecca. 2020. "What Is the Role of Teachers in Education?" Classroom. https://classroom.synonym.com/role-teachers-education-6509642.html

Desli, Despoina, and Anastasia Dimitriou. 2014. "Teaching Mathematics and Science in Early Childhood: Prospective Kindergarten and Primary School Teachers' Beliefs." *Review of Science, Mathematics and ICT Education* 8(2): 25–48.

Dewar, Gwen. 2018. "Why Toy Blocks Rock: The Benefits of Construction Play." Parenting Science. https://www.parentingscience.com/toy-blocks.html

Dewey, John. 1942. *The School and Society*. Chicago: University of Chicago Press.

Dover, Grace. 2018. "Benefits of Constructivist Learning Design." Smart Sparrow. https://www.smartsparrow.com/2018/02/28/the-benefits-of-constructivist-learning-design/

Edison Innovation Project. 2020. "Looking to Encourage Innovation through the Ages." Edison Innovation Foundation. https://www.thomasedison.org/

Edwards, Carolyn, Lella Gandini, and George Forman, eds. 1993. *The Hundred Languages of Children: The Reggio Emilia Approach to Early Childhood Education*. Westport, CT: Praeger.

Exploring Your Mind. 2018. "Divergent Thinking: What It Is and How to Develop It." Exploring Your Mind. https://exploringyourmind.com/divergent-thinking-what-it-is/

Farr, Virginia. 2003. "The Role of Celebration in Building Classroom-Learning Communities." Doctoral diss. Johnson City, TN: East Tennessee State University. https://dc.etsu.edu/cgi/viewcontent.cgi?article=1928&context=etd

Fountas, Irene C., and Gay S. Pinnell. 1996. *Guided Reading: Responsive Teaching across the Grades*. Portsmouth, NH: Heinemann.

Furner, Joseph M., and Nancy L. Worrell. 2017. "The Importance of Using Manipulatives in Teaching Math Today." *Transformations* 3(1): 1–25.

Generation Genius. 2021. "Read About Simple Machines." Generation Genius. https://www.generationgenius.com/simple-machines-reading-material/

Getting Smart and Teton Science Schools. 2017. *Quick Start Guide to Implementing Place-Based Education*. Jackson, WY: Teton Science Schools. https://www.gettingsmart.com/wp-content/uploads/2017/02/Quick-Start-Guide-to-Implementing-Place-Based-Education.pdf

Gibson, James J. 1979. *The Ecological Approach to Visual Perception*. Boston: Houghton Mifflin.

Global School Play Day Teacher Resources. n.d. Global School Play Day. https://docs.google.com/document/d/1oOTo2qjNNhJTfX-92PEcBMsf9m5LF-BAoBLp-GdmMrc/edit

Goodman, Stacey. 2015. "Fuel Creativity in the Classroom with Divergent Thinking." Edutopia (blog). https://www.edutopia.org/blog/fueling-creativity-through-divergent-thinking-classroom-stacey-goodman

Goodwin, Anita. n.d.a. "10 Ideas for Mini Green Screens." Goodwinnovate. https://www.goodwinnovate.com/10-ideas-for-mini-green-screen-in-the-elementary-classroom/

Goodwin, Anita. n.d.b. "Green Screen in the Classroom: Getting Started." Goodwinnovate. https://www.goodwinnovate.com/green-screen-in-classroom-getting/

Gray, Peter. 2013. *Free to Learn: Why Unleashing the Instinct to Play Will Make Our Children Happier, More Self-Reliant, and Better Students for Life*. New York: Basic Books.

Griffiths, Janel B. 2019. "5 Awesome Tools for Teaching Robotics in the Classroom." We Are Teachers. https://www.weareteachers.com/classroom-robotics-tools/

Gull, Carla. n.d. Loose Parts Play. Facebook group. https://www.facebook.com/groups/LoosePartsPlay/

Gull, Carla. 2013. "Natural Weaving." Inside Outside Michiana (blog), November 2. http://insideoutsidemichiana.blogspot.com/2013/11/natural-weaving.html

Gull, Carla. 2015. "16 Ideas for Animal Play." Inside Outside Michiana (blog), March 4. http://insideoutsidemichiana.blogspot.com/2015/03/16-ideas-for-animal-play.html

Gull, Carla. 2016. "Adding Plants to an Outdoor Classroom." Inside Outside Michiana (blog), August 21. http://insideoutsidemichiana.blogspot.com/2016/08/adding-plants-to-outdoor-classroom.html

Gull, Carla. 2017a. "30 Plus Ways to Approach Loose Parts Play!" Inside Outside Michiana (blog), May 16. http://insideoutsidemichiana.blogspot.com/2017/05/30-plus-ways-to-approach-loose-parts.html/

Gull, Carla. 2017b. "Light Painting." Inside Outside Michiana (blog), December 14. http://insideoutsidemichiana.blogspot.com/2017/12/light-painting.html/

Gull, Carla. 2017c. "Rocks as a Loose Part." Inside Outside Michiana (blog), November 19. http://insideoutsidemichiana.blogspot.com/2017/11/rocks-as-loose-part.html/

Gull, Carla. 2018a. "15+ Ways to Find Inexpensive Loose Parts." Inside Outside Michiana (blog), February 6. http://insideoutsidemichiana.blogspot.com/2018/02/15-ways-to-find-inexpensive-loose-parts.html/

Gull, Carla. 2018b. "Approaches to Loose Parts Play." Loose Parts Nature Play (podcast), February 6. https://loosepartsnatureplay.libsyn.com/approaches-to-loose-parts-play

Gull, Carla. 2018c. "Cultivating the Early Years Loose Parts." Paper presented at the 2018 Early Years Loose Parts Conference, Sheridan, IL, October 6.

Gull, Carla. 2018d. "Lights and Reflection as a Loose Part." Inside Outside Michiana (blog), February 27. https://insideoutsidemichiana.blogspot.com/2018/02/lights-and-reflection-as-loose-part.html

Gull, Carla. 2018e. "Loose Parts Clean Up: 11 Tips." Inside Outside Michiana (blog), October 16. http://insideoutsidemichiana.blogspot.com/2018/10/interested-in-listening-to-this-with-my.html/

Gull, Carla. 2018f. "Loose Parts Handout." Inside Outside Michiana (blog), December 31. https://insideoutsidemichiana.blogspot.com/2018/12/loose-parts-handout.html

Gull, Carla. 2018g. "Nature Art Inspiration." Inside Outside Michiana (blog), January 31. https://insideoutsidemichiana.blogspot.com/2018/01/nature-art-inspiration.html

Gull, Carla. 2018h. "Nature Play Fun: Creating Temporary and Mobile Nature Play Spaces." Loose Parts Nature Play (podcast), October 24. https://loosepartsnatureplay.libsyn.com/nature-play-fun-creating-temporary-and-mobile-nature-play-spaces/

Gull, Carla. 2019. "Intaking Loose Parts." Loose Parts Nature Play (podcast), November 23. https://loosepartsnatureplay.libsyn.com/intaking-loose-parts/

Gull, Carla. 2020a. "7 Day Loose Parts Challenge." Online lecture series, Goshen, IN, May 25–31, 2020.

Gull, Carla. 2020b. "Developing a Loose-Parts Mindset." Lecture in the 7 Day Loose Parts Challenge, Goshen, IN, May 25–31.

Gull, Carla. 2020c. "Electricity as a Loose Part." Loose Parts Nature Play (podcast), January 20. https://loosepartsnatureplay.libsyn.com/electricity-as-a-loose-part

Gull, Carla. 2020d. "Learning Outdoors." *In Middlebury Magazine*, July 7. https://issuu.com/melissatroyer/docs/inmiddleburymagazine_july2020/

Gull, Carla. 2020e. "Loose Parts Bingo." https://drive.google.com/file/d/1l7uW0EuLCTyFRWtwVBnmxEFv1izfHb9y/view

Gull, Carla. 2020f. "Loose Parts Starts." Loose Parts Nature Play (podcast), July 10. https://loosepartsnatureplay.libsyn.com/loose-parts-starts/

Gull, Carla. 2020g. "Math and Loose Parts in Nature." Inside Outside Michiana (blog), September 5. http://insideoutsidemichiana.blogspot.com/

Gull, Carla. 2020h. "Rolling into Physics: Ramp Investigations." Loose Parts Nature (podcast), April 16. https://loosepartsnatureplay.libsyn.com/rolling-into-physics-ramp-investigations

Gull, Carla. 2020i. "Minecraft IRL (in real life)." Loose Parts Nature Play (podcast), July 23. https://loosepartsnatureplay.libsyn.com/minecraft-irl-in-real-life

Gull, Carla. 2020j. "Rube Goldberg Machines." Loose Parts Nature Play (podcast), February 4. https://loosepartsnatureplay.libsyn.com/

Gull, Carla. 2020k. "Storytelling, STEM, and Simple Machines in Outdoor Classrooms." Presentation at the Nature-Based Early Learning Virtual Conference, July 29–31.

Gull, Carla. 2020l. "Tinker Carts." Loose Parts Nature Play (podcast), March 3. https://loosepartsnatureplay.libsyn.com/tinker-carts

Gull, Carla, and Chris Whitmire. 2015a. "Loose Parts Planning Options." Inside Outside Michiana (blog), April 15. http://insideoutsidemichiana.blogspot.com/2015/04/loose-parts-imagination-creativity.html/

Gull, Carla, and Chris Whitmire. 2015b. "Loose Parts Planning Worksheet." Inside Outside Michiana (blog), April 15. http://insideoutsidemichiana.blogspot.com/2015/04/loose-parts-imagination-creativity.html/

Gull, Carla, Jessica Bogunovich, Suzanne Levenson Goldstein, and Tricia Rosengarten. 2019. "Definitions of Loose Parts in Early Childhood Outdoor Classrooms: A Scoping Review." International Journal of Early Childhood Environmental Education 6(3): 37–52.

Gull, Carla, Suzanne L. Goldstein, and Tricia Rosengarten. 2020. "Bridging Research and Practice: Seven Loose Parts Myths Busted." Exchange 42(6): 34–38.

Hale, Christy. 2012. Dreaming Up: A Celebration of Building. New York: Lee and Low.

Hand, Jamie. n.d. "How to Teach Preschoolers to Think Like an Engineer in 3 Easy Steps." Preschool STEAM. https://preschoolsteam.com/engineering-for-preschoolers/

Hand2Mind. n.d. "Benefits of Manipulatives." Hand2Mind. https://www.hand2mind.com/resources/benefits-of-manipulatives#:~:text=Research%20indicates%20that%20using%20manipulatives,the%20environment%20in%20math%20classrooms

Hatten, Stephanie. 2014. "Engage Elementary Students with Stop Animation!" ISTE (blog), August 15. https://www.iste.org/explore/Toolbox/Engage-elementary-students-with-stop-animation%21

Hauser, Jill F. 1997. Super Science Concoctions: 50 Mysterious Mixtures for Fabulous Fun. Charlotte, VT: Williamson Publishing.

Heavin, Amy. 2018. "A Vertical Build—A Lego Wall Built for Our Makerspace." Fractus Learning. https://www.fractuslearning.com/makerspace-lego-wall/

Heroman, Cate. 2017. *Making and Tinkering with STEM: Solving Design Challenges with Young Children*. Washington, DC: NAEYC.

Hesmondhalgh, Tom. 2011. "10 Reasons to Take Learning Outside the Classroom." Creative Education (blog), June 6. https://www.creativeeducation.co.uk/blog/learning-outside-the-classroom/

Holman, Cas. 2020. "Getting Started: Facilitator Support." Rigamajig. https://www.rigamajig.com/getting-started/

Holmes, Andrew G. 2019. "Constructivist Learning in University Undergraduate Programmes. Has Constructivism Been Fully Embraced? Is There Clear Evidence that Constructivist Principles Have Been Applied to All Aspects of Contemporary University Undergraduate Study?" *Shanlax International Journal of Education* 8(1): 7–15.

Houser, Natalie E., et al. 2016. "Let the Children Play: Scoping Review on the Implementation and Use of Loose Parts for Promoting Physical Activity Participation." *AIMS Public Health* 3(4): 781–799.

Hunter, Robin. 2004. *Madeline Hunter's Mastery Teaching: Increasing Instructional Effectiveness in Elementary and Secondary Schools*. Thousand Oaks, CA: Corwin.

Imagination.org. n.d. *Global Cardboard Challenge*. https://cardboardchallenge.com/

Interaction Design Foundation. 2020. "What Are Affordances?" Interaction Design Foundation. https://www.interaction-design.org/literature/topics/affordances/

International Society for Technology in Education (ISTE). 2021. *ISTE Standards for Students*. https://www.iste.org/standards/for-students/

Iowa Regents' Center for Early Developmental Education. n.d. *Ramps and Pathways*. Cedar Falls, IA: Iowa Regents' Center for Early Developmental Education, University of Northern Iowa. https://regentsctr.uni.edu/sites/default/files/activity_sheets/Ramps_and_Pathways_Activity_Sheet_2018.pdf

Iowa Regents' Center for Early Developmental Education. 2021. "Ramps and Pathways." Iowa Regents' Center for Early Developmental Education. https://regentsctr.uni.edu/ramps-pathways/ramps-pathways

Kable, Jennifer, and Juliet Robertson. 2010. "The Theory of Loose Parts." Creative Star Learning Company. http://hfweb.co.uk/cpnl/wp-content/uploads/2011/04/Loose_parts1.pdf

Kaplan Early Learning Company. 2021. "Using Block Play to Promote STEM in the Classroom." Kaplan Early Learning Company. https://www.kaplanco.com/ii/block-play-stem

Kerr, Sherryl. 2017. "Why Is Elementary Education So Important?" Education versus Literacy. http://www.the-education-site.com/why-is-elementary-education-so-important/#:~:text=Elementary%20school%20is%20the%20most,to%20act%20on%20their%20own

Kiewra, Christine, and Ellen E. Veselack. 2016. "Playing with Nature: Supporting Preschoolers' Creativity in Natural Outdoor Classrooms." *International Journal of Early Childhood Environmental Education* 4(1): 70–95.

Kodo Kids. 2019. "Introducing Simple Machines: Low-Tech Tools." Kodo. https://kodokids.com/introducing-simple-machines-low-tech-tools/

Koralek, Derry. 2015. "Ten Things Children Can Learn from Block Play." *Young Children* 70(1). https://www.naeyc.org/resources/pubs/yc/mar2015/ten-things-children-learn-block-play

Lego Education. 2016. *Lego Education WeDo 2.0 Curriculum Pack*. Lego Education. https://le-www-live-s.legocdn.com/sc/media/files/user-guides/wedo-2/science-teacher-guides/scienceteachersguide-en-us-v1-a927149dcfc792a230cdc8b918381ba0.pdf

Lego Education. 2020. "Grants and Funding." Lego Education. https://education.lego.com/en-us/grants-and-funding

Lehrhaupt, Adam, and Deb Pilutti. 2018. *Idea Jar*. New York: Simon and Schuster.

Lesley University. n.d. "Empowering Students: The 5 E Model Explained." Lesley University. https://lesley.edu/article/empowering-students-the-5e-model-explained/

Lester, Stuart, and Wendy Russell. 2010. *Children's Right to Play: An Examination of the Importance of Play in the Lives of Children Worldwide*. Working paper 57. The Hague, NL: Bernard van Leer Foundation. https://www.researchgate.net/publication/263087157

Levenson Goldstein, Suzanne. 2007. "Teachers' Perceptions Regarding Teaching Effectiveness, Skill Mastery, and Students' Attitudes Toward Reading." Unpublished dissertation manuscript. Thousand Oaks, CA: California Lutheran University.

Lipp, Michelle. 2021. "Math and Loose Parts Play." Fantastic Fun and Learning. https://www.fantasticfunandlearning.com/math-and-loose-parts-play.html

Loose Parts Play Facebook Group. 2020. "If you were to go into a typical elementary classroom." January 3, 2020. https://www.facebook.com/groups/LoosePartsPlay/permalink/2877647602256841

Lynch, Erin. 2018. "10 Ways Teachers/Principals Can Celebrate Student Success." Sadlier's English Language Arts Blog (blog), October 31. https://www.sadlier.com/school/ela-blog/5-ways-to-celebrate-student-success

Maes, Ann. 2015. "The Theory of Loose Parts: The Right to be Creative." Little Worlds. http://littleworldsbigadventures.com/theory-of-loose-parts/

Martinez, Sylvia Libow, and Gary Stager. 2013. *Invent to Learn: Making, Tinkering, and Engineering in the Classroom.* Torrance, CA: Constructing Modern Knowledge Press.

Maslyk, Jacie. 2016. *STEAM Makers: Fostering Creativity and Innovation in the Elementary Classroom.* Thousand Oaks, CA: Corwin.

McClure, Marissa, Patricia Tarr, Christine M. Thompson, and Angela Eckhoff. 2017. "Defining Quality in Visual Art Education for Young Children: Building on the Position Statement of the Early Childhood Art Educators." *Arts Education Policy Review* 118(3): 154–163.

Montessori, Maria. 1912. *The Montessori Method: Scientific Pedagogy as Applied to Child Education in "The Children's Houses."* New York: Frederick A. Stokes.

National Coalition for Core Arts Standards. 2015. National Core Arts Standards. Dover, DE: State Education Agency Directors of Arts Education. https://www.nationalartsstandards.org/

National Governors Association Center for Best Practices, Council of Chief State School Officers. 2010. "English Language Arts Standards, Reading: Literature." Common Core State Standards Initiative. Washington, DC: National Governors Association Center for Best Practices, Council of Chief State School Officers. http://www.corestandards.org/ELA-Literacy/RL/

Neddo, Nick. 2020. *The Organic Artist for Kids: A DIY Guide to Making Your Own Eco-Friendly Art Supplies from Nature.* Beverly, MA: Quarry Books.

Nelson, Eric. 2012. *Cultivating Outdoor Classrooms: Designing and Implementing Child-Centered Learning Environments.* St. Paul, MN: Redleaf.

Next Generation Science Standards. n.d. "The Three Dimensions of Science Learning." Next Generation Science Standards. https://www.nextgenscience.org/

Nicholson, Simon. 1971. "How NOT to Cheat Children—The Theory of Loose Parts." *Landscape Architecture* 62: 30–34.

O'Connell, Cathal. 2018. "Technologies Inspired by Nature." *Cosmos*, July 9. https://cosmosmagazine.com/technology/technologies-inspired-by-nature/

Patt, Michelle B. 2018. "It's Not a Mess." Explore Inspire EC (blog), August 28. https://exploreinspireec.blogspot.com/search?q=it%27s+not+a+mess

PBS and WGBH Educational Foundation. n.d. *Goals for the Understanding of Balls and Ramps.* PBS Learning Media (video). https://unctv.pbslearningmedia.org/resource/tdpd12.pd.sci.ballgoals/goals-for-the-understanding-of-balls-and-ramps/

Peterson, Jordan, and Austin Craig. 2017. *The New Creatives: Patrick Rochon.* Provo, UT: BYUtv (video), July 26. https://www.byutv.org/post/d84c106f-d95c-423c-a940-806df80eb5b0/the-new-creatives-patrick-rochon

REFERENCES AND RECOMMENDED RESOURCES AND READINGS

Piaget, Jean. 1923/1926. *The Language and Thought of the Child.* Trans. by Marjorie Worden. New York: Harcourt, Brace.

Play Safely Forum. n.d. "Risk-Benefit Assessment Form." Playlink. https://playlink.org/risk-benefit-assessment-form.html

Playwork Principles Scrutiny Group. 2005. "The Playwork Principles." The Playwork Foundation. https://playworkfoundation.org/the-playwork-principles/

Raudys, Justin. 2018. "11 Real Ways to Build a Positive School Culture." Prodigy (blog), November 19. https://www.prodigygame.com/main-en/blog/school-culture/

Recess Revolution. n.d. "Recess Revolution: Enriching Environments, Engaging Minds Unstructured Free-Play with Loose Parts. https://www.recessrevolution.org/

Reed, Catherine. n.d. "A 1st Grade Morning Work Alternative." The Brown Bag Teacher (blog). https://brownbagteacher.com/a-1st-grade-morning-work-alternative/

Robertson, Juliet. 2017. *Messy Maths: A Playful, Outdoor Approach.* Carmarthen, Wales, UK: Independent Thinking Press.

Roche, Leigh. 2018. "The Power of Choice for Toddlers: A Rationale for Implementing Choice Theory in the Early Childhood Classroom." *International Journal of Choice Theory and Reality Therapy* 37(2): 50–55.

Sear, Margaret. 2016. "Why Loose Parts? Their Relationship with Sustainable Practice, Children's Agency, Creative Thinking, and Learning Outcomes." *Educating Young Children* 22(2): 16–19.

Shefelbine, John. 1995. "Learning and Using Phonics in Beginning Reading." *Thrust for Educational Leadership* 25: 8–9.

Shilling, Richard, and Julia Brooklyn. n.d. "What Is Land Art?" Land Art for Kids. https://www.landartforkids.com/what-is-land-art.html

Smith, Gregory A. 2017. "Place-Based Education." *Oxford Research Encyclopedia of Education.* July 27. Oxford University Press. https://DOI:10.1093/acrefore/9780190264093.013.95

Smith-Gilman, Sheryl. 2018. "The Arts, Loose Parts and Conversations." *Journal of the Canadian Association of Curriculum Studies* 16(1): 90–103. https://jcacs.journals.yorku.ca/index.php/jcacs/article/view/40356/36367

Sousa, David A., and Tom Pilecki. 2013. *From STEM to STEAM: Using Brain-Compatible Strategies to Integrate the Arts.* Thousand Oaks, CA: Corwin.

Spencer, Rebecca, et al. 2019. "Educator Perceptions on the Benefits and Challenges of Loose Parts Play in the Outdoor Environments of Childcare Centres." *AIMS Public Health* 6(4): 461–476.

Stanchfield, Jennifer. 2016. *Tips and Tools: The Art of Experiential Group Facilitation.* 2nd ed. Oklahoma City, OK: Wood N Barnes Publishing.

Stanley, Emily. 2011. "The Place of Outdoor Play in a School Community: A Case Study of Recess Values." *Children, Youth and Environments* 21(1): 185–211.

Stanovich, Keith E., Anne E. Cunningham, and Barbara B. Cramer. 1984. "Assessing Phonological Awareness in Kindergarten Children: Issues of Task Comparability." *Journal of Experimental Child Psychology* 38(2): 175–190.

Stoltzfus, Marcos. 2019. *Kinderforest: Connections to Indiana Academic Standards*. Wolf Lake, IN: Merry Lea Environmental Learning Center of Goshen College. https://www.goshen.edu/merrylea/wp-content/uploads/2020/10/kinderforest_white_paper_final.pdf

Suskind, Diana. 2019. "International Stonework Play Day." Nurture in Nature Australia. https://nurtureinnature.com.au/international-stonework-play-day/

Sutton, Mary Jo. 2011. "In the Hand and Mind: The Intersection of Loose Parts and Imagination in Evocative Settings for Young Children." *Children, Youth and Environments* 21(2): 408–424.

Swartz, Clay. n.d. "How to Make a Rube Goldberg Machine." *Scout Life*. https://boyslife.org/hobbies-projects/projects/159359/how-to-make-a-rube-goldberg-machine/

Tallamy, Doug. 2009. *Bringing Nature Home: How You Can Sustain Wildlife with Native Plants*. 2nd ed. Portland, OR: Timber Press.

Thornhill, Michelle. 2017. "Loose Parts and Intelligent Playthings Categorized by Schema." https://brucecounty.on.ca/sites/default/files/Loose%20Parts%20By%20Schema_0.pdf

Tompkins, Gail E. 2017. *Literacy for the 21st Century: A Balanced Approach*. 7th ed. Boston, MA: Pearson Education.

Topal, Cathy W., and Lella Gandini. 1999. *Beautiful Stuff! Learning with Found Materials*. Worcester, MA: Davis Publications.

University College Dublin. n.d. "Constructivism and Social Constructivism in the Classroom." Open Educational Resources of UCD Teaching and Learning, University College Dublin. http://www.ucdoer.ie/index.php/Education_Theory/Constructivism_and_Social_Constructivism_in_the_Classroom/

University of Toronto. 2017. "Emergent Curriculum." Early Learning Centre, University of Toronto. https://elc.utoronto.ca/about-us/emergent/

Vacca, JoAnne L., et al. 2003. *Reading and Learning to Read*. 5th ed. Boston, MA: Pearson Education.

Van't Hul, Jean. 2010. "Land Art for Kids: Richard Shilling on Land Art for Kids." The Artful Parent. https://artfulparent.com/richard-shilling-on-land-art-for-kids/

Veselack, Ellen, Dana Miller, and Lisa Cain-Chang. 2015. *Raindrops on Noses and Toes in the Dirt: Infants and Toddlers in the Outdoor Classroom.* Lincoln, NE: Dimensions Educational Research Foundation. https://dimensionsfoundation.org/wp-content/uploads/2016/07/it-paper-cec_final.pdf

Viluma, Ilona. 2020. "Cognitive Benefits from Playing with Building Blocks." Gigi. https://www.gigibloks.com/blogs/news/cognitive-benefits-from-playing-with-building-blocks

Waldorf, Sarah, and Annelisa Stephan. 2020. "Getty Artworks Recreated with Household Items by Creative Geniuses the World Over." The Iris (blog), March 30. http://blogs.getty.edu/iris/getty-artworks-recreated-with-household-items-by-creative-geniuses-the-world-over/

WNET Education. 2004. "Constructivism as a Paradigm for Teaching and Learning." Concept to Classroom. https://www.thirteen.org/edonline/concept2class/constructivism/index.html

Wolfe, Patricia. 1987. 'What the "Seven-Step Lesson Plan" Isn't!' *Educational Leadership* 44(5): 70–71.

Wood, Jill. 2020. "Adventure Play." The Parish School. https://www.parishschool.org/campus-life/adventure-play/

Ying, Joel. 2019. "The Decline of Play—Peter Gray." Living the Present Moment. https://livingthepresentmoment.com/the-decline-of-play-peter-gray/

Yopp, Hallie K., and Ruth H. Yopp. 2000. "Supporting Phonemic Awareness Development in the Classroom." *The Reading Teacher* 54(2): 130–143.

Zakarin, Jordan. 2013. "Michelle Obama Makes Surprise Oscars Appearance, Reads Best Picture." *The Hollywood Reporter*, February 24. https://www.hollywoodreporter.com/general-news/michelle-obama-at-oscars-2013-424051

Index

N

O